PENG

A SPORTING CHANCE

Writer and broadcaster Titus O'Reily was born in Melbourne and raised by the Sisters of Collective Misery, a kindly but sombre order who placed an emphasis on sport above all other things, including religion. As a writer, Titus has carved out a reputation for inaccuracy and being difficult to work with. His unique take on sport has been hailed by some of the most respected figures in sport as 'awful', 'childish' and 'barely comprehensible'.

titusoreily.com

Also by Titus O'Reily

A Thoroughly Unhelpful History of Australian Sport

A SPORTING CHANCE

AUSTRALIAN SPORTING SCANDALS AND THE PATH TO REDEMPTION

TITUS O'REILY

PENGUIN BOOKS

PENGUIN BOOKS

UK | USA | Canada | Ireland | Australia
India | New Zealand | South Africa | China

Penguin Books is part of the Penguin Random House group of companies
whose addresses can be found at global.penguinrandomhouse.com.

Penguin
Random House
Australia

First published by Penguin Random House Australia Pty Ltd, 2018
This edition published by Penguin Books, 2019

Cover design by Alex Ross © Penguin Random House Australia Pty Ltd
Cover photograph courtesy Getty Images/PA Images Archive
Typeset in Sabon and Brandon Grotesque by Midland Typesetters, Australia
Printed and bound in Australia by Griffin Press, part of Ovato, an accredited
ISO AS/NZS 14001 Environmental Management Systems printer.

A catalogue record for this
book is available from the
NATIONAL
LIBRARY   National Library of Australia
OF AUSTRALIA

ISBN: 978 1 76089 285 2

penguin.com.au

MIX
Paper from
responsible sources
FSC® C009448

CONTENTS

FORGIVING THE
GOOD BLOKES

It will come as no surprise to Australia's 24 million sports fans that our sunburnt continent is home to one of the most dominant predators the world has ever seen. In our tropical rainforests, grasslands, eucalyptus forests and dry deserts, bounded by the Indian and Pacific oceans, this predator is king – free to roam without the restrictions that hold back many other species living in this ancient land.

That creature, of course, is the Star Athlete.

Star Athletes have always flourished in this country, because they supply the people with the one thing they need to survive: sporting glory.

Some of these athletes enjoy stellar careers and go on to become model citizens. But others are caught in an all-too-familiar cycle of winning, crisis and forgiveness. These athletes are a mutation known as the Good Bloke, a dangerous subspecies of the Star Athlete, much like Indominus rex, the hybrid dinosaur in *Jurassic World*.

The Good Bloke has usually won a lot of silverware or has huge potential, and is also friends with lots of other sportsmen and media commentators. They are always forgiven for making fools of themselves, and suffer no consequences for indiscretions that would result in the rest of us being escorted from our workplace by someone with 'People and Culture' in their title.

Once upon a time the Good Bloke lived a free and easy life, but times are changing. This once impervious predator is now in danger. New, strange and terrifying threats have risen: smartphones, social media, integrity units, women in positions of power.

These changes raise questions that once seemed unthinkable. Is there no longer a place for the loveable larrikin in Australian sport? Does the rise of the nanny state mean photographing a model in the shower against her will and sending those photos to mates will begin to have serious consequences? Is the path to forgiveness as open as ever, or are our Star Athletes just one ball-tampering incident away from extinction?

ANATOMY OF THE SPECIES

In 2010, Rugby League legend Mal Meninga was a happy man. He had just coached Queensland to a 3–0 series whitewash in the State of Origin.

This wasn't anything new; New South Wales losing the State of Origin was an annual occurrence, like the coming of autumn, or Sam Stosur being bundled out in the first round of the Australian Open. In fact, ancient peoples used NSW losing the State of Origin series as the sign to start preparing the land for planting, and there's a pillar at Stonehenge that aligns with the sun each year at the exact moment NSW lose.

In 2010, though, Meninga had won all three games in the series, the first time he'd achieved that as coach. As he answered reporters' questions in the afterglow of a hard fought 23–18 victory, he waxed lyrical about what made his Queensland team so great.

'Their belief is fantastic and their mateship, which is really important, is second to none as well. They'll do everything they possibly can for their mate to be successful.'

Unintentionally, Meninga had identified both the building blocks of a great team and the worst excesses of the Star Athlete.

Mateship, or friendship on steroids, is a uniquely Australian obsession. It places equality, loyalty and friendship – usually between men – on a pedestal so high it is technically in low-Earth orbit.

So powerful is our idea of mateship, so bound up with the ANZAC spirit, sport and the adversity of colonial times, that in 1999 John Howard seriously considered including it in the Australian Constitution. Drafted by Les Murray, Howard wanted this preamble added:

> Australians are free to be proud of their country and heritage, free to realise themselves as individuals, and free to pursue their hopes and ideals. We value excellence as well as fairness, independence as dearly as mateship.

In many ways mateship is an admirable trait, but Howard's line of thinking polarised people and was ultimately knocked back, showing a remarkable level of common sense compared to, say, the United States, where the right to shoot people is enshrined in the constitution.

Howard's attempt to raise mateship to a holy tenet even led Les Murray* to observe that mateship was 'blokeish' and 'not a real word'.

Richard Walsh, in his 1985 essay 'Australia Observed', wrote, 'The ultimate accolade in Australia is to be a "good bloke", meaning someone who is gregarious, hospitable, generous, warm hearted, and with a good sense of humour. In Australia it availeth a man nothing if he makes himself a fortune and is not a good bloke!'

---

* Not Mr Football Les Murray, of SBS fame, but poet Les Murray. Sorry for mentioning a poet in a sports book, *especially considering* such an excessive amount of government funding goes to the arts, starving the sporting community of much-needed cash.

On the surface this sentiment seems fine, but in the pressure cooker of the sporting world, mateship gets a bit twisted. It can exclude people, mainly women, and lead to an atmosphere so suffocating it's hard to think outside the group. So powerful is the distortion field created by mateship in a high-pressure environment, it can even make appointing David Warner vice-captain of the Australian cricket team seem like a good idea.

Like many good things, mateship can become toxic in high doses.* In the framework of a team, where everything is about achieving something together, every part has to be dedicated to the greater whole. This extends beyond the players to coaches and administrators, and even the million-dollar businesspeople who get seduced by the glamour of sport.

Let's face it, achieving something together is a lot easier if everyone conforms to a shared world view, and that's certainly the case for teams that pull off great victories.** It's even easier if everyone likes each other and believes that they're among a great group of blokes. (It also means your premiership reunions won't be as awkward as that time John Howard had a bowl on national television.) The default response to any challenge becomes 'do everything you can for your mate to be successful'. That's why Meninga thought mateship was so important.

A problem emerges, however, when a member of a close-knit group of mates does something awful, ridiculous or plain stupid. And in sport, that's not uncommon. The us-against-them mentality, so useful on the field, is then extended well beyond the boundary line.

---

* Even West Coast Coolers can be toxic in large amounts, something I discovered on Alan Bond's yacht once, while in the company of the singer Sade. It's a long story.
** As a member of a sports team, you can only do superficially non-conforming things, like having a funny haircut. Anything deeper than that threatens this conformity. Tattoos used to be non-conformist but are now so common that not having one is the way to stand out.

Usually the result is a full-throated defence of the player in question. It's not entirely disingenuous either, as it must be hard to believe that a teammate you achieved so much with on the field, who you've seen do great things, who's had your back, would be seriously lacking in some other area of their character. After all, if your teammate isn't a good bloke, what does that say about you?

INEVITABLE APOLOGIES

'With hindsight, I can see how others may have felt like it was a hostage situation.'

'At the time, I was unaware the site has significant cultural and historical importance.'

'Obviously, I owe a pretty big apology to the members of both Cold Chisel and The Veronicas.'

Does it mean you're mates with people who aren't good blokes? Are you, yourself, not a good bloke? Talk about an existential crisis.[*]

This is why, on various NRL and AFL panel shows, you'll often hear a player say something like this about a teammate: 'Yeah, Davo's disappointed with himself for fighting those four guys and all the public urination, but he's a great bloke and he knows he's messed up. Of course, coming hot on the heels of his sexual assault conviction, it isn't ideal. This is all so out of character.'

Then, sometime in the following week, the player who has transgressed delivers an apology that isn't really an apology. And once the dust has settled, a media outlet will probably sign Davo to a lucrative contract to provide special comments for their coverage that are usually anything but special. Give it a few years and everyone will be referring to Davo as 'a bit of a loveable rogue' or 'one of the game's great characters'.

That's because the sports media has as many Good Blokes roaming wild as sports teams do. It's an industry dominated by ex-players and reliant on maintaining good relationships in the sporting world.

---

[*] Apologies for using the word 'existential' in a book about sport. And no, I don't know what it means either.

So players and the media instinctively team up to offer defences of the Good Blokes in their midst.

The result of this group defence is that the term 'good bloke' no longer means what it says. Like 'fun run', it often actually means exactly the opposite.

The combination of this group defence and fans' desire for success means sports stars get away with things that would be unthinkable in any other industry. Try joking with a bunch of blokes at your work about drowning a female peer and see how long you stay employed.

AN INDUSTRY LIKE NO OTHER

People involved in sport – whether playing it, running it or covering it in the media – often do terrible things. They're risk-takers by nature and not necessarily good at decision-making off the field – just look at the sporting world's abundance of mullets, sleeve tattoos and fondness for Daryl Braithwaite's 'Horses'.

A small snapshot from *The Archives of Sporting Missteps* might include cheating the salary cap, violence against women, accepting money from bookies, setting entertainers on fire, taking performance-enhancing drugs, getting into compromising positions with dogs, dyeing horses with human hair dye and allowing the Hawthorn Football Club to keep designing new away jumpers.

Finding an industry that gets even close to these levels of unethical behaviour is very difficult. No, wait: banking. Banking is worse.

The only difference between sportspeople and bankers is that we tend to forgive sportspeople.* The royal commission into the banking, superannuation and financial services industry is like a sporting crisis, except we already dislike the people involved.

---

* I suppose we start off liking sportspeople, or at least when things go wrong we live in hope that they will turn things around and deliver us some glory.

Yet sport can still challenge banking for moral turpitude, especially if we consider the case of Matthew Lodge.

In October 2015, Lodge, a promising twenty-year-old League player, was on holiday in New York. At 4 a.m. after a big night out, he physically harassed Carolin Dekeyser, a German tourist, on a street in the Upper West Side, while asking her, 'Do you think you're going to die? This is the night you're going to die.'

I'm probably going out on a limb here, but in my opinion that's not normal behaviour. But Lodge wasn't finished.

Dekeyser, desperate to get away, started randomly pressing buttons on the intercom at one of the apartment buildings nearby. Joseph Cartright was at home with his wife, Ruth Fowler, and their nine-year-old son Henry, and he came to Dekeyser's aid, letting her into the lobby. Lodge followed the two of them in and began assaulting Cartwright. He then entered the apartment and locked out Cartwright.

Inside, Ruth and Henry huddled in fear behind a locked bathroom door as Lodge proceeded to smash everything in sight before trying to punch through the bathroom door. Henry yelled out to Lodge through the door, 'I'm too young to die.'

Only the arrival of armed police prevented Lodge from doing any further damage. It took some three years for Lodge to finally pay some of the $1.6 million he'd been ordered to by a US civil court.[*]

What organisation would take such a person back into the fold?

The answer is the Brisbane Broncos and the National Rugby League, who have allowed Lodge to return to play in 2018, despite the simple fact that he assaulted people, leaving them traumatised, and has failed to show any remorse for his actions.

On top of this, many in the League community have responded in less than impressive fashion to Lodge's return. Cronulla-

---

[*] This was only after a huge backlash from the media and the public after he re-joined the NRL.

Sutherland Sharks captain Paul Gallen said, 'I don't know. We've let blokes back in the game who have touched women – or hit women – I wouldn't put him in that class. We got blokes like that still playing so let's just move on.'

As Gallen eloquently points out, the bar is already so low, why make an exception in this case? That's depressing in itself, even if he didn't realise what he was saying. Gallen later hit reverse on these remarks so quickly you could smell the burning rubber down in The Shire.

The boys' club closing tight around the imperilled athlete was very predictable. But in this case, there was an alarming development. The world has changed, and new voices are now occasionally allowed in the mix. The most terrifying voices of all. *Women's* voices.

NRL CEO Todd Greenberg, who rubberstamped Lodge's return, found himself in an interesting position when he went on the Fox Sports program *League Life*. He was interviewed by a panel of four respected sports journalists: Lara Pitt, Jess Yates, Yvonne Sampson and Hannah Hollis. Once, this would have been unheard of – an all-female panel quizzing the top boss on why he was allowing a player like Lodge back into the League.*

That interview is one of the most brutal things I've ever seen, and I saw Port lose to Geelong in the 2007 grand final by 119 points *and* I've heard Daryl Somers sing live. Greenberg had answers, but none of them were good. Each path he headed down, his interviewers tore apart his flimsy excuses with breathtaking ease.

Jess Yates nailed Greenberg on something that comes up time and time again when it comes to fallen Star Athletes: that a second chance is simply par for the course. 'But it's not even a second chance,' Yates said. 'It's a third, fourth, fifth chance. I would argue that his second

---

* In fairness to Lodge, he has shown that when it comes to terrifying people, he's an equal-opportunity offender, covering off men, women and children.

chance is not being in jail and making something of his life away from the game.'

Never before has a senior sporting administrator so publicly come out of their boys' club and walked smack-bang into the modern world. You could actually see Greenberg's shock as he tried to compute that not everyone thinks like he does.

The day after Greenberg's grilling, with timing that shows the universe has a dry sense of humour, the NRL celebrated International Women's Day, tweeting, 'Happy International Women's Day! #PressforProgress'.

Perhaps 'press for progress' was an acknowledgement of what four journalists had done to Greenberg the night before.

To add to the whole mess, Matt Lodge also made his return to the field for Brisbane on that International Women's Day. It was the most tone-deaf moment in sport since Wayne Carey appeared on Channel Seven's AFL coverage for White Ribbon Night.

At the conclusion of the game, St George player James Graham walked over to Lodge, extended his hand and said, 'Welcome back.' But then, you have to take into account that Graham once copped a twelve-match ban for biting opponent Billy Slater's ear in a grand final, so he may not be truly representative of how all NRL players feel.

Perhaps most telling is that while the boys' club that runs League had considered it acceptable for Lodge to return, the public certainly judged the situation

EQUALITY NOW?

While women are massively under-represented when it comes to Good Blokes, there may be hope the girls' club will stick up for each other as blindly as the blokes do.

When Collingwood's Sarah D'Arcy was reported for kicking an opponent in February 2018, it was instantly reported in the media as 'out of character'. The Western Bulldogs' Ellie Blackburn said D'Arcy was 'not like' that, despite fairly conclusive video evidence to the contrary.

another way. They booed Lodge mercilessly. It was a moment that clearly showed how our sporting administrators, so cocooned from reality, so protected by mateship and groupthink, had failed to recognise the changing landscape.

Things got no better for the NRL and the Brisbane Broncos when it was revealed, not long after his return, that in 2016 Lodge had pleaded guilty to a charge of common assault against an ex-girlfriend, which contradicted his claim that he had never 'hit any woman or assaulted any'.

The NRL and the Broncos response was again completely tone-deaf, simply pointing out that they already knew about this incident. 'What's the big deal?' seemed to be their take on what was a rather significant new piece of information that undercut their message that New York had been a one-off incident for Lodge.

To be fair, this is an extreme case. Rugby League isn't out on its own like the Robinson Crusoe of sporting organisations in Australia. The reality is that there are crises everywhere, and there have been ever since the British Empire decided to set up an expansion club on the shores of Port Jackson.*

THE ANATOMY OF A SPORTING CRISIS

Trawling through our chequered sporting history reveals that not only do the players who bugger things up fall into a few recurring character types, there are tried-and-true ways of apologising for those incidents or covering them up, some more successful than others. It's clear this is a lively cottage industry with its own way of operating.

'Davo' always falls into one of three categories: the Wayward Champion, the Colourful Racing Identity or the Cashed-Up Businessman. Show me a scandal and I'll show you one of these

---

* Like more recent expansion teams in the Sydney area, the locals were either indifferent or outright hostile to the idea.

archetypes at its centre. Get two or more of these archetypes involved at once and you have a CRISIS.

The types of scandals are easy to identify too – drugs, sex, violence, inappropriate dog-handling, the list goes on – but each scandal brings its own challenges. In this book we'll examine them all, providing a kind of Richter scale of scandals, so you can instantly know how much trouble your favourite player is in.

Of course, a scandal is nothing without a comeback, and the path to redemption is so well-worn it's deeper than the Grand Canyon.

There's the unapologetic apology, the trip to the overseas rehab centre, blaming a woman for your actions and the tell-all interview with family members explaining how this isn't the Davo *they* know, while also promising that 'he's learnt a lot and definitely changed'.

After studying all this, I've pulled together all the best-practice steps for making a comeback, in a helpful guide for the sportspeople among you. You know, just in case you suddenly find yourself living with outlaw motorcycle gang members, or in an astounding coincidence seventeen different women accuse you of sexual harassment.

But beware, while the path to redemption is well mapped, it's not always smooth. While most make it back, there are some who are never forgiven, and we'll examine where they went wrong.

The rise of women's sport is another factor to consider. Will this make our sporting clubs bastions of equality and dignified behaviour? Or will female sport stars let fame and success go to their heads so that they too must front a media conference to apologise for 'having offended anyone' by setting someone on fire during Mad Monday celebrations? Will the sisterhood become the new mateship?

After all, won't true equality occur only when a female athlete can resist arrest on Mad Monday and still get a commentary role with a major broadcaster on Tuesday? Do we dare to dream that equality is close at hand?

So, with integrity units lurking and drug testers circling, let us examine the Good Blokes in our sporting history, from Young Griffo in the 1890s to today's Australian cricketers. Let's go behind the scenes of notorious scandals to find out why we have so frequently given players a sporting chance. And to learn if we, the fans, will continue to do so.

PART I

THE ARCHETYPES

THE WAYWARD
CHAMPION

When a sportsperson's talent seems to exceed what should be humanly possible, it captures our imagination. There's something magical in witnessing someone turn a sport on its head because the laws of physics don't seem to apply to them. We can't help but be in awe.

That's because it taps into something deeper than sport. On some level we are always fighting for control of our lives, to bring order to what we sense is the underlying chaos of existence. And to see a Wayne Carey, a Shane Warne or a Matthew Johns dominate a game is to see someone tame the most chaotic of situations, rising above it and shaping the world into how they would like it to be.

This is what we love. Wouldn't we all like to be able to bend situations to our will? Exist seemingly beyond the constraints everyone else experiences?

To do that you need the pure physical talent, but you need other things too: relentless drive, a risk-taking personality and an unhealthy amount of belief in yourself. This is why so many of our sporting heroes seem to have equal measures of sporting talent and poor decision-making skills.

The pattern of sporting glory followed by scandal and then forgiveness is a constant in Australian life. The Wayward Champion is an eternal character. Our first ever Wayward Champion of note was boxer Albert Griffiths who, in the nineteenth century, was the first Australian sport star to attract as much controversy as he did praise.

Every Wayward Champion in Australian sporting history is simply following in the footsteps of 'Young Griffo' – prodigious sporting talent ensuring forgiveness is always on offer. This pattern continues today, with examples like Shane Warne, arguably our most famous Wayward Champion. Warne's indiscretions are different to Griffiths', but the forgiveness is still there.

JUST ANOTHER NIGHT

A man sat at the bar in Young Mitchell's saloon in San Francisco, nursing what was certainly not his first drink of the evening. Short and carrying a bit of weight around the middle, he wasn't much to look at. No one would give him a second glance; just another drunk at the bar.

As he sat there, a man entered the saloon and made a beeline for him.

The bartender, sensing danger, warned the man at the bar. 'Here he is now, Griff – that fellow who is looking for you.'

The normal reaction to being told someone is about to confront you in a bar is to at least turn around, but 'Griff' seemed not at all interested.*

Sensing some action, the crowd parted before the newcomer, and as he got within striking distance of Griff he cocked his fist and swung with all his might, aiming for a king hit from behind. But Griff, who seemed to be oblivious, just moved his head slightly, causing the knockout blow to sail past harmlessly.

The aggressor swung again and again, but the man kept ducking each punch, never turning around and instead watching his attacker

---

* My reaction to being told someone is about to confront me in a bar is to run, screaming hysterically.

in the giant mirror behind the bar. After a few minutes of this, with not a punch landed, the attacker slumped to the floor exhausted and said, 'You win, Griffo. I was going to knock your block off, but you haven't got one. I'm licked without being hit.'

The Australian man, Albert Griffiths, or 'Young Griffo' as he was known in boxing circles, didn't even respond. He resumed his drinking as if nothing had happened.

WHAT JUST HAPPENED?

It was day two of the first test of the 1993 Ashes series and at the crease stood the English batsman Mike Gatting. Gatting was known as a terrific player of spin, famous for it in fact, and he was facing a young kid who had played just eleven tests before this one at Old Trafford.

The young kid, Shane Warne, was about to bowl his first ball in an Ashes series. He was a leg spinner, a type of spin bowling that had been in decline for a long time. As he took a few steps before releasing his first ball, no one was expecting much from the peroxide-blond Warne.

When he released it, the ball travelled straight down the pitch before drifting to the right in the air and taking a nasty dip. Gatting took a step forward but when the ball hit the ground, far out from leg stump, it quickly spun to the left, completely in the opposite direction. It spun all the way back to clip the top of off stump, meaning it had moved sideways about 23 centimetres, a huge amount for spin bowling and almost impossible for the batsman to play.

Gatting was bowled. He stood there for a moment, completely unsure of what had happened, a look of pure shock on his face. He shook his head in disbelief and wandered off the ground in a daze.

That delivery has been called the ball of the century. It signalled the arrival of a talent that was difficult to comprehend. Just four runs later, Warne took another wicket. England went on to lose the test, with Warne finishing with eight wickets and named man of the match.

Warne went on to terrorise batsmen for years to come.

ON THE ROCKS

Albert Griffiths was born on 31 March 1871. Probably. His gravestone, in the Bronx, lists his birthdate as 1880. Back in the nineteenth century, record keeping was about as accurate as that of the Essendon Football Club in 2012.

What is known for certain is that Griffiths was born in Millers Point, Sydney, just next to The Rocks. By the time Griffiths arrived on the scene, these were tough suburbs of a rapidly expanding Sydney. The Rocks was littered with brothels, pubs and opium dens, and there was a good chance you'd be assaulted and robbed by the roaming street gangs.*

Griffiths' childhood was struck by tragedy when his mother died. His father, a wharfie, sent him out to be raised by neighbours but took him back once he'd found a new wife.

Schooling wasn't a priority for Griffiths and he began working early, as a paperboy and runner for the *Sydney Morning Herald*, an assistant to a tailor and later on helping out a horse trainer.

Griffiths wasn't exactly the 'hold down a steady job' type, though. He liked to have fun and hang out with his mates. In The Rocks, that meant joining one of the many street gangs that operated in the area.

THE PUSH

Wandering through Sydney's The Rocks today, in the shadow of the Sydney Harbour Bridge, it's hard to imagine it as a hotbed of gang

---

* While this wasn't great, at least Sydney had a nightlife back then.

crime. These days, the only street robbery is the prices tourists are being charged.*

Yet in the late nineteenth century, its thriving gang culture gave us some of the greatest names in the history of crime. At the time a gang was known as a 'push' and there were plenty around Sydney, including the Millers Point Push, the Argyle Cut Push, the Glebe Push, the Straw Hat Push,** the Forty Thieves from Surrey Hills and the Gibb Street Mob. There was even a Catholic gang, the Green Push, and a Protestant one, the Orange Push. Spoiler alert: those two didn't like each other.

These gangs were so well known that both Henry Lawson and Banjo Paterson immortalised them in verse. Henry Lawson's 'The Captain of the Push' begins:

> As the night was falling slowly down on city, town
> and bush,
> From a slum in Jones' Alley sloped the Captain of the
> Push;
> And he scowled towards the North, and he scowled
> towards the South,
> As he hooked his little finger in the corners of his mouth.
> Then his whistle, loud and shrill, woke the echoes
> of the 'Rocks',
> And a dozen ghouls came sloping round the corners
> of the blocks.***

The Rocks Push was the most famous of these gangs and they ran the suburb from the 1870s until the late 1890s. During this time

---

* I bought a bottle of water there in 2003 and should have it paid off in late 2019.
** Just the phrase 'Straw Hat Push' frightens me to this day.
*** I realise I've now both mentioned a poet and included some poetry in a book about sport. I'm not sure what's wrong with me either.

even the police risked being robbed if they entered the area, so mostly they didn't. When members of a Push weren't robbing the public they were usually fighting, either other gangs or each other.

Despite being made up of 'unruly youths' there was a strict hierarchy to these gangs. The Rocks Push chose their leader through bare-knuckle boxing matches. I believe that's a tradition our political parties still use to select their leaders.

Bare-knuckle boxing was also used to decide quarrels between gangs, with the leaders squaring off. The unintended consequence was that this gang culture became a hothouse for Australia's nascent boxing community. It was like a high performance centre for the sweet science well before anyone said things like 'high performance centre'.

In the same year Albert Griffiths was allegedly born, 1871, Larry Foley, the leader of the Catholic Green Push, faced off with the leader of the Protestant Orange Push. The fight lasted a mere 71 rounds before the police arrived and broke it up. Those in attendance awarded the fight to Foley, despite the early finish.

Foley was such a gifted boxer that he made a small fortune bare-knuckle fighting, despite it being illegal at the time.

On 20 March 1879, Foley fought the London-born Victorian Abe Hicken for the first unofficial boxing championship of Australia. The fight was conducted on the Victorian side of the Murray River. Twenty New South Wales policemen, who had been tipped off about the fight, sat watching from across the river, unable to intervene as the other bank was out of their jurisdiction.

A large crowd saw Foley knock out Hicken after 16 rounds. Back then, no one really worried about the long-term effects of being repeatedly belted in the head, or the fact that fights went on indefinitely until someone couldn't box anymore.

For his victory, Foley pocketed £600, a fortune in those days. A reporter asked him how he felt. 'Very, very happy,' said Larry.

When the reporter asked the punters in attendance how they felt – the majority having bet money on Foley – they said, 'As happy as Larry,' and an iconic Australian phrase was born.

For the twenty New South Wales police hoping to arrest the boxers, the day was a disappointing one. The crowd and the boxers disappeared into the Victorian bush. Even worse, although they didn't know it at the time, Australia's most wanted man was in the crowd: Ned Kelly had robbed the bank at Jerilderie just six weeks earlier.

Flush with cash from a successful career bare-knuckle fighting, it was time for Foley to do what all Australian sportsmen eventually do: he retired and bought a pub, the White Horse Hotel in Sydney's George Street. His fighting and gang days over, he set up a boxing gym out the back and called it 'the Iron Pot'.

The gym was so successful in turning out boxing champions, that Foley became known as 'the Father of Australian Boxing'.[*] And when a seventeen-year-old by the name of Albert Griffiths walked into the Iron Pot, Larry recognised a true genius.

THE NATURAL

Before his sixteenth birthday Albert Griffiths had become the leader of The Rocks Push. These were tough times and Griffiths lived in the toughest area. There was no avocado on toast for these nineteenth-century millennials, just petty theft and fistfights. These weren't random fights though; despite being illegal they were well organised and publicised, and involved prize money and hundreds of people watching and wagering on the outcome.

---

[*] The Rocks Push's reign only really ended in 1900 when, due to the conditions in the area, the bubonic plague broke out. The government decided it had better step in, which it did by demolishing hundreds of decrepit buildings. Larry Foley established a very successful demolition company that did much of that work. The idea of a former gang leader who had significantly contributed to the problems in The Rocks taking government money to address the consequences of those problems caused no public outcry. In many ways, this is still business as usual in Sydney today.

Griffiths was so skilled in the art of bare-knuckle fighting he regularly defeated much larger and older opponents.* He was a natural and didn't fear anyone. On one evening he fought four men, one after the other, drinking beer between each fight and still winning easily.

His talent didn't go unnoticed by the emerging boxing community in Sydney. After bouncing around a few of the gyms in the area, Griffiths finally ended up at the Iron Pot with Larry Foley.

What struck Larry and everyone in the Iron Pot was that Young Griffo was impossible to hit. It turns out that regular street fighting, while incredibly dangerous, can really teach you a thing or two about the art of boxing. The fact that your opponent isn't wearing gloves tends to focus the mind on not getting hit. A slight feint here, a move of the shoulders there, and Griffiths would make even the most experienced boxers look silly. What was even more astounding was that he did this while barely moving his feet during the entire fight, often not shifting them outside a space that could be covered by a handkerchief.

Under Larry's tutelage – one former gang leader teaching another – Griffo rattled off a succession of impressive victories, then turned professional.

It was a rapid rise. In 1889 he fought Nipper Peakes for the Australian featherweight title in front of a crowd of about a thousand people at the Apollo Hall in Melbourne's Bourke Street, winning on points in eight rounds. He defended the title several times and, in 1890, he fought world featherweight champion 'Torpedo' Billy Murphy in Sydney.

Murphy was a New Zealander with a deadly right, known as his 'torpedo punch'. He'd won the world title earlier that year at

---

* In the late nineteenth century, bare-knuckle boxing was banned in much of the world. It opens up cuts on fighters' faces very easily, making it look barbaric. The response was to box with padded gloves, which some now argue is worse – it stops the cuts, but means fighters can go on getting punched for longer, causing brain injuries. My view is you should avoid being hit in the head by pretty much anything: bare fists, padded fists, shoes, tyre irons, cricket bats. Avoid them all, I say.

the California Athletic Club in San Francisco, against the Irish-born American Ike Weir.

Weir had dominated the match until the fourteenth round, when, confident of victory, he excited the crowd by performing a backflip. This turned out to be a tactical mistake. As soon as Weir landed, Murphy unloaded his torpedo punch, resulting in a knock-out. It was an important but possibly unnecessary reminder for other pugilists: don't do a backflip in the middle of a boxing match.

Upon his return to New Zealand, Murphy agreed to fight a young Australian who seemingly couldn't lose. The bout was recognised as a world title fight by the British and the Australians. But the Americans, being Americans, refused to recognise it as such because it wasn't being held in America,* although years later that decision was reversed.

Murphy certainly had a significant power advantage over Griffiths and, in the first three rounds, knocked Young Griffo down twice. Then Griffo's skill started to shine through. As the fight wore on, Griffo's ability to make Murphy miss his punches tired out the world champion, to the point that, after Griffo landed a right on Murphy's jaw in round fifteen, the New Zealander threw off his gloves and conceded defeat.

Suddenly, the leader of the most notorious street gang in Sydney had become the world champion. Boxing and criminals have, of course, rarely overlapped since. But it was not the last time that organised crime and sport have become entangled.

HONEST JOHN

It was September 1994 and Australian batsman Mark Waugh was in Sri Lanka for the Singer World Series, an ODI tournament that saw the Australian team take on India, Pakistan and Sri Lanka.

---

* Luckily, these days America has moved past such an insular view of world.

A mercurial batsman, Mark was the twin of future Australian captain Steve Waugh and, early in his career, Steve's shadow loomed large. At one stage Mark picked up the nickname 'Afghan' in reference to the Soviet Union's invasion of Afghanistan, often referred to as 'the forgotten war'.[*]

But things worked out pretty well for Mark; he carved out a very successful career as a sublime batsman and superb slips fielder. Things didn't work out quite as well for Afghanistan.[**]

During that 1994 tournament in Sri Lanka, the Australian team was staying in Colombo, at the Oberoi Hotel. There Mark bumped into an Indian man who introduced himself simply as 'John'. John explained that he was someone who bet a lot on cricket and had won a lot of money over the years.

Instead of saying 'that's nice' and moving on, Mark kept chatting. John asked if he'd be willing to provide information on things like the Australian team selection, strategy and the weather and pitch conditions. In exchange, John would give Mark $4000.

Mark wasn't so keen on revealing the team selection and strategy; after all, he had principles. But sure, he would help out with the other stuff for this random 'John' whose surname he didn't even know.[***]

Doubling down on this stunning piece of bad judgement, Waugh also agreed to introduce John to Australia's star player, Shane Warne, who just happened to be gambling at a casino nearby.[****]

---

[*] It's one of the rare examples of a clever Australian sporting nickname. The norm is to just add an 'o' or a 'y' to a surname and call the job done.

[**] Although, Afghanistan's national cricket team has been on the rise in recent years, being granted test status in 2017. Cricket has often been the best way to heal international conflict. Just look at how well Pakistan and India get along.

[***] To quote Bill Watterson's comic strip *Calvin and Hobbes*, 'I don't know which is worse . . . that everyone has his price, or that the price is always so low.'

[****] Warne had actually been told the casino in question was an unsavoury place, but he seemed to have taken that as an endorsement rather than a word of caution.

You'll be surprised to learn that 'John' wasn't actually this Indian gentleman's real name,* it was in fact Mukesh Kumar Gupta, and he turned out to be a very interesting character.

A RAPID RISE

Gupta was hurrying home after work along the lanes of Old Delhi. It was 1984 and his rather meagre bank clerk's salary meant he lived in a rundown home in a very poor area. As he moved between the markets that lined the streets and lanes of the old city, Gupta came upon a large group of men betting on cricket. Cricket was enjoying a resurgence in India as they had defeated the mighty West Indies the year before in the World Cup, at Lord's no less.

Gupta was astounded by the amount of money being wagered and, as he began to chat to a few of the men placing bets, he was amazed at how little they knew about cricket or the specific games they were betting on. It looked to him like there was money to be made.

As Gupta stood there, taking it all in, an idea began to form in his mind. It was an idea that propelled him to becoming an incredibly rich man, and it brought the sport of cricket to its knees.

AN EDUCATION

Gupta's realisation was that to do well betting on cricket, he just needed to know more than anyone else about the matches being played. Overnight, he became consumed with gathering as much information as possible.

At first this meant reading everything on cricket he could get his hands on, and listening to the BBC World Service a lot, paying close attention to weather reports. He also began talking to anyone he could about cricket, in the hope that he could find a scrap of information or insight.

---

* It turns out that, counterintuitively, John is not actually a popular name in India – it doesn't even crack the top 1000.

Gupta was obsessive. In a report released years later, it was revealed he rang one of his overseas contacts seventy times in one day, just to gain as much information as possible and stay up to date on a single match.*

The mid 1980s were pre-internet days, so the information Gupta was able to pull together gave him a huge advantage. A simple thing like a forecast of rain, which might cause a drawn match, wasn't instantly available to everyone like it is now.

Placing smart bets, Gupta found that he was making large amounts of money. Soon he took over a jewellery business while continuing to move up in the betting world. Eventually he moved into bookmaking himself.

Yet, despite doing well, Gupta's hunger for cricket information was not sated. Like so many Wall Street inside traders discovered in the eighties, information no one else has is its own form of currency. He wanted more.

In 1988, Gupta was watching a club match in Delhi in which Indian national team player Ajay Sharma played particularly well. Gupta approached Sharma and, praising his performance, gave him money as well as his phone number and said that he would be happy to help out with any problems he ever faced. Two weeks later, Sharma rang Gupta and provided him with information on pitch conditions, injuries, team selections and weather. It was the beginning of a beautiful friendship.

Sharma introduced Gupta to other cricketers from a range of international teams, who provided similar information and more. This meant Gupta often knew who was injured and who wasn't, who would be dropped and who would be the replacement, and a range of other insights, sometimes about both teams in a given match. He regularly knew what tactics both teams would employ,

---

* Even I now understand that ringing someone seventy times in one day is excessive. I even have a court order that says that.

GREAT EXCUSES IN HISTORY: IAN HEALY

In 2015, after the Australian cricket team was bowled out by England for a mere 60 runs in 18.3 overs, commentator Ian Healy had an interesting excuse for the collapse: 'All their partners are here and some of the most respected cricketers I played with hated that distraction. They weren't allowed on tour until after the series had been won. Your mind needs to be completely focused on it. Cricket is a sport that requires complete concentration. You need everything going for you and I'm not sure they're pushing for that hard enough.'

Typical women! Plus, their pheromones probably wafted down from the stands and weakened those poor male cricketers.

meaning he would know more about a game than the coaches and players of either team.

Around this time, at the height of his powers, Gupta made a couple of Australian mates. He would later say that once he became an insider in the cricket community, he was shocked by how easy it was to make friends with professional cricketers. By the mid nineties, he was arguably the most influential man in world cricket, it's just that not many people knew it.

But, as is so often the case, it's when Australian sportspeople come into contact with the wider world that strange things start happening.

THE LAND OF THE FREE

By 1892, Griffo had done everything he could possibly do in Australia, having risen to the elite tier of both boxing and gang crime. If he wanted to take on the top fighters of his day, he'd have to go to the United States.

It was a move that filled him with some trepidation; after all, it must have been hard to give up living in the plague-nurturing slums of Sydney. When he first set sail for the United States he lasted about five minutes. Five minutes into the sea voyage, that is. Having second thoughts, Griffo dived off the ship and swam back to shore.*

He tried again the next year, 1893, and managed to stay on board this time. Landing in the States, the young boxer made his way to Chicago, which, unlike Sydney, has never had any problems with organised crime.

Despite being in a new country, Griffo felt right at home in the ring. On 13 November 1893, he fought a boxer known as 'Young Scotty'.** Griffo was so confident of his skill, early in the match he challenged Young Scotty to try to hit him – Griffo would not punch back. For several minutes he bobbed and weaved, and Scotty failed to land anything significant.

Once he started throwing punches, Griffo won the fight, impressing the American crowd with his almost supernatural ability.

It was around this time that the American boxing media started to notice Albert's somewhat irregular training habits. That is, he had none. Like most people, Griffiths hated training. The difference being that he was a world class boxer. Not until Nick Kyrgios did another Australian sportsperson get so far by skating through purely on talent.

Not only did Griffo hate training, he loved drinking.*** Stories emerged of the boxer preparing for a fight by drinking all through the night before. One newspaper reported that for his bout against Young Scotty, Griffo had to be located and removed from a bar right before the fight, making his defensive display and easy win even more remarkable.

Nat Fleischer, the founder and editor of the enormously influential *The Ring* magazine, said, 'He never was one to take his professional career seriously. Training was a nuisance to him and he

---

* This would be my reaction too if I ever found myself on a cruise ship.
** I like this naming convention. I would be 'Middle-Aged Titus' if I were a boxer.
*** This doesn't seem that strange to me, but I'm told it's not an ideal lifestyle for elite sports.

preferred hanging around bar rooms and guzzling his liquor. Seldom indeed was Griffo sober for a fight, yet so amazingly clever was he that regardless of his physical and mental condition at the moment, he invariably held his own or could and did whip his opponent.'

Griffo quickly established himself as one of the best boxers in the United States, but his love of carousing was starting to overwhelm his professional life. Hopeless with money, he would often earn the cash he needed for booze by challenging bar patrons to hit him in the face. Griffo, of course, always won the bet.

The truth is Griffo was an alcoholic. It would haunt him all his days. Later, when his life had gone truly off the rails, he said that all his trouble started when he made it big in the United States – he found that everyone wanted to have a drink with him.[*]

In one instance, just before a fight with the rising Jimmy Dime, Griffo was found in a hotel room, passed out and surrounded by empty champagne bottles. He was hurriedly awoken and rushed to the fight, which he was still able to win comfortably.

While there were plenty who were willing to take advantage of Griffo and send him out to fight in terrible shape, there were many others who tried to help him. But the task proved impossible. A former trainer, Tim McGrath, said Griffo had a complete lack of ambition. 'Glory and money meant little to him. He loved his good times, and it was impossible to get him into condition. No manager ever did. He never took a fight seriously and was never in condition for one that I know of.'

WINNING STREAK ENDS

While Young Griffo's private life may have been spinning out of control, his boxing career was not. Griffo was adored by the crowd. The American press anointed him the 'Australian Will o' the Wisp'

---

[*] This is a pitfall I've managed to avoid, in that no one wants to drink with me.

because he was so difficult to hit. The tales of his drinking added to his reputation rather than diminishing it. He would attract attention by announcing before a fight in which round he would knock out his opponent, a practice picked up by Muhammad Ali almost a century later.

In January 1894 he fought the future world featherweight champion Solly Smith to a draw. In March of the same year he took on Ike Weir, the man Torpedo Bill Murphy had beaten for the world title. A crowd of five thousand people showed up at the Second Regiment Armory in Chicago to watch the fight.

A once again inebriated Griffo knocked Weir down twice in the third round. The newspaper the *Inter Ocean* described the fight as 'three of the fastest, fiercest and most brutal rounds ever fought in an American prize ring'. Officially the fight ended in a draw, as the police stopped the fight in that third round, but almost all in attendance awarded the fight to Griffo. Not long after the fight, Weir retired from boxing.

At this stage in his career, Griffo was still undefeated. Depending on who you believe, he had fought somewhere between 115 and 174 bouts.

In August that year, at the Seaside Athletic Club in Brooklyn, Griffo faced a legend of the boxing game in Jack 'The Napoleon of the Prize Ring' McAuliffe, in a bout scheduled for ten rounds. The Irish-American McAuliffe came out hard against Griffo, but once again, Albert made one of the all-time great boxers look foolish, knocking him down in the sixth round. McAuliffe managed to get up and continue.

Upon the final bell all in attendance agreed Griffo was the clear winner. All except Maxwell Moore, a close friend of McAuliffe's, who just happened to be the referee. Moore announced McAuliffe as the winner and then quickly escaped the building as the crowd turned ugly.

After the fight, Moore claimed he had erred in counting the points, admitting Griffo should have won. But it was too late. Young Griffo had officially lost his first professional fight.

FREE MONEY

Shane Warne was in his natural habitat: a casino. That night the roulette wheel had not been kind and he was on his way to losing US$5000. As he sat there watching the money pour down the drain, Mark Waugh approached and introduced his new friend John.

The trio chatted away. John mentioned that he was a big fan of Warne's and that over the years he'd won a lot of money betting on him. Warne felt comfortable enough with John to visit him in his hotel room the following day. Nothing strange about that; who among us hasn't visited a man, who we know only as John, in a hotel room the day after meeting him in a casino?

John proceeded to tell Warne again what a big fan he was and gave him US$5000 to cover his gambling missteps from the night before. Warne took the money, later explaining that he believed it came with 'no strings attached'.* He said that he didn't know John was involved in bookmaking or he wouldn't have taken the money. Rob O'Regan QC, who investigated the incident for the Australian Cricket Board (ACB), said Warne certainly did know at the time that John was a bookie.

Either way, Warne left John's hotel room with the US$5000 and promptly lost it all at the casino.

A FEW CALLS AND A PROBLEM

From that meeting in John's hotel room in September 1994 until February 1995, John called Shane Warne three times for information on weather, the state of the pitch and the make-up of

---

* Anytime someone says the phrase 'no strings attached', assume there are strings attached.

the Australian team. Warne, perhaps sensing this wasn't exactly a brilliant idea, responded in general terms, to the point where John stopped calling him.

Mark Waugh turned out to be a bit more useful, with John calling him ten times over that summer.[*]

It must have seemed fairly easy to both cricketers – a few phone calls, just providing information that wasn't too sensitive. But rumours had begun swirling about betting and match-fixing in the cricket world. Those pesky media types were starting to write stories about it.

In fact, behind the scenes, journalists were warning the ACB about rumours of players being involved with bookmakers. Like many organisations, the ACB only began worrying about something once it appeared the media was onto it, despite being vaguely aware of the issue a long time before journos.

More recently we've seen this in the painfully slow and awkward response Cricket Australia mounted to the ball-tampering scandal in South Africa.

Back in the nineties they decided they'd better find out what was going on before the media did. They started asking questions and pretty quickly unearthed Waugh and Warne's sub-optimal decision making. There was only one sensible thing to do in response: cover the whole thing up, obviously.

MORE CERTAINTY

Like any good businessperson, Mukesh Kumar Gupta knew that uncertainty was an impediment to growth. Uncertainty made planning and investment difficult. Even though he probably had more information on cricket than anyone else on the planet, it hardly made betting on the game risk free.

---

[*] Perhaps Mark was just lonely.

Leaving anything to chance is sloppy business practice, so the obvious next step for Gupta was to remove any doubt about the result of matches. In an orderly manner, he began organising the outcomes. This created the largest ever controversy in cricket and, indirectly, led the ACB to cover up Warne and Waugh's relationship with 'John'.

Gupta was hardly alone in fixing matches. By this point a network of bookies and big gamblers, mainly from India, were loosely working together to gather information and influence the outcomes of cricket matches. Gupta later claimed to have paid money to a wide range of cricketers, either for information or to influence matches, but his refusal to co-operate with any cricketing authority makes it difficult to substantiate many of those claims.

What is clear is that the operation was extensive. Many of Gupta's claims were proven to be true, including Warne and Waugh taking money, and most famously South African captain Hansie Cronje fixing matches, for which he was banned from cricket for life.

In 1994, in this hotbed of corruption, the Pakistani player Salim Malik approached Warne, Waugh and their teammate Tim May, asking them to throw matches. The three Australians refused and, despite Warne and Waugh having recently accepted money from 'John', decided to report him to the authorities.*

For Warne and Waugh, things had just become complicated.

SEVERAL BAD DECISIONS DESERVE SEVERAL MORE

There were two amazing things about the ACB's decision to cover up Waugh and Warne's indiscretions. The first, you'd have to say, was that they decided to cover it up at all. After all, they'd been

---

* In 2000, Malik received a life ban for fixing matches, although a Pakistani court overturned this ban in 2008 on a technicality. Doing the research for this book, what was surprising was not how often people get caught but how often they get off on a technicality.

THE PREPARED STATEMENT

There is no better way to show how sorry you are for your actions than to read a prepared statement written by a committee of lawyers and spin doctors.

The entire purpose of the prepared statement is to prevent the person doing the apologising from saying what they actually believe or doing any thinking. More often than not it finishes with 'I will not be making any further comments and I hope you respect my privacy at this difficult time.'

Imagine if in the middle of a fight with your partner, you read from a prepared statement and then announced you won't be taking any further questions.

tipped off about the rumours by journalists, which is hardly a good starting point for keeping something confidential.

The second amazing thing about the cover-up is that they actually managed to keep the incidents quiet until December 1998, almost three years later. When the ACB investigated the matter in 1995, Waugh and Warne quickly confessed, and each wrote a statement about what had gone on. Waugh was fined $10 000 and Warne $8000. That was it. No more was to be spoken of it, the ACB decided. They didn't even miss any matches.

Think about that for a second. They found out players had taken money from a bookie and as a punishment basically all they did was ask them to pay back the money, with a bit of interest.

Compare that to the sanctions handed out to David Warner, Steve Smith and Cameron Bancroft in 2018 for ball tampering – they were banned from international and domestic cricket for between nine and twelve months. Smith and Warner also lost Indian Premier League contracts worth millions of dollars.* It makes the

* For the full story on that, see page 188.

fines handed out to Warne and Waugh in 1995 seem even more ridiculous.

There were lots of reasons why the ACB decided to cover up the whole mess, but none of them were good or intelligent reasons. One was that the public pressure to suspend Warne and Waugh for a significant period of time would have been immense, and that would affect their chances of winning tests, the key criteria in all ACB decisions. Besides money, I mean.

Another reason for keeping the affair quiet was the rather awkward fact that Warne and Waugh had just reported Pakistani captain Salim Malik to the authorities for attempting to pay them to lose matches. The ACB thought the pair's credibility as witnesses in that case would be damaged if it was known they had taken money from arguably the biggest peddler of corruption in cricket, Mukesh Kumar Gupta.

It was potentially even worse than that too. Although the ACB didn't know it at the time, Gupta was paying Salim Malik to fix matches for him. While it's difficult to tell if Gupta was behind that particular approach from Malik to the Australians, it wouldn't have taken a genius to realise the cases might be linked. By covering up Warne and Waugh's involvement with Gupta, the ACB delayed the sport confronting the widespread corruption that had overtaken it.

In a pattern that repeated itself throughout Warne's career, what is astounding is that they all would have got away with it if not for those pesky journalists.

In 1998, in the middle of an Ashes series, Malcolm Conn, a journalist at *The Australian,* found out about the whole thing. When Conn told the new ACB CEO Malcolm Speed that he was going to publish the story, the ACB quickly released a statement about the fines, but they didn't name the players in question.

It was another strange way to manage an incident that had been terribly mismanaged from the start. The move won the ACB no favours in the media and Conn named the players the next day anyway, breaking the whole mess wide open and earning Conn a Walkley Award.

RAISE THE DRAWBRIDGE

Once the world knew Warne and Waugh had taken money from 'John' and that the ACB had tried to bury the whole affair, the saga moved from cover-up to damage control.

Damage control mainly involves minimising media access to those at the heart of the scandal and instead pushing out friendly voices to defend them. This isn't hard to do for Good Blokes, as the power of mateship, forged in the pressure cooker of competitive sport, means a group defence mechanism kicks in. It's like the herd surrounding a wounded member to shield them from the lions, except the lions are an angry public and the media, and the wounded animal is really well co-ordinated and rich.

In this case, the first step was to put Warne and Waugh in front of the media in the most controlled manner possible. This meant getting them to read from a prepared statement. In a room packed by media, they made the point that they hadn't fixed any matches, just provided 'innocent information' in return for money.

They both put this massive bit of misjudgement down to being 'naive and stupid', hardly an earth-shattering concession at this stage of proceedings.*

To top off the press conference, it was announced the pair wouldn't be taking questions. The journalists in attendance were irate, given the prepared statements gave such a flimsy explanation of events. Warne and Waugh's management must have concluded that no matter how angry it made journalists, this was far better

---

* I think they were arguing they were 'naive and stupid' only on this occasion, but a lot of people extrapolated it beyond that.

than letting their naive and stupid clients actually answer questions. This was probably not bad reasoning, but it did add to the sense that there was more to the story than what had been said.

The next step in the damage-control playbook is to get the defenders out there, and for Warne and Waugh it was an impressive list.

Tim May, who had reported Salim Malik with Waugh and Warne, was now head of the Australian Cricketers' Association, and he pledged the players the union's full support. He described them as 'outstanding servants of Australian cricket', which is an odd thing to say about two cricketers who took money from the most corrupting influence in cricket.

Some fine upstanding members of the cricket fraternity stood by Warne and Waugh. Former captain Allan Border defended them and Richie Benaud, the doyen of cricket commentary, also down-played the incident. Even Don Bradman, the greatest cricketer of all time, said Warne was one of the best influences on the game and that the scandal did not change that.

Yet the media was not so easily won over by this full-throated defence from the old-boy's network. In an editorial in *The Weekend Australian*, Warwick Hadfield and Brian Woodley offered wise counsel: 'Warne is in need of some good advice, but not from business managers and PR folk too happy to tell him how wonderful he is in order to flog a few more videos, books, pairs of duds, sports shoes or anti-smoking ads.'

Warne's coterie of yes-people was not moved. The sense that he had not done anything that serious was only reinforced. Warne later said he only gave John the sort of information he'd also give to any journalists. If that was the case, he should have stopped to think about why John was happy to pay him for such readily available information.

Years later, in an interview with Michael Parkinson – which Warne co-produced – he made a series of statements playing down the affair and directly contradicting statements he'd made to the ACB's independent investigation into the scandal.

While spin bowling came to Warne with superhuman ease, accepting responsibility for his rather regular stuff-ups would prove a herculean task.

EVERYONE GETS AWAY WITH IT

Sometimes all the spin doctoring in the world can't protect you. Mark Waugh had to play a few days after the story broke and, as he walked onto the field to bat, the Australian crowd responded with white hot anger. It was the sort of hostility usually only seen at a family Christmas. As for Warne, with the luck that seems to cling to him just as tightly as controversy, he was injured and unable to play in that match, so avoided the wrath of the public.[*]

The tough times ended there for Waugh. He stayed in the national team for almost another four years, became a highly paid commentator for the Big Bash League and was until recently a national selector for the Australian cricket team. Truly a cautionary tale for any player thinking of taking money from a bookmaker.

Cricket Australia missed an opportunity to teach its players right from wrong, to show that there would be consequences for actions. The fact that they didn't set the tone for years to come, with the 2018 ball-tampering scandal the nadir of that legacy.

As for Gupta, he later confessed his role in a range of match-fixing operations to India's Central Bureau of Investigation. This blew the lid off the corruption endemic in international cricket, but Gupta refused to co-operate with any cricket authorities in helping them prosecute or investigate the cricketers involved. Meaning we

---

[*] As Warne watched Waugh walk out to that reception, he may well have thought that he couldn't afford any more scandals, but it turns out he could.

don't know the true extent of the corruption, and it would appear there are cricketers who were complicit who got off scot-free.

In 2011, the Delhi High Court dropped the match-fixing criminal proceedings against Gupta. The man who had engineered cricket's biggest ever scandal, known as John to his close friends, walked away from it all a free man.

THE PEAK OF HIS POWERS

Despite suffering his first loss, Griffo was still a superstar, both in America and back at home. Promoters were eager to book him and he was making good money, although he couldn't count and was regularly taken advantage of financially. His habit of regularly shouting the bar didn't help. He burnt through cash at an astounding rate.

In 1894 and 1895 Griffo took on world featherweight and bantamweight champion George Dixon in three epic bouts.

Dixon, a black Canadian boxer, was later named by *The Ring* as the greatest featherweight of all time. Born in Nova Scotia, he was the first black boxer to hold a world championship belt. When he defeated a white boxer in front of a predominantly white crowd riots often broke out, not an uncommon occurrence at the time for black boxers.

Dixon was hailed as one of the pioneers of 'scientific boxing', the careful study of an opponent and a disciplined style in the ring. He trained extensively, unlike Griffo, and was said to have invented shadow-boxing as a training exercise.

Despite Griffo's alternative training regime of late nights, heavy drinking and more heavy drinking, he fought the best boxer in the world to a standstill in each fight. *The Brooklyn Daily Eagle* described their first fight as a 'battle that bristled throughout with glittering skill and generalship' and twenty years later *The Washington Post* described their second fight as 'an encounter

AN OUTLIER

Boxer Anthony Mundine is one sportsman who doesn't receive much forgiveness. In a controversial career, he's said some interesting things.

He claimed homosexuality and Indigenous culture were incompatible, posting on Facebook: 'Watching redfern now [the TV Show] & they promoting homosexuality! (Like it's ok in our culture) that ain't in our culture & our ancestors would have there [sic] head for it! Like my dad told me GOD made ADAM & EVE not Adam & Steve.'

It was pointed out to Mundine that Adam and Eve are not really compatible with Indigenous culture. Since then Mundine has converted to Islam – a key part of Dreamtime, I assume.

On the 9/11 terrorist attacks, he said: 'They call it an act of terrorism, but if you can understand religion, and our way of life, it's not about terrorism. It's about fighting for God's law, and America's brought it upon themselves.'

On Cathy Freeman: 'Cathy Freeman. She sold out, toeing the line. And that ain't me. I'm not a fake' and 'As far as being a leader, that's not her anyway, a man can only lead.'

Statements like these, and constant claims to be one of the greatest athletes of all time, mean the majority of the sporting public show Mundine outright hostility. It seems defeating a few plumbers in the ring doesn't get you the respect you deserve.

between two boys who have certainly never been excelled, and probably never equaled'.

Perhaps one of the reasons Young Griffo was able to last the whole twenty-five rounds of that second fight was that his manager, Hughey Behan, organised for him to be jailed before the bout to ensure he would be sober in the lead-up. I think this is a tactic many modern-day coaches could use to great effect.

In later years, George Dixon also succumbed to alcoholism, which was not an uncommon outcome in those days. Boxers fought hundreds of long fights in their careers, with little or no concern for the damage they were doing to themselves.

Less than a month after his third fight with Dixon, Griffo took on Joe Gans in the African-American's home town of Baltimore. Gans went on to be rated the greatest lightweight boxer of all time; today there's a bronze statue of him in Madison Square Garden. Yet against Griffo, Gans could only manage a draw, in what was seen as a lacklustre match by both boxers.

Gans and Griffo fought again in 1897, but a lot happened in the intervening two years. Young Griffo descended into a downward spiral that was astounding even in the tumultuous world of sport.

DESCENT

Griffo's alcoholism hadn't significantly hurt his boxing career up until this point, although it's stunning to think how good he might have been if he'd trained and been sober. But in 1896, the wheels really started to come off outside the ring.

In April, Griffo was drinking at a casino on Long Island, which he frequented regularly. A few drinks had become a lot and he assaulted a town official, William Connors, resulting in his arrest. Of course he was quickly released, because he already had a fight scheduled, which he subsequently lost. Even back then, the courts had their priorities right.

But just two months later, Griffo was arrested again, this time for driving intoxicated and behaving in a disorderly manner. In this instance the judge decided twenty-five days in prison would sort Griffo out. It didn't.

In fact, Griffo already had another court date in the diary, for a sexual assault he'd committed on an eleven-year-old boy in Brooklyn back in 1895.

This time, Albert was not shown any leniency for his boxing prowess. He pleaded guilty and was sentenced to a year in prison.

Up until this point, Albert's antics had been seen as mainly self-harming. But surely this was a step too far, even for the sports world.

Thankfully, upon his release, boxing promoters turned Albert away, announcing they would prefer to send a strong message about sexually assaulting children than make money.*

The year in jail may have done Griffiths some good physically, in that at least he dried out a bit. In 1897 he managed a fifteen-round draw in a rematch with Joe Gans, and the fight was considered another classic. Despite all his problems, it seemed that Young Griffo could still match it with the best in the world in the ring.

Griffo had now entered a familiar routine. A month after the Gans fight, he was arrested in St Louis for vagrancy, after several nights of drinking. Once again, he was released from jail for a fight.

But the drinking was now starting to impact Griffo's boxing. While being drunk in the ring was hardly new for Griffo, in a fight against Tom Tracey he rolled out of the ring in the first round and walked away. The fight was judged a no contest. It emerged that, on his way to the fight, the car Griffo was travelling in had been cleaned up by a streetcar. Despite injuring his shoulder in the crash, Griffo had shown up to the fight, albeit only briefly.

TRAGEDY

In 1898 Griffo fought Joseph Devitt, who went by the name 'Bull' McCarthy. The fight was the third meeting between the two and while McCarthy presented Griffo with a challenge, it was nothing the Australian couldn't handle. In the twentieth round, Griffo won by knockout.

McCarthy, however, didn't get up. He was rushed to hospital but died later that night, as a result of brain concussion.

---

* Well, not really; they loaded him up with fights soon after his release and showed not the slightest concern at all. One would like to think this wouldn't be the case these days, but it's jarring to think someone could be so quickly forgiven for something like that, even back then.

Griffo took the news hard. He proceeded to drink himself silly and was then taken into custody on charges of manslaughter. At the bail hearing he was described as 'helplessly intoxicated' but the judge ruled the death was not malicious and that McCarthy's death was the result of an 'accident in a friendly contest'.

Griffo never recovered mentally from McCarthy's death. He continued to fight, but only because it was the only way he could make money to fund his drinking.

A few months later Griffo was found running naked down a major street in Chicago. He assaulted three police officers as they made the arrest. His relationship with the Chicago police force already strained, a few months later he tussled with an officer who was throwing his mate out of a pub at two in the morning.

When he was brought before the court, one officer testified to finding Griffo in a saloon jumping over tables, talking to himself and fighting imaginary foes. At the detention hospital where he was being held he began every morning by shouting a list of names. 'They are the names of horses at the track,' Griffo explained. 'I win money on them.'

The doctors at the hospital declared him insane and the Chicago judge sentenced him to time in an asylum. When the sentence was read out, Griffo attacked the judge.

EXPENSIVE SHERRY

Albert Griffiths took up residence in the Cook County Insane Asylum in Dunning, Chicago. In 1899, it housed over a thousand people, made up of those deemed insane, drunkards or sometimes just poor.

The boxing world had not forgotten Griffo, though. A boxing manager by the name of George Dawson visited Griffo and was surprised to find him coherent and keen to get out of the asylum. Griffo had a simple message for Dawson: 'For Heaven's sake, get me out of here.* I'm not crazy but I will be if I'm kept here with this mob of lunatics much longer.'

Moving heaven and earth and pulling in many favours, in 1900 Dawson managed to get the state to agree to release Griffo, provided he stumped up $3000 as an indemnity against any damage he might do in the community. Dawson set about putting in place a series of exhibition fights that would see Griffo earn enough money to get him back on his feet and then some.

His opponents were carefully chosen and by no means difficult for a fighter of Griffo's standard. Nonetheless, these fights showed Griffo, now sober, was still one of the best boxers in the world. Boxing venues around the country fell over themselves trying to book him. So lucrative was this comeback, even boxers holding championship belts struggled to match Griffo's popularity and earnings.

Part of this run of fights included a third bout against Joe Gans. Up against a boxer at the peak of his powers, it was clear that the years of alcohol abuse had caught up with Griffo. He went down in the eighth round.

Despite the loss, his indiscretions and his criminal record, which included the sexual assault of a child, Griffo's popularity with fans knew no bounds. Over the next year Dawson, now Griffo's manager, arranged $10000 worth of exhibition fights, a huge sum. John Whitbeck, a Chicago restaurateur and a friend of Dawson's, described the fights as 'not hard matches but easy exhibitions with a sparring partner and guaranteed purses ranging from $300 to $1000'.

Dawson, who was keeping a close eye on Griffo, introduced him to polite society and kept him away from his old haunts. Not surprisingly, Griffo found this life constricting. One night before the string of lucrative fights kicked off, an old friend convinced him to

---

* Surely a TV show called *I'm a Celebrity . . . Get Me Out of This Insane Asylum* is not far away.

partake in a glass of sherry. Suddenly Griffo was gone, disappearing back into his old ways.

Years later, Whitbeck recounted how some 'fool friend of Griffo's insisted on him taking a glass of sherry and it was all off'.

> All the sporting fraternity knows how he went to pieces and how Dawson, in disgust, had to cancel all the $10 000 worth of engagements. No pugilist, aside from a heavyweight champion, had such an opportunity to reap such a golden harvest. Those $10 000 engagements were only a beginning. If he had kept sober, Griffo could have virtually coined money for two or three years to come.

Dawson, who had done so much to walk Griffo back from the brink, was heartbroken. He told a friend that giving money to Griffo was as good as throwing it in the sewer.

Whitbeck was harsher in his assessment. 'Young Griffo is a degenerate of the worst type. It is absolutely impossible to keep him in respectable condition. Given five hundred dollars tonight, he will be broke tomorrow, and no inducement, not even the guarantee of $10 000 for twenty minutes' work with the gloves, would make him forego a drinking bout with the lowest of levee characters.'

THE FINAL BELL

With Dawson no longer around to manage him, Griffo kept fighting, but in less lucrative bouts, and continued getting into trouble. In September 1901, he was arrested for armed robbery and the following year he served time at the Bridewell Prison Farm in Chicago. He escaped imprisonment at the farm, only to be found in a nearby vacant lot, freezing, his hands so cold there was real fear he could lose them to frostbite.

Over the next few years he was sent either to the Cook County Insane Asylum or the prison farm for a variety of minor charges. In between some of these stints he would fight to earn a bit of money. Around this time he was instructed to retire from boxing due to a 'valvular affection of the heart that may bring death to him in the ring at any time'. Unsurprisingly, Griffo ignored this advice.

Fighting off and on, he still managed to mix it with some top fighters, but the combination of alcohol, hard living and more than 200 fights was starting to take its toll. In 1904, in Chicago, Griffo had his last ever fight. Squaring up against Tommy White, it was soon obvious to onlookers that, at thirty-three, Griffo had kept boxing well past his use-by date. The same realisation obviously came over Griffo – before the first round was over, he simply gave up and left the ring, never to return.

DOWN FOR THE COUNT

No longer able to box, Griffo bounced around various asylums and poorhouses, occasionally being arrested for begging.

He spent most of the last fifteen years of his life outside New York's Rialto Theatre, on Broadway, where the wife of a former opponent allowed him to beg.

Friends occasionally organised benefits for him, but he was too hard to pin down. Relatives in Australia tried to have him arrested to save him from himself, and get him off the booze, but with no success. On 7 December 1927 he was found dead in the boarding house he was staying in on New York's West Side. He had passed away from heart disease at the age of fifty-six.

Griffo had no descendants and a local boxing promoter covered the costs of his funeral, which was attended by many old boxers.

JUST HOW GOOD?

Newspapers across the United States and Australia ran articles about Griffo's death. For his contemporaries, there was no doubt Griffo was a boxer of unique ability.

While it's hard to have much faith in the accuracy of the records of the time, it appears that out of 232 fights, Young Griffo only lost nine. Back then, many of the fights officially ended in a draw if both boxers were still standing at the end, even if one of them had been awarded more points by the judges.

Ring magazine founder Nat Fleischer said, 'Griffo was the greatest ever boxer I have seen in over fifty years of watching fights and fighters.'

Perhaps the highest praise came from the dominant boxer in Griffo's weight division, 'The Old Master' Joe Gans, who had fought Griffo three times. Recounting their first fight, Gans said, 'I trained for three weeks for the bout, and when I got a flash at Griffo in his corner I noticed that a fold of fat wobbled over his belt. He was in fit condition for a sanatorium instead of a prize ring.

'You would naturally think that a man in his condition would steer away from a punch, but he crowded me from the first tap of the gong. He clearly outboxed me. It's a pity that a boxer of his talent never took care of himself, as he was the greatest defensive boxer that ever lived.'

Young Griffo was very much a sportsman of his time. He never ran out of forgiveness, even the sexual assault of a child was glossed over – or perhaps fans just didn't know – but ultimately he ran out of money, something the champions of today have a better chance of avoiding.

A TROUBLESOME DOUBLE CHIN

Shane Warne sat at the hastily arranged media conference on the eve of the 2003 ODI World Cup in South Africa. The room was full to capacity as the world's cricket media buzzed with anticipation. Surely the rumours couldn't be true?

Just three years earlier the spin bowler, a genius on the field, who made the cricket ball defy physics, had been named as one of Wisden's five cricketers of the century. For cricket fans the *Wisden Cricketers' Almanack* is the closest thing to holy scripture, so naming Warne on this list meant he had been anointed a cricketing saint.

As Warne began the media conference in South Africa, this towering reputation appeared to be about to collapse. He was about to announce he had just tested positive to a banned substance. Surely there'd be no coming back from this.

Yet nothing was ever sure with Warne. He had form with scandal, and he had even better form with always bouncing back. He'd faced many personal challenges in his career but, unlike Griffo, he had the money and friends in the media to see him through.

While Warne had avoided a significant suspension during the John the Bookmaker affair, he was not so lucky when he returned a positive drug test. Although the routine test had been conducted a few weeks earlier, the results came in just before Australia's first game in the World Cup.

Warne had tested positive for a diuretic called Moduretic, a prescription drug used in treating high blood pressure and fluid retention. Why would someone take such a thing when it's not prescribed to them? In Warne's version of events, it was given to him by his mum to get rid of a double chin he'd developed after a few too many late nights and bottles of wine.

The idea was that the diuretic would help with fluid loss, effectively allowing Warne to lose weight faster. Future events would display Warne's obsession with his own appearance and made this excuse eminently believable.

However, others* might argue that diuretics are often used by drug cheats to get traces of performance-enhancing drugs or steroids

---

* By 'others', I mean cricket fans in every country but Australia. It's amazing how un-Australian people who aren't Australian sometimes are.

out of their system as quickly as possible. The rapid fluid loss they induce effectively flushes any evidence of doping from the body.

In Warne's case, the cynic's argument was that he was recovering from a shoulder injury at the time and, because certain banned substances can speed up healing, he had a motive for taking a diuretic besides dealing with his double chin.

Warne's response to the positive test was strange in its inconsistency, to say the least. At first, he claimed publicly that this was the only time he'd ever taken a diuretic, even threatening to sue one media outlet who reported he'd done it before. But a week later, when he fronted an ACB hearing, he admitted he had taken Moduretic more than once.

In fact, Warne's entire performance at the ACB hearing was shambolic. He made a big deal of the fact that he'd never read the anti-doping code but this ignorance-is-bliss defence wasn't given much weight. While everyone readily accepted the claim that he hadn't bothered to read the code, they didn't accept it as an excuse.

Warne also tried a variant of the dog-ate-my-homework defence, claiming the Moduretic packaging was torn and he couldn't read the ingredients. It was a strange argument, given he'd admitted he didn't know what substances were banned.

The ACB inquiry was not impressed. 'Much of Warne's evidence on these issues was unsatisfactory and the committee does not accept he was entirely truthful in his responses to questions about his knowledge of the ACB anti-doping policy. Coupled with that is his vague, unsatisfactory and inconsistent evidence about the extent of using a Moduretic.'

Warne was found guilty and given a twelve-month ban. Even here he was lucky – the prescribed penalty for such a breach was two years.

Despite the lenient suspension, the whole affair is instructive in how the old-boys' network still comes to the fore when one of their own is in trouble. It also showed once again how accepting responsibility seems to be something Good Blokes have trouble doing.* Warne responded to the finding by claiming he was 'a victim of the anti-doping hysteria [...] a 12-month suspension is a very harsh penalty for not checking what I took with anyone'.

While Warne had received significant support from teammates following the John the Bookmaker controversy, this time the bonds of mateship were stretched.

Glenn McGrath wrote, 'As much as the boys are right behind Warney 100 per cent, for someone of his experience, he should have known the risks [...] Shane has brought this on himself.' Captain Ricky Ponting was blunter, stating that professional sportspeople needed to check everything before taking it. 'For Warnie, who's been playing international cricket for a decade, to ignore that approach is madness.'

Dick Pound, who was president of the World Anti-Doping Agency at the time, slammed Warne's 'I didn't know' approach, saying, 'You cannot have an IQ over room temperature and be unaware of this as an international athlete.'

In saying this, Pound had unintentionally identified one of the core reasons Warne manages to repeatedly come back from such incidents: people figure he was simply acting out of stupidity, not cheating or operating in a Machiavellian manner.**

In fact, Warne seemed to endorse this view, saying of the drug controversy, 'Whether you hate me, you like me, you love the way I play or whatever, the facts of the matter are that I don't read much, I don't take a lot of interest in the outside world . . . I just play cricket.'***

---

* This is a strange phenomenon. On the field, coaches and clubs insist on personal accountability as a key to success. But off the field, they consider it dispensable.

** I believe Niccolò Machiavelli played for Carlton in the seventies and was known for his devious tactics off the half-back flank.

*** Warne's insistence that he didn't pay much attention to anything beyond cricket was certainly confirmed when he questioned the theory of evolution, saying on *I'm a Celebrity . . . Get Me Out of Here!*, 'If we've evolved from monkeys, then why haven't those ones evolved? Because, I'm saying, aliens. We started from aliens.'

Much like the controversies early in Young Griffo's career, Warne is considered benign. Someone who's just not very well equipped to handle life off the pitch, naive rather than a cheat.

Contrast this to, say, cyclist Lance Armstrong's years-long doping. He's seen as a manipulator because not only did he know very well what he was doing, he was calculated in how he went about destroying the lives of people who accused him of wrongdoing.

While Warne's teammates offered some harsh feedback, he was hardly left out in the cold. Channel Nine quickly offered him a commentary role for the year he was suspended, quite an extraordinary thing to do on the face of it, given the suspension was for taking a banned substance.

After the suspension, Warne successfully returned to cricket. The idea that he was a well-meaning but error-prone good bloke had saved him again, and it saved him again even after his cricketing career ended.

AN UNSTEADY FOUNDATION

Much like Griffo, Warne's career always marched to the steady beat of scandals. While Warne had the benefit of money and post-retirement career options, he lives in a time of phones and cameras, invasive tabloid press and social media. Every misstep is captured.

From countless incidents of infidelity, an astounding number of erotic text messages becoming public, on-field clashes and getting caught smoking while being sponsored by Nicorette, Warne went through a lot.

His ability to rebound from those scandals was astonishing, but also somewhat understandable. Like Young Griffo before him, most thought he was a good bloke who liked a fun time but just couldn't manage his impulses, someone whose judgement was as terrible as his sporting talent was extraordinary.

The perception was that there was nothing malicious about Warne. That more often than not his troubles ended up hurting him more than anyone else. But when you start having to use a spreadsheet to keep track of your self-inflicted scandals, it could be argued there's a pattern there that can't simply be explained away as 'not being a details person'.

At some point, we all have to take responsibility for the detail.* Warne's most recent scandal showed he hasn't learnt a thing from his past mistakes. And once again, it was those pesky journalists who caused everything to come crashing down.

In 2011, Fairfax Media's *The Sunday Age* started poking around the Shane Warne Foundation, which raised funds 'to help enrich the lives of seriously ill and underprivileged children and teenagers in Australia'. What they discovered was that Warne's foundation didn't publish any accounts.

To get a better sense of the landscape, Fairfax examined how the charities of seven prominent sporting figures were managed. It turned out none of them published annual reports on their websites but, in response to Fairfax, many offered financial statements to show how they raised and spent money.

Two things probably piqued Fairfax's interest in Warne's charity. The refusal to offer any detailed financial statements and that its CEO was Shane Warne's brother, Jason, who refused to disclose his own salary. It was later revealed to be $80 000 a year. Not excessive for the CEO of a charity, but it smacked of nepotism.

Perhaps if Warne's foundation had been more forthcoming the journalists would have moved on. But the lack of transparency and the fierceness with which the foundation tried to block the release of any financial reporting only fuelled their interest.

The original 2011 article had attracted little public interest,

---

* Try the 'I'm not a details person' defence on the Australian Tax Office and see how you go.

but behind the scenes the battle for the foundation's financial records continue to be fought as hard as many of the Tests Warne played in. In September 2015, *The Sunday Age* attempted to get access to the foundation's reports through a disclosure provision in Victoria's *Fundraising Act 1998*. This could not have come at a worse time for Warne as the state regulator for charities, Consumer Affairs Victoria (CAV), had started doing their own digging just a few months earlier.

In a last-ditch attempt to hold off Fairfax, the foundation attempted to get the Australian Charities and Not-for-profits Commission (ACNC) to use its powers to declare the foundation's financial records confidential. This is usually invoked by charities that deal with sensitive issues like family violence, which the Shane Warne Foundation did not.

While the ACNC considered this, the Fairfax request under the Fundraising Act had given the foundation just twenty-one days to disclose its annual reports or it would be in breach of the law. The clock was ticking and the ACNC would not decide in time.

The foundation decided to provide *The Sunday Age* with some reports and asked for more time to disclose the full range of documents. Then, in an amazing coincidence, *The Sunday Age*'s major competition, Melbourne's *Herald Sun*, was given an exclusive story in which the foundation explained it had some cash-flow issues and high costs but had a detailed plan to sort it all out.

The next day *The Sunday Age* went ahead and published what they had anyway, revealing that, between 2011 and 2013, from every dollar raised the Shane Warne Foundation had only distributed 16 cents to beneficiaries. On top of that, it was revealed the foundation was renting office space in a building owned by Warne's parents. Further details showed the foundation had also struggled in 2014–15, with only 24 cents in every dollar raised making it to beneficiaries.

Warne's response to these revelations followed the same script as the bookmaker and drug scandals. He attacked those who criticised him, contradicted events that had clearly been proven to have happened and took no personal responsibility.

Appearing on Channel Ten's *The Project*, Warne told critics, 'You can all get stuffed if you want to have a go at us for it but we are very proud of what we have been able to achieve.'

Following the *Sunday Age* story, Warne told the *Herald Sun*, 'We have no problems with anyone going through our books at any stage.'

Taking him at his word, Consumer Affairs Victoria appointed KPMG to do an independent audit of the foundation. The audit only looked at whether it had complied with sections of the Fundraising Act pertaining to reporting requirements and appropriate internal controls. The findings showed that Warne's foundation failed at both.

So poor was the record keeping that the audit found it was possible 'fraud, error or non-compliance may occur and not be detected'.* KPMG also concluded that it could not determine if the foundation had 'completely recorded' the amount of cash it had received since 1 July 2012, although Warne would have had nothing to do with that.

To be fair, Warne's foundation was not alone in discovering that their way of raising money was difficult – holding big glitzy events and gala dinners means high costs that eat into the donations they generate. In recent years, many charities have moved away from that model for precisely this reason.

It's hardly a hangable offence to admit your charity's fundraising model isn't working. The ACNC itself has stated 'having higher administration costs does not necessarily indicate that a charity is ineffective and poorly run'. Perhaps if the foundation had admitted

---

* Good news for everyone who hates paperwork: avoiding it may help protect you in the future.

these problems earlier, it may have avoided the public-relations firestorm that eventually came its way.

Warne claimed it was all a witch-hunt. He announced he would be shutting the foundation, portraying the decision as down to him being tired of the 'unwarranted speculation'.

CAV director Simon Cohen, however, characterised the decision differently. He said he'd considered deregistering the foundation but found it to be unnecessary after the foundation gave an undertaking to CAV that it would wind up as soon as possible.

But Warne's draw as a sports superstar meant the media reported the outcome very favourably, with the *Herald Sun* running the headline 'Shane Warne Foundation cleared of wrong-doing'.

Warne's reaction to this debacle – like the drug and bookmaking affairs before it – underlines how sport stars tend to believe they are above scrutiny. Scrutiny that would be considered normal for anyone else for them takes on the proportions of a 'witch-hunt'.

Warne's decision to set up a charity, with good intentions, doesn't absolve him from the responsibility of running that charity properly. He appointed his brother as CEO and located the office in a building his parents owned; it doesn't take an overpaid communications consultant to see that wasn't a good look, even if there was no intent to deceive.

Warne just seemed upset he was being questioned at all. He never seemed to understand that when you're raising money for charity people expect a high level of transparency. The fact that your overall aims might be incredibly worthy has no bearing. No charity is above that.

It was the same with the drug scandal a decade earlier. The banned substances list is there for a reason and no one is above following those rules, nor should they be.

Warne, despite this trifecta of major scandals – which would clean bowl anyone else – still occupies the crease as an Australian

IT'S A WITCH-HUNT!

If you find yourself in a bit of trouble, a fun thing to do is claim anyone asking reasonable questions is on a 'witch-hunt'. This is the equivalent of playing the man not the ball.

It's a proud tradition and one Lance Armstrong used a lot before finally admitting to the doping that saw him stripped of seven Tour de France titles. Before he conceded everything people were saying about him was true, he said, 'Over the past three years, I have been subjected to a two-year federal criminal investigation followed by Travis Tygart's unconstitutional witch hunt.'

Cricket Australia Chairman David Peever did the same after the ball-tampering scandal, saying, 'Circumstances like this are not the time for witch-hunts.'

Perhaps the master of the witch-hunt is News Limited columnist Andrew Bolt. He claimed the AFL's finding of bringing the game into disrepute against the Essendon Football Club was 'a kind of witch-hunt justice'. He also said of Israel Folau being criticised for homophobic comments: 'Everything about this "scandal" smells of a witch-hunt by hypocrites.'

National Treasure and Fox Sports commentator, after years at Channel Nine. Because he's 'Warnie', and stuffing up is part of his brand.

THE INEVITABLE COMEBACK

While Young Griffo's alcoholism and descent into regular incarceration was enabled by managers, promoters, venues and fans forgiving him time and time again, his post-fighting career was particularly bleak.

After retiring Griffo ended up begging and living in poorhouses because in the earliest years of the twentieth century there was no TV commentary career to take up, no deodorants or pointless vitamin supplements to endorse, and very few jobs in the boxing industry at large.

His modern-day equivalents have more options, and because their stardom has currency beyond their sporting careers they are often forgiven for misdeeds even well after they retire.

Former footballer Ben Cousins' life has had a trajectory very similar to Griffiths'. They both performed at the highest level before substance addiction ruined their lives.

Cousins played 270 games for the West Coast Eagles and Richmond, winning the Brownlow Medal and a premiership with the Eagles. Journalist Mike Sheahan named him as one of his top fifty players of all time.

Like Griffo, Cousins served time in prison – in 2017 he was sentenced to twelve months for drug possession and breaching a violence restraining order relating to his ex-partner. He served ten months of his sentence in Perth's Acacia Prison before being released, in part because the Eagles gave him a job in their community and game development department.

Many saw that as his former club trying to make good for not providing more support when Cousins was playing for them, although you could argue that a place that failed him so badly is not the ideal environment for recovery. His time there did not last long.

Young Griffo never had opportunities for recovery like that after he retired. In some ways it's a welcome development that there's now a support network for ex-athletes, but equally the fact that the various codes always seem willing to take someone back, no matter what, sends the broader message that the actions of their stars don't have real or long-term consequences.

Does someone with Cousins' history of stalking their partner* really deserve another chance with the same employer? No other industry so eagerly awaits the moment a disgraced member is

---

* Despite the restraining order he attempted to contact her over 2000 times. Two thousand times is a lot.

DEFENDING THE GOOD BLOKES

[Coach, teammate, close friend, sibling] says [player's name] is a 'ripper bloke' despite [punching someone, urinating in public, using social media inappropriately, trafficking drugs].

'Sure, he's done something here that's reprehensible but he's just a loveable larrikin when you get to know him,' says [coach, teammate, close friend, sibling]. 'What people don't see is that when he's not [belting people, abusing teammates, hanging out with gangland figures, sexually assaulting someone], he's great fun to get drunk with.'

allowed back into the fold, with the possible exception of the entertainment media.

With big names – like cricket's David Warner, the AFL's James Hird and Brendan Fevola, the NRL's Andrew and Matthew Johns, and swimming star Grant Hackett – there never seems to be any doubt they'll be allowed to return. The talk in the media moves quickly from being about the scandal itself to when would be an appropriate time for the sport to welcome them back.

All of those players have been involved in incidents that would make them unemployable in almost all industries, yet almost all of them are either thriving in high-profile media roles or on the pathway to redemption.

BAD GOOD BLOKES

Shane Warne's ability to bounce back from scandal is astounding, but at least it sort of makes sense. There are other Good Blokes who have received forgiveness in ways that defy comprehension.

There wouldn't be too many of us who can say, hand on heart, that we haven't tried to headbutt our way out of the back of a police car while handcuffed at least once in our life. But we probably have little else in common with North Melbourne great Wayne Carey.

Carey is arguably the AFL's greatest ever player, winning two premierships and being named All Australian seven times, but he's best known for sleeping with the wife of his teammate and best friend. Even people with no interest in the AFL have heard that story.

Is sleeping with your best friend's wife an unforgivable offence?* In many ways, for Carey it's been the hardest thing to find forgiveness for. If you consider all the other things he's done, that's astounding. I'm not saying sleeping with your best friend's wife is a small thing; I imagine if you're one of the people involved it's a fairly intense experience. But considering Carey has resisted arrest in both the US and in Australia, and was found to have traces of cocaine on his clothes when entering Barwon Prison to mentor Indigenous inmates (although he denied having used it), it's amazing that sleeping with someone else's wife is the thing that stands out in the public's memory.

His history with women is even worse than his history with law enforcement. He once grabbed a woman's breast in the street as she passed and artfully posed the question, 'Why don't you get a bigger pair of tits?'

In 2007, Kate Neilson, Carey's girlfriend at the time, reported to Miami police that he hit her in the face with a wine glass, cutting both her neck and mouth. Carey later claimed he intended to throw the glass over Neilson's head and didn't mean to make contact with her. We've all done that, accidentally glassed someone. With co-ordination that bad, it's amazing he was such a good footballer! Poor old clumsy Wayne.

When the Miami police arrived at his hotel room, Carey was not thrilled to see them, given it was just a common slip with a wine glass. He kicked a female officer in the mouth and elbowed another in the face, presumably in a clumsy attempt to submit to the arrest.

---

* Former AFL player Garry Lyon certainly felt the public opprobrium of this crime, when it was revealed he was in a relationship with the wife of Billy Brownless, his best mate. This led to Brownless saying, 'It's just wrong, mate – you don't touch a man's wallet, you don't touch his wife.' I'm no expert on either, but there do seem to be a few differences between a wallet and a wife. Still, best to avoid touching both.

Lieutenant Bill Schwartz of the Miami Police Department told *The Age* that once handcuffed and finally placed in the police car, Carey 'used his head as a battering ram and tried to smash a hole between the front compartment of the police car and the prisoner compartment'.

Carey was convicted for assaulting the officer, but Neilson didn't press charges of her own.

With this incident following a string of problems, Carey was dropped from Channel Nine's *Footy Classified* and a range of other media gigs. Many thought that was the death of Carey's media career. And maybe it would have been if Carey had been a fringe player. But being one of the greatest players ever makes Carey a star, and stars exert their own gravitational pull – a pull that media companies can't resist.

In 2010, the AFL signalled that Carey was being brought in from the cold, inducting him into the Australian Football Hall of Fame. Carey was no longer radioactive and the opportunities came quickly. Soon he was back on Triple M radio, he joined Channel Seven's matchday commentary team and *Talking Footy*, and he began writing for *The Age*.

Although it followed the familiar pattern of forgiving the Good Blokes, Carey's case is notable for a few reasons. How much do we take into account a person's upbringing, or alcohol and drug dependencies? Carey certainly had a tough upbringing, his father was in and out of prison and a violent man at home, and he has openly discussed his problems with alcohol and cocaine in the media.

But the legal system doesn't take these things into account when it comes to serious crimes. You can be empathetic towards someone struggling with substance abuse or having a terrible childhood, but it doesn't lessen the crime or its impact on victims, and so it shouldn't lessen the consequences.

Theories of justice are helpful here.* There are many different ones, but most break down the aims of punishment into three areas.

The first is to remove someone from the community for the public's safety if deemed necessary. Hence sending someone to prison or short-term stays in police cells. This is about keeping someone locked away until they are no longer a threat, so it could be just a few hours while they sober up or, in extreme cases, for decades.

The second aim is to impress upon the offender that society disapproves of what they did and, in so doing, show the community that justice has been done, that punishment has occurred. This also serves to send a message of deterrence to others. These days, things like community service, fines and prison have replaced more draconian measures.**

The final area of punishment – and a more modern addition – is rehabilitation. Trying to change the person so they're safe to re-enter the community.

In a simple sense, Carey or any other Wayward Champion could be judged against these three elements. Have all these things happened? If so, it would be unfair to punish them further.

But the celebrity factor introduces complexity. The fact is that these people are returning to privileged positions in their community. Being handed a platform of huge influence sends a message that is not necessarily linked to forgiveness, it's a separate issue.

Being found guilty of some crimes disqualifies you from certain jobs – it's part of the punishment. Company directors can be banned from being directors, even if the rest of their freedoms are restored; lawyers can be disbarred and doctors can lose their right to practise. All because these are privileged positions.

---

* I'm aware introducing theories of justice in a book about sport is almost as bad as those early mentions of poetry.
** Tar and feathering was an example of this, it's both highly public and unpleasant. A bit like reality TV.

It seems in the sports world, though, people in privileged positions are held to a lower standard.

At the Cats vs Bulldogs match in July 2016, the AFL was hosting White Ribbon Night event dedicated to highlighting the scourge of violence against women: in Australia, one woman a week is murdered by her current or former partner. White Ribbon Night is an annual mass participation campaign to raise critical funds for family violence prevention programs.

As Channel Seven gave it their full 'we're doing lots for this issue' treatment on the night, there in the middle of the screen was Wayne Carey. To me it seems to lessen all the AFL has done to try to progress this issue. It makes you question the integrity of Channel Seven and *The Age*'s commitment to this.

The other component of Carey's case is whether he has been forgiven by the general public or just the boys' club of the football community and media. I'm yet to meet anyone who's forgotten or forgiven Carey for his extensive rap sheet.* At the end of every online article about him it said, 'Comments are not open on this article.' Presumably to stop the comments being filled with invective.

Do I blame Carey for taking the jobs he's been offered? Not really. But the fact that they were offered to him shows that for the people who run media outlets and sporting organisations what someone has done on the field is more important than what they do off it. This also seems to be more important than whatever support these organisations give to social issues.

This is the value of a stellar sporting career in Australia: it has the power to overcome the standards that other people are held to.

Wayward Champions still benefit from this. When news broke in April 2018 that the former Essendon champion Mark 'Bomber' Thompson had been charged with seven drug-related offences,

---

* This is based on my experience of talking with footy fans, which is extensive but hardly a scientific measure – it's more the vibe.

including trafficking and possession, the media focused on what a bad place he was in and how terribly sad it was.

This may well be true, but the same media are the first to demonise any other citizen when it comes to drug charges. Many of the same outlets campaign hard against safe injection rooms or any measures for dealing with drug addiction based around rehabilitation rather than criminalisation. Yet when it came to Thompson, empathy and concern for the enigmatic premiership captain and coach – a lauded risk-taker in a football sense – was the order of the day.

Bomber Thompson is just part of a long legacy of Wayward Champions, going back to Young Griffo and stretching through Shane Warne, Wayne Carey and countless others.

But to witness forgiveness on a massive scale, we need to head to the racetrack.

THE COLOURFUL RACING IDENTITY

Horseracing was the first sport to figure out that the sport itself isn't that important. It's the distractions around it that take centre stage and bring the punters.

These days, all the sporting codes are following this lead, making the matches shorter and increasing the opportunities for drinking and betting. The Big Bash League, Rugby Sevens, NRL 9s and AFLX are all attempts to provide as much distraction from the actual sport as possible. Who wants to watch sport when you can watch fireworks exploding next to poorly co-ordinated 'breakdance crews' while BMXs jump over them both?

However, racing still has them covered. The old saying 'I went to the races and didn't even see a horse' is as accurate as ever.* A trip to the races is made out to be glamourous, but really the attraction is the implicit permission to behave in ways that you wouldn't in normal society, and that's embraced by people who attend one day a year and those who are involved regularly.

I remember a friend telling me once that I had to watch the zombie show *The Walking Dead*. After I watched an episode, they

---

* Once I went to the races and only saw a police horse. Unfortunately, it also saw me. I was promptly arrested for not wearing a tie in the Chairman's Club. To this day I don't know how the police horse got in there, but the crime was serious enough for it to trample me.

asked if I was terrified. 'No,' I replied. 'I've been to Oaks Day, I've seen what the complete breakdown of society looks like.'

At the races everyone is drunk, and in the last few hours of the day all inhibitions are gone. I've seen people do all kinds of horrible things they would never do normally in public. Once – and I apologise for sharing this disturbing image with you – I saw a drunk bloke, right in front of everyone, wearing brown shoes with a dark suit. I mean, what makes a person do something like that?[*]

Racing has always had its 'colourful characters'. From its earliest days in Australia, horseracing has brought respectable society, celebrities, sporting stars and the criminal class together under the one lavishly themed corporate marquee, united in the opportunity to win big and to take risks.

For a long time, the racetrack was the only place you could place a bet in Australia. Off-track betting was not allowed and betting on other sports was illegal.[**] So the racetrack offered something that the other sports didn't, and the betting element attracted those from the shadier side of life.[***] And with that came the opportunity to launder cash and engineer results.

While our Wayward Champions have been forgiven for some pretty exciting stuff, it doesn't even come close to what the horseracing community will forgive. For an industry that revolves around betting – and therefore the need for people to believe in the integrity of the sport – an enormous amount of goodwill is shown towards those who manipulate or try to fix races.

Racing has always had a culture that encourages bad behaviour: the incentive of large windfalls of hard-to-trace cash and the

[*]   Poor breeding is the most obvious explanation.
[**] Unlike today, when you can bet on anything, all the time. I even know someone who used their phone to place bets while at a funeral. After losing a lot of money, they no longer had to fake being sad.
[***] It will be interesting to see how much other sports change as they excitedly embrace the cash brought in by gambling, and the trouble that follows. In this context, 'interesting' is code for 'worth sitting back and watching this unmitigated disaster unfold'.

heady mix of the respectable and the not-so-respectable has led to the emergence of the Colourful Racing Identity.

The phrase came to prominence in the late twentieth century. It's used to describe someone who frequents the races and is suspected to be up to something not exactly on the right side of legality, anywhere on the spectrum from 'slightly dodgy' to 'running an extensive criminal enterprise'. It's still popular with journalists today, who are worried that if they said 'massive criminal' they would be sued.[*]

Instead of treating those who are caught breaking the rules – or the law – as a threat to the industry, they are not only forgiven but often celebrated. Perhaps with so many questionable characters, and so many scandals, most people in racing have a vested interest in providing forgiveness. After all, who knows when they might need the same kindness extended to them?

A BROAD CHURCH

St Jude's Anglican Church at Randwick in Sydney was full to the brim for one of the most interesting funerals ever held there. It was 6 February 2018 and the mourners were assembled to farewell Jack 'The Bird' Sparrow, a legendary punter on Sydney's racing scene.

As Jack's son Adam put it on the day, his father had lived 'always on the fringes of controversy'.

'Fringes' might have been generous. Jack was banned from racecourses for a good chunk of the sixties, as he associated with some of the more criminally connected characters of the racing scene. These associations were certainly reflected by those in attendance at his funeral, with the Reverend Andrew Schmidt telling the assembled, 'This is my first colourful racing identity funeral.'

He was certainly not wrong about that. John 'Sheriff' Schreck, the Australian Jockey Club's chief steward in the eighties, said

---

[*] Australia has some of the toughest defamation laws in the world, which is why my lawyer has had three heart attacks. She is thirty-seven.

of racing: 'It is about the only business that attracts high-class businessmen, politicians, prostitutes and pimps, and they all congregate together every Saturday.' And now here they all were in St Jude's Anglican Church.

In attendance was Robbie Waterhouse, husband of famous trainer Gai and father of betting millionaire Tom. Robbie had been banned from racecourses in the eighties for prior knowledge of the wonderfully shambolic Fine Cotton affair,* and only allowed back in 2001.

Also there were underworld figures Graham 'Abo' Henry** and convicted drug dealer Bruce 'Snapper' Cornwell***. Melbourne underworld identity Mick Gatto was to be one of the pallbearers. As proceedings dragged on, Mick leapt to his feet and the crowd got excited, thinking he was over the rather long speeches. Instead, he was helping Mr Sparrow's sister-in-law, who had fainted.

Perhaps the most interesting racing identity in attendance was Victor Spink. He had been one of the biggest punters Sydney had ever seen, and in the eighties and nineties he was at the centre of one of Australia's biggest racing scandals: the 'Jockey Tapes'.

But the phenomenon of the Colourful Racing Identity goes back to well before it was ever given a name. In fact, the man who invented the prestigious Melbourne Cup was one of the first colourful racing personalities this country produced.

---

* The Fine Cotton scandal involved a group of men trying to swap a bad horse for a good one. The problem was, the good one was a different colour. So they dyed it with human hair dye from the supermarket and painted its legs white with house paint. Surprisingly, this sophisticated scam didn't work and they all got caught.

** Graham 'Abo' Henry had been Arthur Stanley 'Neddy' Smith's bodyguard. Smith was made famous in the ABC miniseries *Blue Murder*. Henry once ran into police prosecutor Mal Spence at the Lord Wolseley pub in Ultimo. He confronted Spence, accusing him of telling other criminals Henry was a dog, and then to prove that he wasn't he stabbed Spence in the stomach and neck. Spence lived but Henry got six years in jail.

*** 'Snapper' had been jailed previously for importing 120 kilograms of cocaine into Australia, worth $20 million.

THE FIRST TUESDAY IN NOVEMBER

As they came around the bend and into the final straight, the crowd of 106 479 rose to their feet. History was on the line on the first Tuesday of November 2005.

With 500 metres to go, Makybe Diva, the champion stayer who had won the two previous Melbourne Cups, was well back and on the inside. Despite carrying 58 kilos, the most she had ever carried, she was the punters' overwhelming favourite.

As the field hit the 400-metre mark, here came Makybe Diva, a clear path down the straight for her, and wasn't she moving. The crowd was losing their collective minds. A day of drinking in the sun tends to make people easily excitable and now the favourite, who so many had backed, had hit the lead.

As the mare crossed the finishing line for her third Melbourne Cup triumph in a row, the Flemington racetrack exploded with cheers, hugs and mistimed high fives.

'A champion becomes a legend!' exclaimed the race caller Greg Miles.

The party was about to go up several notches. The Melbourne Cup, one of the biggest stages in world sport, had once again delivered a moment that would become part of Australian folklore.

But despite the glamour and prestige it now attracts, the Cup's origins encapsulate the at times murky intermingling of racing, high society and criminal elements.

A STRIKE TO THE HEART

On a December night in 1987, thieves broke into the exclusive, male-only Melbourne Club. Several threads of history were all coming together on that one night.

The thieves cut a hole into the back gate of the building on Collins Street, a site the club had occupied since 1858. There were no clues left behind and they broke in without raising any suspicion, a rather amazing feat in itself.

Under the cover of darkness, the thieves entered the building. They made their way to the ornate main dining room, where Melbourne's powerbrokers and captains of industry have run the state of Victoria for over a century.* They found what they were looking for: two solid-gold Melbourne Cups.

The famous icon of Australia's best-known race, these elegant yet simple trophies were each valued at $150 000, but worth much more, culturally.**

Despite the cups resting in the heart of this exclusive Melbourne establishment, which sold itself as being close to impossible to get into, they were easily spirited away. The trophies were never seen again and no one was ever caught.

It wasn't the first time the Melbourne Cup and crime had been brought together under the venerated Melbourne Club roof. Back in 1883 one man not only pulled those same threads together, he held them tight.

A MAN BY ANOTHER NAME

As the ship swung away from the dock, Francis C. Selwyn looked back at the English coast, where, it would be fair to say, things had gone pear-shaped fairly quickly.

It was 1852 and Francis was off to the Australian colonies, but not by choice. Few people of his stature went there by choice. He was fleeing moneylenders who were after him for some rather substantial debts.

---

* In Melbourne, the establishment will always ask, 'What school did you go to?' Like there's nothing weird about fifty-year-olds still caring about where they spent their teenage years. I didn't even care what school I went to back when I went to school, let alone now. I prefer to ask, 'What nightclubs did you go to?' It will tell you more about a person.

** The famous three-handled cup was designed in 1919. It's been presented every year since, except during World War II, when the winner received war bonds valued at £200.

That's why Francis C. Selwyn wasn't his real name, it was Frederick Charles Standish. He was the son of Mr Charles Standish, of Standish Hall, Lancashire. His father was a gentleman of significant means and connections, a member of Parliament and a close companion of the late King George IV. He would have been appalled by this turn of events.

Charles had used his considerable power and patronage to give his son every opportunity in life. He'd obtained a commission in the Royal Artillery for him, where Frederick had served for nine years, attaining the rank of captain. As well as helping his son carve out a military career, he purchased Yorkshire's Cayton Hall for him.*

Life was good for Frederick; he was well liked, a man of the establishment who was good company and enjoyed the finer things in life. His chief passion in life was horseracing and, more specifically, gambling on horseracing.

On English racetracks, there was no more popular punter. Not only did Frederick back horses with huge sums of money, he also had an almost supernatural ability to lose. The bookies loved him.**

While his father's fortune covered some of Standish's gambling losses, on a captain's salary it wasn't long before he was deeply in debt. His problem seemed to be that because he was so likeable, people kept extending him lines of credit long past the point where it was sensible to do so.

By 1852, things were dire. He'd mortgaged Cayton Hall to the hilt and now people were starting to come looking for him. Not fun people, either.

---

* Even back then, housing affordability was no big deal, so long as your parents were rich enough to just buy you one.
** Bookies are wonderful people – the bigger a loser you are, the more they like you. This was not the case with my ex, Sharon, who did not use the phrase 'you're the biggest loser I've ever met' with affection.

Sensing his time was up, Frederick sold Cayton Hall to fund his escape and boarded a ship for Australia, where a man could go missing.

Standish didn't know it, but he was fleeing to a place that would be fertile ground for his worst habit. The colony of Victoria was about to go through one of the biggest economic booms in world history.

GOLD! GOLD! GOLD!

It's hard to overstate the impact the discovery of gold had on the young colony of Victoria, which had only recently separated from New South Wales. In late 1851, gold discoveries in Bendigo and Ballarat saw the frontier outpost explode into one of the richest places on earth. In just two years, the colony's population went from 77 000 to 540 000. And to think that Australians complain about population growth these days.

Arriving in Melbourne, Standish,[*] a man looking to get lost, headed to the goldfields. He was seeking work and the opportunity to fade into a community made up of transient people.

However, these were not easy days for Standish. He had lived his whole life as a gentleman and manual labour was a foreign experience. The goldfields were basically like the worst music festival you've ever been to. Lots of hairy blokes, no real showers or toilets to speak of and mud, lots of mud. Unlike a music festival, you didn't get to go home after three days.

Standish bounced around from diggings to diggings, staying at Heathcote, Fryerstown, Castlemaine and Beechworth. He proved to be as successful at prospecting as he had been at gambling. Destitute, he began illegally selling grog on the goldfields under the guise of a

---

[*] Once ashore, Standish went back to using his actual name because, in the colonies, no one cared.

ginger-beer business, an odd occupation for a man who a few years later became the police commissioner of the entire colony.

But two years into his Australian adventure, Standish had no prospects. It was a stunning fall from grace for a man born into enormous privilege. If only back then they'd had those ads that tack 'gamble responsibly'* on the end, that would have fixed everything.

AN OLD FRIEND

In 1853 an old army buddy of Standish's, Andrew Clarke, arrived in the colony as the new surveyor-general.** Clarke and Standish had attended the Royal Military Academy at Woolwich together back in 1840 but now the two men couldn't have been at more different points in their lives.

Clarke would spend five years in Victoria. He was a respected figure and set up the foundations of local government in the colony, the first electric telegraph in Victoria, helped plan the first railways and established the Roads Board and the Victorian Constitution. When he left, it was to become inspector-general of fortifications in England.

Standish, on the other hand, was on the run, broke and unemployed. At the lowest point of his life, he was desperate. Two years living on the fringes of society had broken him. Clarke was the only lifeline he had.

In 1854, they caught up at Clarke's two-storey stone house in what is now the suburb of Northcote.*** Over a night of reminiscing

---

* 'Gamble responsibly' must be the weakest warning in the history of time. 'I was a degenerate gambler and then they started saying "gamble responsibly" at the end of ads really quickly and my entire life turned around.'
** The surveyor-general's duty was to measure and determine land grants for settlers in Victoria. Lucky no one lived in Australia before all the white people showed up, huh?
*** A suburb which Clarke named after his close friend, Sir Stafford Northcote. Northcote is now hipster central in Melbourne and Clarke Street, which is named after him, is two streets away from where I'm writing this.

and heavy drinking, Standish poured his heart out to Clarke. His old friend promised to use his connections to help Standish.

He was true to his word. Within months, a man on the run from gambling debts was the new assistant commissioner of police on the Bendigo goldfields.*

A RAPID RISE

Standish now had a foot in the door at the Victorian public service. While he had struggled with manual labour, he did understand power, patronage and the politics of the establishment.

He could drink with the best of them, play cards, knew the top brothels and was good fun to have around. These were the key selection criteria in the Victorian public service, so not much has changed.

Within a short period of time, Standish had ingratiated himself not only with the Victorian police force but with the key bureaucrats and powerbrokers of the colony. By 1855, he was promoted to Protector of the Chinese in Bendigo, a role that mainly involved keeping the Chinese miners confined in their own areas, collecting money from them and stopping the white miners from attempting to beat them up or worse.

In 1857 he was again promoted, this time to Warden of the Goldfields at Sandhurst, where he stayed until 20 August 1858, when he wrote in his diary: 'Heard about 4.30 that I had just been appointed by the Executive to the C. C. of Police.'

In just six years the man who had fled England under a false name to avoid substantial debts, the former purveyor of sly grog on the goldfields, become the chief commissioner of police. Think about that if you're struggling to get a promotion at work.

---

* Another white man appointed on merit.

Standish's rapid rise was a testament to his prowess as a networker. He instinctively understood where the power centres of the colony were and did everything to integrate himself.[*]

The first group of influence was the police force and the Victorian public service more broadly. This was a world Standish knew, full of well-bred gentlemen who enjoyed the finer things in life.

The second was the Freemasons of Victoria. Despite being born into a family of Roman Catholics – sworn enemies of the Freemasons – Standish rose to the position of district grand master of the Victorian Freemasons, giving him access and standing among all the key people who ran Victoria at the time. It wasn't enough for Frederick Standish to merely join these groups, he had to end up in a position of power within them.

The third power centre he joined was the Melbourne Club.

WHERE THE ELITE MEET TO EAT

The Melbourne Club was originally formed in 1838 as a place where squatters – those men who had occupied large tracts of Crown land and treated it as their own – could stay while in the city.

In 1858 the club moved into 36 Collins Street, where it remains to this day. That's also when the newly appointed chief commissioner became a member, right as the club began to develop into the social headquarters of Melbourne's upper class.

Standish felt right at home and tales of his all-night drinking sessions and fights became well known

> **DID YOU KNOW?**
>
> Even racehorses can be Good Blokes. Phar Lap once ran a sophisticated art forgery ring. It was covered up after his death.

---

[*] He was like the person at work you hate because they never do any work but are always going to lunches and conferences and actually post things to LinkedIn, which psychiatrists agree is the clearest indicator that someone is a sociopath.

around town. He was there so often that by 1872 he had moved in, and he lived there until his death.

His time at the Melbourne Club was not without incident.

At one stage, after a card game went south, Standish was 'severely horse whipped' in a drunken fight by fellow Melbourne Club member Captain Robert Machell.

In 1882, in even more spectacular fashion, Standish was thrown through a window by Colonel Craigie Halkett after Standish called him a 'provocative name'.* Standish declined to press charges, instead opting for a far more serious punishment: Halkett was forced to resign as a member.

Despite the drinking and fighting, Standish was now a man of significant power in Victoria and he used this to fuel his greatest passion, horseracing.

VICTORIA TURF CLUB

While some police commissioners make the bold choice of focusing on policing, there is no doubt horseracing was Standish's priority. Once again gainfully employed and part of the elite, he fell back into old habits of losing a lot of money on horses.

But being police commissioner made it a little harder for people to pursue him over his debts. In fact, having the police commissioner owe you money was probably not a bad thing.

Standish was quick to join the Victoria Turf Club. At the time, it was one of the two bodies that competed for control of racing in Victoria, the other being the Victoria Jockey Club. And as with all institutions he joined, it wasn't long before he was a leading figure.

When Standish joined, he decided the Turf Club needed a

---

* No record exists of what the provocative name was, but it must have been good to get him thrown through a window. I once got called a provocative name at a club, but instead of throwing the person through a window I took myself home and cried for several days. Both are good options.

schedule of races that rivalled the Jockey Club's popular program, which included the 2000 Guineas Stakes, the most prestigious race in the colonies at the time. In 1861, Standish gave notice that at the next meeting of the club, 'he should move that a race similar to the Chester Cup at home, to be called the Melbourne Cup, be run annually at the spring meeting of the club'.

Standish's lifetime of gambling gave him an excellent insight into what punters wanted. The Chester Cup was a handicap race, where the better horses were given bigger weights to carry to make the race more competitive. This meant more horses would enter the race, leading to higher prize money and more betting.

Standish was a genius when it came to promoting and organising races, and he was the driving force in the industry for decades. He remained a terrible gambler.

THE FIRST MELBOURNE CUP

The first Melbourne Cup, held on Thursday 7 November 1861, saw seventeen horses enter the 2-mile race. It attracted a crowd of 4000, which was a large crowd for the time but less than had been hoped for. Days earlier the city had been plunged into mourning by the news of the deaths of explorers Robert O'Hara Burke and William John Wills.

On the morning of the first Cup, the *Age* newspaper printed Wills' last diary entry and many of the government buildings were draped in black cloth. Not the sort of thing that gets people heading out to the races for a day of frivolity.

Here, again, Standish found himself at the centre of events. His friend and saviour Andrew Clarke was on the exploration committee for the expedition, and Standish himself was Burke's commanding officer and a close friend.

In fact, Burke wrote to Standish just before setting out on his ill-fated trek, ending his letter:

I am confident of success and willing to accept the alternative of success or disgrace, although failure is possible. This self-imposed task (as you call it) is no sinecure, and I think it will take the sting out of me if I see it out.

Good-bye my dear Standish.

From yours, ever sincerely, R O'Hara Burke.

Standish would be a pallbearer for Burke at his state funeral in 1863, which was attended by 40 000 people.

Despite the tragedy, the 1861 Melbourne Cup went ahead, with Standish acting as a steward on the day. The race was not without incident, with one horse running off before the start and three horses falling during the race. Two of them died, a tradition that stays with us to this day.

The winner was a horse called Archer, from New South Wales, which gave the older colony significant bragging rights over Victoria. This tension between the two colonies soon spilled over in spectacular fashion.*

TROUBLE

The Melbourne Cup was run the following year and again Archer won easily – eight lengths in front – denting Victorian pride for a second year in a row. This dominance by New South Wales set up a crisis that threatened to end the Melbourne Cup in just its third year.

Etienne de Mestre, Archer's trainer, had his eyes set on a third victory in 1863 and duly sent off his application for the race by telegram. Unfortunately, the telegram arrived on a public holiday in

---

* To be honest, tensions between New South Wales and Victoria are always spilling over, especially in the sporting world. It's why all the other states hate them, they're so needy. You're both very good, relax.

Victoria and didn't make its way to the stewards until the following day, when they promptly ruled it as having missed the deadline.* Needless to say, Standish was one of the stewards.

A sensible approach would have been to accept the telegram had been lodged on time, but the inter-colony rivalry seemed to get the better of all involved. Archer was unable to race, leading every New South Wales trainer to boycott the race and vow to never participate again.

As a result, just seven horses competed in the 1863 Melbourne Cup. The future of the race looked bleak.**

The Victoria Turf Club's problems didn't end there. Competition with the Victoria Jockey Club was sending both institutions broke. Neither could continue as they were, dividing the punters and the horses, spreading them too thin.

Standish was again in the thick of the action as a solution was sought. Both clubs agreed to cease operating and instead formed a new body, the Victorian Racing Club (VRC), to oversee racing in Victoria, which included running the Cup.

Standish – never one to miss an opportunity to accrue power and influence – was a founding member of the new club. He was heavily involved until his death, holding almost every position imaginable, including committeeman, handicapper, steward, treasurer and finally chairman. In his excellent history of the VRC, *A Century Galloped By*, John Pacini reports Standish was the club's 'most skilful race and programme framer' and among the most knowledgeable and experienced racing men in Australia.

The restructure also provided a chance to reset relations with New South Wales. Bridges were quickly mended. A big part of the healing was the appointment of Robert Bagot as secretary

---

* Good to know the 'I only just saw your message' excuse was around even back then.
** This was before the success of the Melbourne Cup was measured by how many brands had marquees at the event.

of the new VRC committee. Bagot was a surveyor and engineer from Sydney who had recently levelled and returfed the Melbourne Cricket Ground, and soon did the same at Flemington.

Once he became club secretary, Bagot built a new grandstand and planted impressive new gardens, turning Flemington into the best racecourse in the country.[*] He also convinced the Victorian government to declare the Melbourne Cup a public holiday, perhaps one of the greatest bits of lobbying anyone has ever done.

Under his watch, and with Standish working tirelessly to advance the VRC's causes, by 1880 the Melbourne Cup was pulling in crowds of 100 000. That's a figure it maintains to this day.

DISTRACTIONS

Sorting out racing in Victoria was Standish's main pursuit, but he did have to do a little bit of policing on the side, given he was the commissioner.

The police force Standish had inherited was not exactly a well-oiled machine. In fact, police tended to drink and frequent brothels so much that in 1854 a special jail had to be built just to hold officers who had broken the law, to keep them away from the general prison population.

Standish was a good cultural fit for this police force. His drinking and gambling were widely known in the colony and he tended to favour men of similar interests, often promoting them above others of greater ability.[**] He also had excellent knowledge of Melbourne's brothels and famously held a dinner party where naked prostitutes with pale skin were made to sit on chairs covered with black cloth, to better showcase them.

---

[*] Flemington still has the best gardens of any racecourse in the country. Throughout the Melbourne Cup carnival you can see people passed out in wonderfully appointed and landscaped gardens.

[**] In this regard he was ahead of his time, as this is now common practice for every modern-day sporting administrator.

This sort of behaviour didn't go unnoticed and, between 1860 and 1863, three parliamentary committees investigated him across a range of issues, almost all stemming from the fact that Standish, with all his various distractions, barely ran the force at all. He was seen to allow corruption in the force to run unchecked and to protect some members of the community who were involved in criminal enterprises.*

Standish, in a warning to potential whistleblowers, refused to reinstate officers he'd sacked, even when instructed to do so by a parliamentary committee.

One of the committees went so far as recommending he be replaced, but the government ignored that, instead getting closer to Standish, seeking out his advice and help on a range of matters. In return, he helped them, often circumventing police hiring policies to get people the government liked into the force.

Standish managed to see off the three parliamentary inquiries in the early 1860s, but another in 1870 looked certain to bring him down. Investigating the quality of the force, this committee found the men that Standish had promoted were 'wholly unfit, as regarded either moral courage or any other qualifications to hold the position which they occupied'. The force was inept at best and corrupt at worst.

But still nothing happened. It was only years later that the reasons for this inaction came to light. The first clue was found in a dairy by journalist James Smith, who wrote:

> Captain Standish – my informant adds – is furnished
> with a report every morning of the number and the
> names of those who have spent the night in the better
> class of brothels. The record must be a curious one

---

* Luckily everyone learnt a valuable lesson and police corruption never happens these days.

and calculated to lift the veil from the secret immorali-
ties of many of the outwardly moral and respectable.

This approach to protecting himself and the force by maintaining
leverage over the powerful was supported in the memoirs of Chief
Superintendent John Sadleir,* who gave a very clear reason for why
Standish had escaped the 1870 parliamentary inquiry:

> A high officer of the State in those evil days, a man
> notoriously of unclean life, was found late at night
> under ambiguous circumstances on the private prem-
> ises of a gentleman residing in one of the suburbs.
>
> The owner of the premises did not wait for an
> explanation. He took the law into his own hands and
> severely punished the intruder, finally kicking him out
> of the place.
>
> Partly to safeguard himself, this gentleman called
> early on the following day on the Chief Commissioner
> of Police, related the circumstances and sought advice
> as to what proceedings he should take.
>
> Then followed such negotiations and interven-
> tions of friends as might have been expected, with the
> result that the matter was hushed up.
>
> The high official recognised, of course, that it was
> the intervention of the head of the police service that
> saved the situation. It saved also the police depart-
> ment, for when the schedule for the disbanding of the
> service came before him he promptly vetoed it.

---

* Sadleir was in charge of the police operation at the Kelly gang's siege of Mrs Jones's hotel
at Glenrowan, where Ned was finally captured.

Having dirt on someone higher up is always handy. The Russians call it *kompromat*, short for 'compromising material'.[*]

FRIENDS IN HIGH PLACES

The idea that a parliamentary committee could take down a man who had inveigled himself so completely into every power centre in Victoria turned out to be fanciful.

Standish was so ingrained into the very workings of the colony, he was asked to escort Prince Alfred, the Duke of Edinburgh and the second son of Queen Victoria, when he toured in 1867–68.[**]

> ## INEVITABLE APOLOGIES
>
> 'I'd like to apologise to the patrons of the bar for my actions, but especially to the children present.'
>
> 'I unreservedly apologise for ruining *Play School* for future generations.'
>
> 'I would never knowingly endanger a penguin colony.'

Prince Alfred was the first member of the royal family to visit the Australian colonies.

Given Standish was also nominally responsible for the prince's security, it made sense for him to take him around town personally. When the prince was not visiting the governor and his family, he was being taken to Sarah 'Mother' Fraser's exclusive brothel by Standish.

Standish also took the prince to the Variety Theatre to drink with the actresses backstage and of course he brought him along to the races, a huge coup for the VRC.

Standish and Prince Albert hit it off so well that during the prince's stay they regularly had dinner together at the Melbourne Club, followed by cards and plenty of gambling. They even spent Christmas together.

---

[*] Isn't it exciting what Donald Trump's presidency is teaching us?

[**] By 'escort', I mean take him to various brothels and then back to the Melbourne Club for a nightcap.

When the prince returned to Melbourne in 1869, this time with no official engagements, he once again joined Standish at the Melbourne Club and at Sarah Fraser's brothel.

THE HUNT FOR NED KELLY

Where four parliamentary committees had failed, Ned Kelly succeeded. Australia's most famous bushranger was effectively responsible for Standish's downfall, exposing the mismanagement and corruption in the Victorian police that had grown under his watch.

In 1878 the Kelly gang, already known to police for livestock theft, assault and robbery, were visited at home by Constable Alexander Fitzpatrick, who was attempting to arrest Ned's brother Dan. In response, Ned shot Fitzpatrick in the arm, then forced him to remove the bullet with a knife so it couldn't be used as evidence, which seems rather excessive. They then let Fitzpatrick leave, making him promise to never tell anyone – a promise Fitzpatrick forgot about the instant he made it to safety.[*]

The Kelly gang was now on the run and the police were in pursuit.[**]

The Kellys fled to the heavily forested Wombat Ranges in Victoria's north east. The area was well known to the gang, giving them a significant advantage over the police. The policemen looking for the gang were camped at some old miners' huts near Stringybark Creek. Despite being the hunted, the Kelly gang knew exactly where the police were and confronted them, killing three officers.

The public outcry was immense. The Victorian parliament passed the *Felons Apprehension Act 1878*, which not only outlawed the gang but made it legal for anyone to shoot them.[***] Despite this, the gang remained on the run for two years, robbing banks in Euroa

---

[*] If you ever shoot someone, don't trust them when they say they won't tell anyone. It's a trap for young players.

[**] Pursuit may be overselling it. 'Bumbling and stumbling behind' might be more accurate.

[***] A lesson for any politicians today who want to be seen as 'tough on crime'.

and Jerilderie and killing a police informer. The inability of the police to capture the Kelly gang in this time highlighted the many failings of Standish's reign.

When Ned Kelly was finally captured at Glenrowan,* in the shootout where he famously wore his homemade armour, Standish's problems were only beginning. In the aftermath of the disastrous manhunt a royal commission, the Longmore Commission, was convened.**

Standish appeared as the key witness before the commission and, despite his sizeable political capital, he could not hide the fact that under his leadership the force had become highly dysfunctional. The commission found that the hunt was mismanaged from the start. Witnesses declared Standish had been uninterested at best, often spending time focusing on racing and his other interests. A rumour, which has never been proved or disproved, was that Standish suspended the hunt when the weights of the Melbourne Cup were declared.

While this may not have been true, it was certainly the image that emerged from the commission. The commission found that the manhunt was 'not characterised either by good judgment, or by that zeal for the interests of the public service which should have distinguished an officer in his position'.

Widespread corruption was also uncovered, with the activities of two officers, Winch and Larner, singled out for involvement with prostitution, gambling and taking money from hotels, all while being protected by Standish.

Reading the writing on the wall, Standish resigned in 1880. He had been police commissioner for twenty-two years.

---

* Kelly would be hung for his crimes, his famous last words being, 'Such is life.' Troubled AFL star Ben Cousins has this phrase tattooed across his stomach, which was probably a bit of an indication he was a troubled soul.
** Royal commissions fix everything.

Despite this public shaming, Standish was still well liked in many circles and in 1881, he became the chairman of the VRC, a position he retained until his death.

AN END TO THE PURSUIT OF PLEASURE

Unlike his police work, Standish's work as chairman of the VRC eventually became stressful. A life dedicated to the pursuit of pleasure meant his health was not the best and in 1883 he died of cirrhosis of the liver and a fatty degeneration of the heart. He was fifty-eight years old.

Standish left behind a most curious legacy.

He had presided over a corrupt and ineffective police force, and yet managed the politics of the colony masterfully. He was a major presence in every centre of power and able to withstand astounding political pressure.

He had also been one of the key forces in the establishment of Victorian racing. A founding member of the VRC, he had worked incredibly hard to build the foundations of the huge racing industry we know today, including establishing the Melbourne Cup.

That's not bad for a debt-ridden bloke who fled England under a false name.

On New Year's Day, the Standish Handicap is run at Flemington in his honour.

THE JOCKEY TAPES

As the most prominent of our early Colourful Racing Identities, Frederick Standish set the standard for racing in Australia – a place where the moral meets the corrupt, where glamour meets the seedier side of life.

By the end of the twentieth century, racing was a large and mature industry, and the links with organised crime had only strengthened. By the seventies and eighties the racetrack had become an increasingly popular place to launder the large amount of drug money that was being generated in Australia.

In the nineties the industry was hit by the 'Jockey Tapes' scandal. Unlike in the Standish era, in this enlightened age the police occasionally tried to catch criminals. In one of these fits of competency, the Australian Federal Police started tapping the phone of a drug dealer named Victor Thomas Spink.

RAID!

Across Sydney, Brisbane and Melbourne, 340 police and customs officers carried out raids across 140 houses, arresting eighteen people. The raids followed the earlier arrest of four people in Hervey Bay, a south Queensland town famous for whale watching.

The police operation was the result of phone taps that had recorded 80 000 phone calls between May 1993 and August 1994, totalling 4000 hours of conversation. The Australian Federal Police were targeting several drug syndicates, who had teamed up to import $225 million worth of cannabis resin, hashish, from Pakistan.

While disrupting the importation of drugs had been the goal of the operation, something else had been caught in the extensive net cast by the phone tapping. As the plotters of the scheme discussed the logistics of importing the cannabis resin, Spink was also caught on tape seeking information from jockeys, with the intent of fixing races.

Spink was amongst the people arrested, but it wasn't until his phone conversations were revealed in 1995 by *Sydney Morning Herald* journalist Kate McClymont* that they became known as 'the Jockey Tapes'.

---

* Kate McClymont is the best investigative journalist working in Australia, having brought down former politician and criminal Eddie Obeid. If you hear she's doing a story on you, probably best to just hand yourself in at the nearest police station and plead guilty.

The most surprising thing about what became one of the biggest scandals in Australian racing history is not the offence itself, but the forgiveness on offer after it.

THE MASTERMIND

Victor Thomas Spink was born in 1944 and by sixteen he had his first conviction for breaking and entering. That kicked off his criminal career, which saw him back in court six times in the next three years.

By the time he was twenty-eight, he'd branched out. Having been jailed in England and deported back to Sydney, in 1977 he was jailed for three years for a mailbag robbery worth $54 000.

Upon his release, though, there were no more arrests. It seemed Spink had either gone straight or worked out how not to get caught, but in fact he had just made his way to the racetrack, the perfect place to mix with like-minded people. He emerged as a small-time punter on Sydney's racetracks, where he was well known and well liked among the regulars of the racing community.

It wasn't long before Spink started betting larger and larger amounts. By the end of the boom times that were the eighties, he was one of the biggest punters in Australia. Perhaps most famously, he once lost $400 000 in a single afternoon at the track.

Spink's style was to back favourites when the best jockeys were riding them. He would often put $30 000 on a horse with the trackside bookies before heading to the tote to put even more on.

What later became clear to police was that the whole exercise was a giant money-laundering operation, with $12 million passing through bookmakers' bags and the tote in just five years.[*]

---

[*] That does seem like a lot. Although we've all gotten a bit carried away at the races at some point. Why, one year I had three 50-cent each-way bets in the one day. I was out of control and am not proud of it.

The money needed laundering because it had come from drug deals, and it was Spink who attracted the interest of police in what became known as Operation Caribou.

A COMEDY OF ERRORS

While the criminals' plan was simple, the execution belonged more in a Coen brothers film. It began with 15 tons of cannabis resin being picked up in Pakistan, near the Indian border. A million dollars had been spent purchasing four boats, specially kitted out to transport the drugs to Hervey Bay in Queensland.

The scheme was doomed from the start, with the Australian Federal Police getting wind of the plan and tapping the phones of the key players. Not that the criminals needed much help in stuffing up the whole enterprise: in transit some of the boats ran aground and another boat's engine gave out while at sea.

The technology installed on their main boat that could unscramble the coded police radio also broke, so when a French surveillance plane flew overhead the crew panicked and dumped 10 of the 15 tons of hashish over the side.*

Even after the arrests, the criminals couldn't catch a break, with police managing to recover the hashish that had been dumped and using it as evidence.

Following the raids, the police froze a million dollars in Spink's bank account and seized ten of the eleven properties he owned in Byron Bay, St Ives, Woollahra, Darling Point and Potts Point. Who says crime doesn't pay?

In sentencing those involved, Judge Blanch identified Spink as one of the 'leading participants'.** He faced the possibility of life in prison, but after pleading guilty he received a sentence of twenty-four years. This was cut several times for what the Court of Appeal

---

* Resulting, I like to imagine, in a lot of marine life getting incredibly stoned.
** I imagine this is like being in the leadership group at a footy club.

explained was 'due to other material relating to assistance to the authorities'.

Spink had flipped and helped the authorities with information in order to reduce his sentence. He was released in 2002 having served just six years.

CAUGHT IN THE NET

While Spink's drug importing scheme came crashing down around him, it was his racing activities that captured the public's imagination with the publication of the Jockey Tapes.

The racing conversations intercepted by the police originally occurred in 1993 and '94 and, while they were not the target of the AFP's Operation Caribou, someone thought them interesting enough to leak to the *Sydney Morning Herald*, who in 1995 published some of the transcripts of Spink's phone conversations.

The tapes implicated ten of Sydney's top jockeys in race-fixing at major Sydney meetings, with Spink paying them for tips on certain races. Here's an example:

> **Mr C:** We should all meet . . . twenty minutes after the first tomorrow . . . round the corner somewhere.
> **Jockey One:** Somewhere, you know, just up that side street from the racecourse.
> **Mr C:** You have to watch that some of those f—ing bookies and those c— don't come by and see us talking.
> **Mr C:** We don't have to worry about what we missed today; what we missed today, we're gonna pick up tomorrow. It's just there's teething stages but we're gonna try and get our act together if we can.
> **Mr C:** But do you think we've got one tomorrow?
> **Jockey One:** Well, I think we have. There's three of us gonna get our heads together.

At the time, the real names were not printed by the paper, but it came out that Mr C was Victor Spink. Of the jockeys involved one stood head and shoulders above the rest in terms of fame and ability. His name was Jim Cassidy.

PUMPER

The 1983 Melbourne Cup came at a time when Australians were feeling pretty good about their sporting prowess, having famously won the America's Cup a month before. On this first Tuesday in November, however, it was a New Zealand horse that claimed victory. The horse was Kiwi, and it had been bought by a New Zealand sheep farmer with the wonderful name of Snow Lupton, for NZ$1000.*

Kiwi was not considered a serious Melbourne Cup contender, as the 10–1 odds would have told you – or just the fact that Lupton had used the horse to round up sheep in the lead-up to the race.

As the field turned the corner at Flemington and into the straight, with 500 metres to go Kiwi was running second last, and only because the last horse had come up lame. But Kiwi was a stayer and this was his style: spending the majority of the race at the back of the field and then exploding down the straight.

And explode he did. At about the 300-metre mark, Kiwi was going so fast it appeared the other horses were running in slow motion. With less than 200 metres to go, the crowd suddenly noticed a blur as this unassuming horse bore down on the leaders. At 100 metres to go Kiwi had them dead to rights, surging past the front of the field, surprising even the race caller. He won by a length.

Riding him home was Jim Cassidy, a relative unknown at the time but soon to be one of the most successful and controversial

---

* New Zealand has a system of currency and does not, in fact, operate on a barter system, contrary to numerous public statements I've made in the past. Yes, I too was surprised to learn this.

jockeys to ever grace Australian shores. Born in New Zealand in 1963 and nicknamed 'Pumper' for the way he pumped his hands on the reins, Cassidy's talent as a jockey cannot be overstated.

His racing CV would be the envy of any jockey: over thirty-five years he won two Melbourne Cups (1983 Kiwi, 1997 Might and Power), two Caulfield Cups (1997 Might and Power, 2000 Diatribe), a Cox Plate (1998 Might and Power) and the Golden Slipper (2001 Ha Ha). On top of that, he won 104 Group One races and is in the Racing Hall of Fame in both Australia and New Zealand.

While Cassidy's record in the saddle is second to none, it's his ability to not only survive scandal but to thrive in spite of it that's been most astounding. His career is a case study of how the racing industry rarely punishes its own.

MAY AS WELL BE IN YOUR POCKET

With the Australian Federal Police listening in, Victor Spink was chatting to Jim Cassidy. Spink was going to give him $20 000 to split between four jockeys who had provided him with information about races.

'It may as well be in your pocket than all those other pockets, or even the bookies' pockets,' said Spink.

'Exactly,' agreed Cassidy.

The transcripts published in the *Sydney Morning Herald* seemed to suggest that race-fixing had occurred, with Spink meeting jockeys before races to get information on who to back. With the conversations now public, the Australian Jockey Club (AJC) was forced to investigate, handing bans to Cassidy (three years), Gavin Eades (one year) and Kevin Moses (ten months).

Interestingly, the claims of race-fixing weren't supported by the AJC. The jockeys argued that they didn't actually fix the races, they had just pretended to go along with the plan rather than actually executing it. While I would never question the findings of a racing body, that does seem rather strange.*

Still, the jockeys in question had taken money for sharing information with Spink, which was very clearly a breach of the rules of racing. Spink confirmed as much when defending himself against the accusation. 'They said I tried to fix races, but all I ever did was ring jockeys and get their tips. There was no racing fixing, I was always ringing jockeys, betting was part of my business back then.'

Cassidy used a rather familiar defence for sporting heroes in trouble, he claimed that while what he did was wrong, everyone else was doing it.

In his autobiography, *Pumper,* Cassidy argued that while he had not obeyed the letter of the law, any jockey who said they didn't provide tips to others was kidding themselves.

If your first line of defence is 'everyone else was doing it', you don't actually have much of a defence. It's just deflection and a tactic even children figure out by the time they're about three.

'But Sabastian, Rainbow and Skylar were doing it too!'

'I don't care, we do not eat gluten in this house!'

'It's a fad! Very few people have a gluten intolerance!'

Cassidy also showed no remorse for what had gone on. When he bumped into Kate McClymont, the journalist who had broken the story, he spat on her and said, 'You f—ing bitch, you've ruined my life.'

He was wrong – she hadn't ruined his life at all. This was racing, where almost everything is forgiven. Cassidy's punishment of three years was downgraded to twenty-one months, meaning he was back in time to win the 1997 Melbourne Cup on Might and Power.

What's amazing about all this is that racing is built on punters feeling they all have an equal chance to win. Yet here were jockeys

---

* 'You see, officer, I was only pretending to embezzle $53 million. Obviously I was going to return it once I'd finished pretending.'

THE MASTER OF THE OVER-APOLOGY

Former Queensland Premier Peter Beattie loves a good apology. He's always keen not just to apologise but to enthusiastically agree with anyone criticising him.

As the chair of the Commonwealth Games organising committee, he was forced to apologise for the closing ceremony not focusing on the athletes. 'Did we stuff it up? Yes. Should [athletes] have been a part of the actual ceremony that was broadcast? Of course. We got it wrong. I can't be more honest about it than that.'

As head of the Australian Rugby League, he had to apologise again when he couldn't identify the Sutherland Shire's NRL team (it's the Cronulla Sharks) despite being given a shortlist of three to choose from. Instead he said, 'I've got to be honest, I wouldn't have a bloody clue.' He then said he'd 'loved rugby league all my life'.

providing inside information to a select few, essentially insider trading. This puts every other person betting on the races at a disadvantage.

And there's no doubt this information is useful. You don't offer $20 000 for tips if they have no relationship to placing winning bets.*

FAT TONY

While accepting money from the mastermind of a drug syndicate and spitting on a journalist were subtle red flags Cassidy lacked a firm moral compass, it was still surprising when in 2008 *The Age* alleged that, from 1997, Cassidy had accepted money from Tony Mokbel.

Mokbel was a drug trafficker who ran a criminal enterprise known as 'The Company', which had an estimated turnover of $400 million a year. 'Fat Tony' achieved fame following the Melbourne gangland wars and his rather interesting choice of wig when he was finally tracked down overseas while on the run.

---

* This is always the best bit when people take money illegally in sport: they pretend it wasn't for any useful information. Like drug dealers and match fixers just hand out big money for information they could read online for free.

The Age wrote:

> Jimmy Cassidy accepted bundles of cash from alleged crime boss Tony Mokbel in return for tips about horses he was riding.
>
> Cassidy, a Sydney jockey who has won the Melbourne Cup twice, accepted more than $50 000 from the alleged crime boss in return for a number of winning tips given from 1997 onwards.

This was a stunning claim by *The Age* given that in 1997 Cassidy was only just back from his suspension for the Jockey Tapes.

The links between Mokbel and racing were extensive.[*] The Purana taskforce, the unit established to investigate the Melbourne gangland wars, believed Mokbel used the races to launder his money. Jim O'Brien, head of the Purana taskforce between 2005 and 2009, said Mokbel used third parties to punt for him by 'breaking down the amounts of those bets so that they weren't subject to Austrac [the anti-money laundering agency] reporting by bookmakers'.

It was also believed that Mokbel paid bookies to enter bets for him after the race had already been run, a novel approach to say the least.[**]

Surprisingly, a lot of the claims made in the *Age* article, and by the Purana taskforce, didn't receive much follow-up from authorities. A 2008 inquiry by former judge Gordon Lewis into Mokbel and the racing industry lacked any real powers and couldn't compel anyone to speak to the inquiry. Stewards, lacking any concrete

---

[*] Mokbel loved betting so much he didn't even stop when he was in Barwon Prison. The authorities intercepted him sending out coded messages to place five-figure bets on big races.

[**] Apparently this option isn't open to everyone. I discovered this after a very frustrating 45-minute call with a betting agency. Even constantly pointing out that Tony Mokbel used to do it didn't get me anywhere.

evidence, were unable to press the matter further and, as a result, no bookmakers or jockeys were charged.

Cassidy's response was once again interesting. When asked to comment on the claims by *The Age*, he responded by telling the journalist, 'Your paper can go f— themselves. And so can you.'*

He later denied taking $50 000 from Mokbel for providing tips, however he did admit to receiving money from him. 'Bundles of cash? That will do me. I would not be so f—ing stupid as to start taking $50 000 off Tony Mokbel. He did give me money. If he won at the casino, he'd give me some money to have a bet. But that was it.'

While Cassidy was keen to draw the line at taking money for information from Mokbel, it didn't stop him launching a full-throated defence of their relationship.

> I've got nothing but respect for him. What he did in his personal life was none of my business but as a person he was fantastic to me.
>
> How do you know what people get into these days? I certainly wasn't doing anything wrong.
>
> I think if you scrutinise all racing people, a lot of media, a lot of the so-called hierarchy in racing, I bet they don't all mix with clean skins.

It was an eerily similar response to the Jockey Tapes scandal, basically using the everyone-else-is-as-guilty-of-this-stuff-as-me defence again.

A counter view might be that getting involved with one drug trafficker is careless, but getting involved with two of them starts to look like you don't really care that they're drug dealers.

I've got no doubt that working in the racing industry would

---

* There are probably a lot of occasions when this would be an appropriate response to a journalist.

make it hard to avoid some of life's more colourful characters, but Victor Spink and Tony Mokbel aren't borderline cases.

GOOD KARMA

When Victor Spink was released from jail for his cannabis resin importation indiscretion in 2002, he returned to a beach-front mansion he had managed to hang on to. He waited three years until his parole allowed him to head overseas, then made a beeline for Zurich, to reclaim US$500 000 he had deposited in a Swiss bank account in 1987.*

He had deposited it under an alias, Mr Black, while using a fake Australian passport with the name George Saunders. Now, attempting to withdraw the money, he not only again offered a fake passport but one that had expired. The Swiss bankers, usually a pretty forgiving lot, suspected something was up. They blocked the release of funds.

This triggered a legal battle that saw a lower Swiss court say that Spink was 'one of the most important drug dealers in Australia', who had been 'linked to organised crime since the 1970s'. They also ordered the money should not be released. However, an appeal to a higher court saw the decision overturned on the basis that the 'initial deposit predated his arrest for drug offences and he had committed no crimes in Switzerland'.

Spink received the US$500 000, plus all the interest it had been earning all that time, proving that karma is a concept limited to inspirational Facebook posts.

As for Jim 'Pumper' Cassidy, he retired in 2015. In a sign of racing's firm ethical footing, the Australian Turf Club honoured Pumper with a tribute race day at Rosehill.

---

* Contrast him being allowed to do this to the Victorian Parliament making it legal for any member of the public to shoot the Kelly gang.

NOT ROBINSON CRUSOE

Even if they don't excuse his behaviour, Jim Cassidy's claims that he was hardly alone when it came to breaking racing's rules have some truth to them.

A big part of the problem is that when racing authorities have had the chance to take a hardline stance on jockeys and bookies who broke the rules, they've frequently chosen not to. They're like banking regulators in that regard. Perhaps the most famous example is the Victorian Racing Club's handling of Damien Oliver, one of the most successful and well-known jockeys Australia has ever seen.

Oliver's victory on Media Puzzle in the 2002 Melbourne Cup was an iconic moment that transcended horseracing, coming just days after the death of his brother Jason, who fell in a race in Perth. With tears streaming down his face after winning the race, Oliver entered the stratosphere of Australian sporting heroes. Here was a story ripped right out of Hollywood, so much so that it actually was made into a movie.

Like Cassidy, Oliver has won the great races in Australia multiple times. He's won the Melbourne Cup three times (1995 Doriemus, 2002 Media Puzzle, 2013 Fiorente), the Caulfield Cup four times (1992 Mannerism, 1994 Paris Lane, 1995 Doriemus, 1999 Sky Heights) and the Cox Plate twice (1997 Dane Ripper, 2001 Northerly).

But on 1 October 2010, Damien Oliver phoned Mark Hunter, a professional punter and former Western Bulldogs player, asking Hunter to place a bet for him. The bet was on Miss Octopussy, the favourite in a race at Moonee Valley. Oliver told Hunter to put $10 000 on the horse.

Interestingly, Oliver was also riding in that race. He was on Europa Point, the second favourite. The race was run and would you believe it, Miss Octopussy won, netting Oliver a tidy profit of $11 000.

Unfortunately for Oliver, the Victorian police were listening in on his call with Hunter, as part of their investigation into the still-unsolved murder of another Colourful Racing Identity, Les Samba. It would be fair to say that, if you're involved in racing, it's probably best to assume your phone is tapped.

It took until 2012 for all this to become public, right in the middle of the spring carnival. The VRC took what can only be described as a perplexing approach to the accusations. They could have stood down Oliver immediately, pending formal charges. Instead, they took three months to investigate. That meant Oliver could still participate in the spring carnival, the most lucrative time of the year for jockeys and the VRC.

The VRC had put themselves in a position where, if things went badly, a jockey facing serious charges might end up winning one of their prestige races, such as the Melbourne Cup. And win Oliver did, twice, in the Victoria Derby on Fiveandahalfstar and the Emirates Stakes on Happy Trails.

Two days after the carnival ended, Oliver confessed to putting the bet on Miss Octopussy. But he claimed he still did his best on Europa Point, despite running sixth.

I'm no expert on these things, but if I had $10 000 at risk on another horse, and stood to win a further $11 000 if that horse won, I'm not sure I would be trying my best to prevent it from winning.

Oliver received an eight-month suspension for placing the bet and another two months for using a mobile phone in the jockey's area. The general reaction was one of shock at how short the ban was. Since then, a similar offence has been increased to a two-year suspension.

Perhaps part of Oliver getting such a low penalty was that he hired Robert Richter QC to defend him, who famously represented Mick Gatto in court and helped him beat a murder charge on the grounds of self-defence. Richter has more recently represented Cardinal George Pell.

In Oliver's case, ten months out meant he would be back in time for the 2013 Melbourne Spring Carnival. And in true racing fashion, Oliver was not exactly shunned upon his return.

He quickly found success, with trainer Gai Waterhouse giving Oliver the ride on race favourite Fiorente in the Melbourne Cup. He got the job done, too, winning the Cup for the third time, although it was slightly less of a fairytale than in 2002.

The VRC had allowed someone who'd bet on another horse in a race he was riding in to participate in their most prestigious racing carnival two years in a row. It was not a popular result with Victoria's racing integrity commissioner, Sal Perna. Of the decision not to stand down Oliver immediately the year before, he said: 'In my examination of the information, I am of the view that the decision taken not to [stand the jockey down] until Oliver made admissions was too conservative and cautious in the circumstances. Such view is not shared by RVL.'

Much like cricket's handling of the Mark Waugh and Shane Warne betting scandal, the complete lack of serious punishment for both Cassidy and Oliver, two of the biggest jockeys in Australia, sent a terrible message.

The cynic in me says the racing officials know exactly what they are doing. If they start throwing huge penalties at everyone who commits these sorts of acts, who knows where it will end. Well, there'd be very few people to ride the horses and to take the bets, one suspects.

Perhaps most concerning is that the racing authorities know something else: the punters just don't care. These cases, and the many others that surround racing, have done nothing to dampen the spirits of the betting public. They keep handing over their money despite the regular reminders that racing isn't all on the level.

This is how much Australians love betting – they do it even if they suspect what they are betting on might be rigged. They love it even if they are losing.

Frederick Standish knew this when he established the Melbourne Cup. Punters just want to feel like they're in with a chance.

Deep down, racing is dodgy, and it always has been. For many people it's part of the charm. It's a place that's more fun and crazy than the sanitised real world. You might lose because your horse is no good, or just because the race was fixed. Either way it's all about the risk, it doesn't matter much what the nature of the gamble actually is.

Racing people understand this subconsciously. It's why the most forgiving of all sports fans are the horserace-loving public. If it ever comes time for me to be judged, I hope it's by them.

THE CASHED-UP BUSINESSMAN

If there's one thing that should get the alarm bells ringing in sport, it's when a rich businessman – and it's always a man – starts to get heavily involved in a club. And the threat level should be raised to the highest possible if that businessman is portrayed as a 'white knight' who will save the club.

The archetype of the Cashed-Up Businessman is interesting on two levels.

Firstly, sporting success can massively influence a businessman's reputation. Alan Bond winning a yacht race negated a lot of the bad parts of his legacy, which should have been a pretty poor one, given what he did with the rest of his life. By contrast Christopher Skase's disastrous ownership of the Brisbane Bears did no such thing for him.

But equally fascinating is sports administrators' willingness to embrace billionaires who show up with a lot of cash, offering to save a club and solve all the problems.

We, the fans, also get sucked in by this archetype. We're generally not too concerned with how a cashed-up white knight got so rich so fast. And we seem to be unable to remember the myriad cases where a rich man riding in on his stallion has just made everything worse.

This is not surprising. Clubs almost always need money – or at least think they need more to remain competitive – and the rich like the level of prestige that, in Australia, only sport can offer.

But the ability to make a lot of money in business does not always cross over to sport. Especially if a fortune has been made taking massive risks or cutting corners.

In this section we'll look at the somewhat dubious contributions made to sport by Alan Bond, Christopher Skase, Clive Palmer, Geoffrey Edelsten, John Elliott, Eddy Groves, Tim Johnston and Nathan Tinkler.

ALAN BOND

THE THREE AMIGOS

It was 2013 and on stage at the Hilton Hotel in Sydney sat former prime minister Bob Hawke, the skipper of *Australia II*, John Bertrand, and Alan Bond. The mood was jovial. It was the thirtieth anniversary of the 1983 America's Cup win and the crowd was lapping up the three men reminiscing about the victory.

Hawke was resplendent in a white jacket with 'Australia' emblazoned across it numerous times and Australian flags in the shape of the continent sprinkled liberally all over it. It was the same jacket Hawke had worn in 1983 at the Royal Perth Yacht Club all-night party, when he famously declared, 'We might as well declare it a national holiday . . . I tell you what, any boss who sacks anyone for not turning up today is a bum.'

In 2013 Hawke was again in full voice as he regularly rested his hand on Bond's shoulder. He told a joke involving an Englishman, a Frenchman and an Australian hiking through the Andes. As the punchline was delivered ('There goes your f—ing canoe') the audience lost it.

Bond laughed too. After all, here was one of the greatest corporate criminals in Australian history, some would say *the* greatest, being feted by a former prime minister and an adoring crowd.

Bond was once asked if it was possible to be a corporate criminal and national hero. He said, 'It seems to be so, doesn't it?'

SORRY, HOW'S THAT?

Today, it's hard to imagine how much the America's Cup win meant to Australians. People born after 1983 probably scratch their heads wondering how the entire country could get excited about rich people racing incredibly expensive sailboats.* But at the time, the victory captured the nation in a way that is unlikely to occur again, given the abundance of sports on offer and the splintered media habits of today.

Hawke, looking back after Bond's death in June 2015, explained: 'We had gone through bad economic times, the country was badly divided. But we united around this marvellous historic victory and we thank Alan Bond for that.'

That was the year one of Australia's toughest droughts broke, and the economic boom that followed set new standards for excess. As a result it can be easy to see the America's Cup victory as some sort of turning point in Australian history, even if correlation doesn't imply causation. The idea that winning a boat race gave Australians the confidence to reach new heights in the economy and on the world stage is perhaps the most Australian thing of all time.

If anyone can highlight the redemptive power of sports in Australia, it's Alan Bond. He lived a life that included being jailed for four years (he'd initially been sentenced to seven) for fraudulently stripping a company, Bell Resources, of $1.2 billion. But on the thirtieth anniversary of a boat race, there was the former prime minister of Australia thanking him. He hadn't even been on the boat! He just paid for it.

---

* Remember, there was no Netflix back then.

But Hawke was hardly alone in praising Bond. Even some of Bond's biggest critics generously described his legacy as 'complicated'.

On one side, we have one of the largest corporate collapses in the history of Australia and numerous instances of illegal or immoral behaviour. Countless Australians lost their jobs and a lot of money.

On the other hand, we have victory in a yacht race.

On balance these things wouldn't seem to cancel each other out, but somehow, they have.

THE PERTH SIGN-WRITER

The America's Cup is the oldest continually awarded trophy in sports, beginning in 1851, and for over a century it was very accurately named. Up until 1962, only Britain and Canada had competed against the Americans for it, and until 1983 the New York Yacht Club won every single time.

It was in 1962 that another rich Australian businessman, media magnate Sir Frank Packer, father of Kerry, decided to challenge with the yacht *Gretel*. While the Americans again won the cup, *Gretel* won one of the match races, the first time America had lost one since 1930.

The Australians had had a taste for it now and kept challenging.

In 1974, a new financial backer entered the fray: Alan Bond, an up-and-coming businessman from Western Australia. The Americans had never seen anything like Alan Bond.[*]

Alan was born to Frank and Kathleen Bond in London, in 1938. They were a working-class family and, deciding they would like their son to see sunlight at some point in his life, they emigrated to Fremantle, Western Australia.

Bond was twelve when he arrived in Western Australia. At fourteen, he showed glimpses of the man he would become, fronting

---

[*]   Neither had the Australians, come to think of it.

court on charges of theft and unlawfully being on premises. He repeated the act as an eighteen-year-old, once again charged with unlawfully being on premises with the intent of robbing them.

Bond had dropped out of school at fifteen and apprenticed as a sign-writer, but he had bigger plans than minor breaking and entering. It turned out that Alan's artistry was not in sign-writing but in convincing people to give him money.

First, Bond set up a company, Nu Signs, and went into competition with the business he had previously been apprenticed to.

In 1960, aged twenty-two, Bond began one of the biggest borrowing sprees Australia had ever seen. He convinced a bank to loan him $30 000 for a property development – what distinguished Alan at the time was his willingness to go into debt at an alarming rate, close deals quickly and not worry too much about paying people back. Here was a template for the eighties, already being formed in the sixties.

By 1967, Nu Signs had become the Bond Corporation,* a company that predominantly operated in property while constantly bolting on different types of businesses. It wasn't an easy time. Being leveraged to the hilt meant Bond was constantly trying to get new deals done to pay off the creditors from previous deals.

Crucially, Bond understood that while success in business was one way to gain respectability, in Australia sport was a much faster way to obtain it. He decided to fund America's Cup challenges just as Sir Frank Packer had. In 1974 and 1977, he challenged with *Southern Cross*, before using the yacht *Australia* in 1980.

As the seventies turned into the eighties, Bond's high-debt approach to business turned out to be wildly successful, at least for a while. In 1981, he purchased Swan Brewery for $164 million and, showing his flair for marketing, had painter Ken Done and golfer

---

* It sounded like an evil organisation from some dystopian future.

Greg Norman do a TV ad together, proclaiming, 'They said you'd never make it . . . but this Swan's made for you!'

To be fair, usually when people say you'll never make it, they're right.

BREAKING THROUGH

Bond's first three attempts at wresting the America's Cup off the Yanks may not have delivered the ultimate glory, but they certainly raised his profile. So much so that, in 1978, our grateful nation bestowed on him an honour no less than Australian of the Year.

He shared the award with Indigenous leader Galarrwuy Yunupingu, who is less well known because he has neither lost lots of people's money nor funded a winning yacht, instead frittering away several decades fighting for Aboriginal land rights and challenging mining companies' exploitation of traditional lands.

For Bond, the earlier yachting defeats had set everything up for the America's Cup of 1983. He was pouring money into this attempt and commissioned a new 'winged keel' design, which was superior to anything the Americans had.

In fact, the winged keel was so good that the Americans challenged the legality of the new *Australia II*, taking their protest to the International Yacht Racing Union.* This only raised the interest in the cup back in Australia, where it was seen as Goliath trying to stop David before the competition had even started.

When the ruling was made in Australia's favour, the country got right behind the effort to topple the Americans for the first time in 132 years. Suddenly, people who had never even been on a boat would say things like, 'They should have got the spinnaker up

---

* I like to imagine the International Yacht Racing Union meets on the high seas, where laws don't apply and protests are settled by a duel to the death using cutlasses. I would prefer it if no one presents me with any evidence to the contrary.

earlier.' This ability to become an instant expert in any sport is an Australian trait that reoccurs every Olympics.

With the Yanks challenging him, Bond was in his element. He flew the Boxing Kangaroo flag and used Men at Work's 'Down Under' as a theme song, blaring it from *Australia II* before races to annoy the members of the New York Yacht Club.

When the time came to actually race, things didn't start well, with the Aussies going 3–1 down in the series. They won the next two races to tie the series, but started poorly in the decider. They recovered, making it competitive, and from there the lead changed three times. Once *Australia II* established a firm lead, the crew of the American *Liberty* did everything to get the lead back, tacking forty-five times in their attempt to reel in the Australians. It was no use. *Australia II* crossed the finish line 41 seconds ahead. The cup was now Australia's.

The come-from-behind victory only added to the legend. The Australians had ended the longest winning streak in sporting history. The New York Yacht Club had actually bolted down the cup in their trophy room, never expecting anyone to take it away, that's how big a surprise it was.*

Australians celebrated the victory with the ferocity usually reserved for the end of a war; that's how Bond saw it anyway, announcing, 'this is Australia's greatest victory since Gallipoli'.**

Australia certainly didn't care about Bond's lack of historical knowledge, awarding him the Order of Australia (AO) for 'distinguished service of a high degree to Australia or humanity at large'. Now who says we take sport too seriously?

AND WE'RE AWAY

Bond's victory catapulted him into the role of national hero, and

---

* There's no word on whether Bond's previous experience in burglary was required to get the trophy off the stand.

** You'll find there's a few problems in that statement.

suddenly there wasn't a person in Australia who didn't want to meet him. So Alan did what he always did: he hit them up for money, lots and lots of money.

It set him off on a borrowing and spending spree the likes of which are rarely seen. Even today the amounts are eye-watering. When he won the cup, Bond Corp's accounts were showing $200 million debt against net assets of $250 million, but the next six years saw him borrowing like an annoying neighbour, with his debts increasing forty-fold to $8.5 billion and his net assets plummeting into the negative.

The reason was simple. For the entirety of the eighties, Bond was spending more than he could ever possibly repay. In his office he had a van Gogh painting, a spiral staircase and – the must-have for any office – a spa.[*] He bought businesses at a phenomenal rate, at one stage even purchasing an entire English village. In 1983, he purchased Castlemaine Tooheys for $1.2 billion, giving him ownership of half the beer market in Australia.

As the government opened up the Australian economy to the world, removing tariffs and floating the dollar, local firms faced increasing competition from larger businesses with more modern practices and greater economies of scale. The deregulation of the economy created a takeover and merger boom, paid for with cheap credit from Australian and international banks who handed it out like pensioners feeding a pokies machine.

Bond now added a wide range of businesses to his portfolio, including spending US$262 million on a controlling stake in Chile's national telephone company.[**]

As the eighties sped towards collapse, Bond sped up too.

---

[*] Forget open plan, give me more spas in offices. Who wouldn't want to spend a meeting in the spa with Roger from accounts?

[**] Everyone should own a Chilean phone company at one point in their life.

RACING TOWARDS THE ABYSS

While he was making all these acquisitions, Bond's status as a national hero gave him access to almost any part of Australian life. One of the stranger moments was his appointment to the presidency of the Richmond Football Club in late 1986.

With no knowledge of Australian Rules, Bond talked up raising money for the cash-strapped club. In one disastrous appearance before the members, he said he'd been a lifelong fan of the red and black (Richmond wear yellow and black) and presented the best and fairest award to 'the club captain, Dale Wineman', whose name was Dale Weightman.

This was unforgivable to the Richmond faithful, and they were hardly more impressed when it leaked that Bond wanted to list the club on the stock market and relocate them to Brisbane.

He was moved on in early 1987, with not a single game being played during his very short time in office.

The year 1987 was a fateful one for Bond, who launched some of the most audacious and foolish purchases in the history of capitalism. That year he bought the American brewer G. Heileman in a plan to take his beers to the world. The purchase price of $1.26 billion was considered to be as much as three times what the business was actually worth.

Even more famously, he set out to buy the Nine Network from Kerry Packer. Letting Bond negotiate with Kerry Packer was like letting a child wander into a lion's den.* Bond later said of the negotiations, 'After much discussion, Kerry thumped the table and said, "Listen, if you can pay me $1 billion, I'll sell them to you, otherwise bugger off."'

---

* Kerry himself would shake up cricket in another example of businessmen throwing their weight around in the sporting arena. But Packer didn't waste time with a single team, he just bought an entire sport.

The deal was done for $1.05 billion, with $800 million of it in cash. Packer knew a man heading for a collapse when he saw one.

Packer hung Bond's cheque in the toilet in his office. He remarked, 'You only get one Alan Bond in your lifetime, and I've had mine.' When Bond went under, Packer bought his network back for a rumoured $250 million. Not a bad piece of business.

Packer was smart enough to get the majority of his cash up front, but most were not so lucky when dealing with Bond. In 1987, Bond purchased Vincent van Gogh's *Irises* for US$54 million, at the time the most ever paid for a painting. In a warning of what was to come, Bond bought the painting using a loan from the auctioneer, Sotheby's New York. He never repaid it.

All these massive deals meant the Bond Corporation was leveraged beyond belief and beyond sensible business practices, which was fine as long as the bull market continued. But guess what? It didn't.*

COLLAPSE

Before the stock market collapsed in October 1987, the Bond Corporation was the world's fifth largest brewer, owned huge media interests, including Channel Nine, and conducted a raft of business in mining, telecommunications, property and who knows what else.

Its labyrinthine structure meant few – even those in the company – really understood what was going on. One thing was clear, though: they had a lot of debt and suddenly the whole financial system was going the wrong way.

At first it appeared Bond would survive the crash, but as the country moved into recession, he couldn't change his ways, continuing to make big plays financed by debt. While other business

---

* The market crashing after a boom is the most predictable thing of all time, yet it seems to catch people by surprise every time.

tycoons were cashing in their chips, in 1988 Bond purchased the Hotel St Moritz in New York and bought shares in the British Satellite Broadcasting company and several other companies.

Corporate raider Robert Holmes à Court sold his company Bell Resources to Bond, his long-time arch rival. This couldn't have happened without the help of the corrupt state government led by Brian Burke, later to be the centre of the WA Inc royal commission. Burke arranged for the government-owned State Government Insurance Commission to form a joint venture with Bond Corporation to buy Bell Resources.

Holmes à Court kept 6 per cent of Bell Group and walked away with $340 million from the sale. It was a horrible deal for both the state and the shareholders of Bell Resources.

The truth of it all was that the Bond Corporation was drowning in debt and it was finding it increasingly difficult to pay off the interest on its loans. Bell Resources, on the other hand, had plenty of cash, so Bond and his lieutenants began siphoning off money from Bell into Bond Corp, ultimately totalling $1.2 billion, the largest bit of corporate fraud Australia has ever seen.

State prosecutor Stephen Hall later described it in court as a fraud 'enormous in its magnitude, audacious in its execution and redolent of the most serious dishonesty'.

Also, it didn't work. Bell Resources was effectively ruined and, in 1991, the Bond Corporation finally collapsed with debts of over $6 billion.

The music had stopped and all that was left behind was a mess that is still before the courts in 2018,* as creditors try to sort through the wreckage in the longest and most expensive legal action in the history of Australia, with more than $500 million flowing to the legal profession.

---

* Yes, you read that right, 2018.

FALLOUT

In 1992, Bond was declared bankrupt, with personal debts totalling $1.8 billion.

The trail of destruction included lost jobs, economic catastrophes and a lot of people, from institutional investors to families, who had lost a lot of money. The Western Australian business community was branded a basket case for years.

Michael Chaney, currently chairman of Woodside Petroleum Limited and Wesfarmers Limited, became CEO of Wesfarmers the same year Bond declared bankruptcy. He said it was a difficult time for business operators. 'I'd say it wasn't until the mid 1990s that people started to take WA business seriously again.'

For his part, Bond spent a fair bit of the nineties in and out of prison.

In May 1992 he was jailed for two-and-a-half years for dishonesty regarding fees relating to the failed rescue of Rothwells merchant bank, but after three months he was acquitted and released.

In 1996 he was jailed again, this time for the sale of an Édouard Manet painting, *La Promenade*. The painting had been purchased by Bond's family company Dallhold Investments in 1983, only to be leased to the publicly listed Bond Corporation for $4.6 million over five years, despite shareholders receiving no benefit whatsoever from the arrangement.

The Bond Corporation, which Alan was running as chairman, then sold it to him for less than its value. He promptly sold it for $17 million and kept the money. The court put him away for three years for corporate fraud.

In 1997 he was sentenced again, this time for stealing the $1.2 billion from Bell Resources.

During all these court proceedings, Bond pretended to be unwell, claiming memory loss due to brain damage. He repeatedly avoided questions about where he had sent money offshore by saying 'I don't recall' and 'I just can't remember' over and over.

After his jail time, his memory seemed to return to normal, in what can only be described as one of the great modern miracles of medicine.

In another 'you couldn't make this up' moment in Bond's life, while serving time at a prison farm, he gave the other prisoners lessons in business.

All up, he served just four years of his seven-year sentence, walking out a free man in March 2000.

A COMPLICATED LEGACY

Paul Barry, the journalist who pursued Bond more than any other, said it was estimated Bond had stashed $50 million offshore, despite his personal bankruptcy. The planning for all this had begun early, in 1974, when Bond put his $10 million mansion into a family trust and also began sending money offshore to Jersey and London.*

Once out of prison, Bond returned to a comfortable life and started investing in oil and diamond-mining schemes in Africa. He even made it back onto the 2008 *BRW* magazine Rich List, before history repeated and the Global Financial Crisis wiped him out. Sad.

He died on 5 June 2015 from complications during heart surgery.

Which brings us to his legacy. Considering the fact that he oversaw the largest corporate fraud in Australian history and caused untold destruction in countless people's lives, you'd think people looking back at his life would be highly critical of him.

But you'd be underestimating the power of a yacht race and the mythic power sport can convey on an individual in Australia.

---

* If there's one bit of advice I can give you from researching this section, it's to start putting money offshore as soon as possible if you are committing some fraud. You'll be glad you did later.

Bob Hawke said:

> Well, let us at the outset acknowledge the downside
> of Alan's record and history, he was convicted of cor-
> porate crime on several occasions. And his actions
> caused a lot of hardship to a lot of people [...] But
> let's remember Alan as a man who lifted the spirits of
> this country in 1983.
>
> On balance, he'll always rank remarkably high for
> the contribution he made to Australia.

Julian Burnside QC, who had represented Bond in court, said, 'For those people who painted him as a villain, I would wish those people might have had a chance to sit down and had a coffee and a chat with him. They might have modified their view of him.'*

Colin Barnett, who when Bond died was premier of Western Australia, the state that had suffered the most at Bond's hands, couldn't even bring himself to completely reflect his true legacy: 'He was a controversial figure but will also be remembered for a proud moment in Australia's history, which also put WA on the map.'

WA opposition leader at the time and current WA Premier Mark McGowan found it hard too: 'I think he himself has said at the same time he's a villain and a hero and I think that's probably the best way of describing the life of Alan Bond.'

Australia II skipper John Bertrand articulated perfectly the power of a sporting success: 'People have very polarised views about Alan in this country – his business empire and its collapse and of course, the America's Cup. From my perspective, through the lens of the America's Cup his contribution was enormous.'

---

* That would have to be a pretty amazing coffee, Julian.

Bond was probably the largest corporate criminal Australia has ever seen, and Australia's leaders danced around his true legacy because of a yacht race.

To see what Bond's legacy would have been without a famous sporting victory, we must look to one of his contemporaries.

CHRISTOPHER SKASE
DON'T OPEN THE ENVELOPE

It was 1986 and the Victorian Football League was expanding outside of Victoria. In reality, it was a cash grab. The VFL was overseeing a competition of broke Victorian clubs and as a way to bring in some money they agreed to sell club licences to private owners, with the money from the sale going into the Victorian teams.

The licences weren't cheap, either: $4 million each. Two teams emerged from the process, the West Coast Eagles and the Brisbane Bears.*

VFL Chief Executive Ross Oakley flew to Queensland to announce the founding of the Brisbane Bears, who despite the name were based on the Gold Coast, with their new owner, millionaire businessman Christopher Skase.

In front of the media, Skase handed Oakley an envelope with the cheque for the licence fee. Years later, Oakley recounted what happened next:

> He handed me the envelope and I thought it was a great media opportunity. I was going to tear it open and hold the cheque up for $4 million.
>
> I went to start to tear the envelope and he leant across to me and said, 'Gentlemen don't open envelopes in public.'

---

* I agree you could argue only one team emerged, plus the Brisbane Bears.

> As soon as the launch of the team finished,
> I ducked into the toilet and tore it open – there was
> absolutely nothing there.

The empty envelope was a sign of many things. The first, that the Bears might not work out, the second, that private ownership was not going to be a huge success for the AFL and, lastly, that Skase might not be all that he seemed.

EARLY LIFE

Christopher Skase was born in 1948 in Melbourne, the son of 3DB radio personality Charles Skase. He started a commerce degree but soon dropped out to work at the stockbroking firm JBWere, before changing careers again and becoming a business journalist at the *Sun News-Pictorial* and the *Australian Financial Review.*

By 1974, Skase was bored with commentating on business and wanted to get in the game. He would never be bored again.

His first move was to start an investment company called Takeovers, Equities and Management Securities, which made the acronym TEAM.* One of his earliest deals was to buy a small Tasmanian tin-mining company called Qintex, which was the corporate entity Skase built his business around.

Much like Bond, Skase was operating at a time when the banks were willing to lend money to almost anyone, regardless of that person's actual assets.**

Skase relocated to Queensland, where he became synonymous with the 'white shoe brigade', the businessmen and developers who enjoyed a close relationship with the corrupt premier Joh Bjelke Petersen.

---

* Clever huh? No, you're right, it's not really. It doesn't even really make the acronym 'TEAM', it's more like 'TEMS'.

** Isn't it good the banks are now reliable, sensible corporate citizens?

When it came to Joh, Skase had nothing but praise for him: 'I think his track record stands on a par with Menzies as one of the two greatest politicians and political leaders and managers that this country has ever seen.'

As the eighties boomed, Skase started to purchase a variety of businesses, including the jeweller Hardy Brothers, the car dealer Nettlefolds, a Brisbane TV station and numerous property developments. Increasingly, he pushed into developing resorts and media assets. His exceptionally well-named Mirage luxury resorts were renowned for their opulence, with marble everywhere and the use of a shade of pink named after his wife, Pixie.

His excess was typical of the eighties, with resort opening parties lasting for days. He once even had his private jet fly from Port Douglas to Melbourne and back just to pick up a dress for Pixie.

With the resorts making money and credit cheap, Skase made his move, purchasing the Seven Network from John Fairfax for $780 million, receiving Sydney's ATN7, Melbourne's HSV7 and Brisbane's BTQ7. Then the next year he purchased Perth's TVW7 and Adelaide's SAS7 from Robert Holmes à Court's Bell Group for $113 million, the same Bell Group that Bond would later pillage $1.2 billion from.

Skase was at the peak of his powers. He owned a major TV network and a string of profitable resorts. And let's not forget the jewel in the crown, the Brisbane Bears.

THE BAD NEWS BEARS

Skase had the idea that the Gold Coast needed a sports theme park and decided that the Bears should be the key tenant. It was a disaster. Not for the last time, the Gold Coast rejected a sporting franchise like a body rejects a foreign organ.

Despite the absence of a cheque at the Bears' media launch, Skase did eventually stump up the money a few weeks later, but the incident was a sign that his cash flow was no longer what it once was; that $4 million was a loan from the bank and not actually Skase's money.

The Bears debut season was 1987, just as the share market crashed. This placed extraordinary pressure on Qintex's debt-laden balance sheet. Like Bond, Skase failed to heed the warning, continuing with his high-risk, high-debt strategy.

One of his big plays in promoting the club was to recruit Warwick Capper* from the Sydney Swans, a side that was owned by businessman Geoffrey Edelsten.** Capper was a flop at the Bears, kicking only 71 goals in 34 games.

By 1988, however, the Bears' poor attendances and performances (they lost to Essendon by 140 points in 1988 and finished second last on the ladder) were the least of Skase's problems. In his three years running the Bears, he lost $27 million at a time when his broader empire was crumbling, forcing him to hand the licence back to the VFL.

THE FUGITIVE

Skase's Brisbane Bears folly was nothing compared to the deal that brought it all crashing down: a $1.5 billion bid for the MGM/United Artists movie studio in Hollywood.

In some regards it made sense. Qintex owned media and resorts, and becoming a major Hollywood player would work well with those assets. But times had changed; in 1989 debt was no longer cheap, as interest rates hit 18 per cent and property prices plunged.

Qintex's shares dived in response to the potential deal and, at the same time, a pilots' strike was reducing income at Skase's resorts.

---

* Capper was known for his flashy lifestyle. In 2017, he got locked in a Perth hotel stairwell after mistaking a fire escape door for the entry to the gym. He spent more than an hour in the stairwell and when he was found he said he thought he was going to die. The hotel later pointed out that the door at the bottom of the stairs is unlocked at all times, given it's a fire exit, so Capper could have left at any time.

** More about him soon.

Skase could no longer borrow money, which meant the $50 million letter of credit to secure the $1.5 billion he needed to purchase MGM/United Artists never materialised. The deal fell through.

With debts of $1.5 billion, Qintex was done, collapsing in November 1989.

Skase himself had personal debts of $172 million and claimed to only have $170 left and a few clothes. By 1991, he was bankrupt and scheduled to face trial on sixty charges, some relating to accusations that he improperly gained management fees when heading up Qintex.

In a move that could be described as a tactical error by prosecutors, Skase had been able to keep his passport. He promptly fled to the Spanish island of Majorca, where he holed up in a rented mansion with Pixie. Skase knew what he was doing – at the time Spain had no extradition treaty with Australia, so he was safe.

The outrage back home was immense, with Skase ending up on Australia's top-ten most-wanted list. Public anger mounted further when it became clear Skase was hardly poor. The ABC's *Four Corners* revealed that Skase had been moving money into overseas bank accounts as early as July 1989, months before declaring bankruptcy. He also sent to Britain two Rolls Royces, fifteen Bang & Olufsen TVs and stereos, marble furniture, a Roman statue and an enormous amount of antiques.[*]

The Australian government and his creditors tried everything to get Skase back into the country and to find his money, but nothing worked. TV host Andrew Denton even ran a public fundraising campaign[**] to hire a bounty hunter from Tombstone, Arizona, to capture Skase and return him home, a scheme that never eventuated but did cause the Spanish government some concern.

---

[*] Just the bare essentials for starting life over.
[**] This was before Gofundme or other online fundraising services. The money would probably be raised in an hour these days.

HELPFUL PHRASES

If you're the CEO of a club and a player does something stupid, draw on these handy phrases.

'out of character'

'genuinely remorseful'

'misunderstood'

'the comments were meant to be light-hearted'

'taken out of context'

'brain fade'/'brain snap'

'wake-up call'

'matured since then'

'a learning process for us all'

'with the benefit of hindsight'

'at all times our players co-operated with the SWAT team'

In 1998, the Australian government tried to bring him home by cancelling his passport, only for Skase to claim he had become a citizen of Dominica, the island republic in the West Indies. Skase famously showed up in Spanish court in a wheelchair and wearing an oxygen mask, claiming to have emphysema. Australians didn't believe him, and soon after he was filmed on Majorca swimming and playing tennis, with no signs of any physical problems. I know, I was surprised too.

DEATH IN MAJORCA

Three years later, Skase was admitted to hospital for chemotherapy to treat stomach cancer and an inoperable lung tumour. Understandably, many Australians still didn't believe he was actually sick, but in August 2001 he proved them all wrong by passing away. His funeral service in Spain was attended by just fifteen people.

Christopher Skase's legacy proved far simpler to define than Alan Bond's. *The Courier-Mail* pulled no punches at the time of his death:

> Has Queensland ever played host to a bigger shonk
> than Christopher Skase?
> Even when he died a lonely and helpless wreck,

many commentators thought it was just another of his elaborate cons.

The Guardian said news of the death of Christopher Skase had been met with antipathy Down Under, going on to say, 'Few people believed the claims he was dying and few expressed much sympathy when he passed away on Sunday night from a virulent stomach cancer. "Good riddance," said one MP.'

Three months after Skase's death, the movie *Let's Get Skase* was released in cinemas and no one considered that to be in poor taste, although the movie itself wasn't very good.

A big reason for the public hatred of Skase was the fact he had fled rather than fronting up in court, as Bond had. Skase's lawyer, Tony Morris, QC, said, 'If he had done what Alan Bond did and returned to face the music, at worst he would have spent time on a prison farm. The end of his life would have been more comfortable than it was.'

Yet Bond's corporate crime had been significantly bigger than Skase's, and affected far more people. Skase was charged with misusing his positions to obtain amounts of $19 million, $7.5 million and $2.85 million for himself. There were other charges for some monthly payments too, but all in all nothing close to what Bond had done – stealing $1.2 billion from a company to prop up his own.

This isn't to say Skase was treated poorly, or that how he's remembered is not an accurate reflection of the decisions he made. The point is that it's amazing Bond's legacy is as good as it is. Sure, he stayed in the country to get a slap on the wrist, but he only served a measly four years on a prison farm. When creditors tried to locate the money he had squirrelled offshore he feigned memory loss on the stand.

The major difference was that Bond had achieved what stands for greatness in Australia. His era-defining sporting triumph blinded many to the reality of his character. In the public reflections upon Bond's death, the 32-year-old America's Cup victory was mentioned in pretty much all of them. Skase had no great sporting triumph to cloud how people remembered him. All he left behind was a basket case of a football club that needed to be propped up by the governing body.

Luckily, sporting administrators have learnt from the heady days of the eighties.

Well, not really. Sports administrators don't really do 'learning'.

GEOFFREY EDELSTEN
THE MOST FORGIVING CLUB IN THE LAND

Cashed-up businessmen don't work alone: sports administrators have an uncanny ability to strike deals that have terrible repercussions for innocent clubs, even though those deals are part of their quest for success.

What's often surprising is that even after serious missteps that leave a trail of destruction, sporting clubs are incredibly forgiving of rich businesspeople. The AFL's history is full of these cases. It says a lot about the VFL that in the mid eighties Alan Bond was president of Richmond, Christopher Skase owned the Brisbane Bears and Geoffrey Edelsten owned the Sydney Swans. And we wonder why privatisation of clubs never worked.

While Bond's and Skase's involvements with the league were brief, Edelsten's has continued until recent times, which is quite astounding. To say Edelsten is a colourful character would be underselling him.

THE WEDDING OF THE YEAR

It was the wedding of 2009. Five hundred guests were invited to Crown Casino in Melbourne to watch 26-year old American Brynne Gordon, former fitness trainer, marry the good doctor, 66-year-old Geoffrey Edelsten.

The guests all looked a bit bemused as they filed in. After all, almost all of them had never met the couple. They'd been surprised when an invitation with a DVD turned up. The DVD was narrated by none other than Jason Alexander, as in, George from *Seinfeld*, and *The Nanny* star Fran Drescher. It told the story of how the couple met, including a remake of a scene from *Pretty Woman*.

With an invitation like that, how could you not attend?

Alexander and Drescher hosted the wedding, too, and Anthony Callea and Daryl Braithwaite* performed. Alexander gave a heart-felt address, even though he'd only met the couple the day before. He'd told a packed media conference that they had quickly formed 'a profound friendship'.

Despite the couple's relationship being only nine months old, it was obvious to everyone attending that this was a marriage built on the most solid of foundations. It was a strange event, the extravagance pitched to capture the public's attention and to send a message that Edelsten was well and truly back, following earlier controversies.**

I'm sorry to inform you that despite this wonderful start, the marriage did not last. But for Geoffrey, the wedding was just another chapter in an eventful life.

THE GOOD DOCTOR

Edelsten was born in 1943 in Carlton, the home of his beloved Carlton Football Club, who he still supports today.

Geoffrey was a high achiever, graduating from Melbourne University with a Bachelor of Medicine and a Bachelor of Surgery in 1966. Naturally, these degrees lent themselves to Edelsten dabbling in the music industry. He owned the record label Hit Productions

---

* I wonder if he did 'Horses'? What am I saying, of course he did. What else is he going to do?

** Not really that different an agenda to most weddings.

and co-wrote songs for the Last Straws including 'I Can't Stop Loving You, Baby' and 'A Woman of Gradual Decline'.

As his medical career took off Edelsten relocated to Sydney, opening a new medical practice in Coogee in 1969. He ran a variety of medical businesses, but his big break came when Bob Hawke introduced Medicare in 1984. Edelsten was certainly clever, and he recognised an opportunity when he saw one. He opened 24-hour 'superclinics' that offered multi-disciplinary medical services. With Medicare in place, he could bulk bill patients so they had nothing to pay themselves, meaning people came in droves. Two thousand patients came through his first clinic every week.

Edelsten knew how to get attention, too, working from the same principles he'd later apply to weddings. His thirteen clinics were not your ordinary doctors' offices. They had chandeliers, grand pianos and mink-covered examination tables.* You know, tasteful stuff.

With the money flowing in, it was time for Edelsten to make his most famous purchase.

BUYING THE SYDNEY SWANS

In July 1985, it was announced that Dr Geoffrey Edelsten had purchased the Sydney Swans for $6.3 million. For the VFL, it was a brave new step into privatising clubs, which would end in disaster for all involved. But, like many things that end badly, at first it was very exciting.**

Since moving to Sydney from South Melbourne in 1982, the Swans had been terrible, like, current Carlton terrible; they were awful on the field but found a way to be even worse off it, a fair achievement.

The VFL put the Swans up for sale and it developed into a two-horse race between Edelsten and a consortium led by businessman

---

* To this day, I refuse to be examined on anything less than mink.
** Like democracy.

Basil Sellers. Sellers' proposal was focused on long-term goals, building steadily, attracting members and having a traditional football structure.

'Boring!' said the VFL Commission. They asked Edelsten for his plans. Edelsten said he wanted to spend a fortune buying the best players and turn the club into an instant success. 'Now that's the sort of short-term thinking we're attracted to,' said the VFL.

Sellers, in the meantime, had looked more closely at the figures and the escalating upfront costs and decided it was not economically feasible. He told the VFL he was pulling out. Rather than wondering if he might have a point about the viability of the entire exercise, the VFL instead asked him to keep it quiet so they could drive Edelsten's bid up even higher.

What is perhaps most astounding is that during the VFL's due diligence, they reportedly uncovered quite a lot of concerning information about Edelsten including rumours that he was involved with a hitman. The VFL believed there wasn't enough evidence to substantiate this information.

In the end Edelsten succeeded and the Swans were his. Upon receiving the news he announced, 'I believe it is a great investment and history will prove me right.' It wouldn't.

SPEND, SPEND, SPEND

Edelsten was certainly true to his word. He spent big on buying stars like Merv Neagle, Bernard Toohey, Gerard Healy and Greg Williams. The money Edelsten was willing to spend was crazy.

Greg Williams said of negotiating with Edelsten, 'My manager came up to him with a stupid

INEVITABLE APOLOGIES

'At least my actions have united the major religions in their anger towards me.'

'I can see how my actions could be seen by some as treason.'

'Clearly smuggling exotic animals was, on reflection, a mistake.'

figure, three times more than I was getting at Geelong. He said "yes" in a heartbeat. They were pretty unreal days.'

Edelsten significantly increased the club's spending on marketing and promotions too, and introduced gimmicks like cheerleaders, the Swanettes. It worked to an extent – crowds rose and performances on the field improved. In 1986 the Swans finished third last but by 1987, they ended the season second on the ladder.

The problem was, there was no money, and Edelsten still needed to pay instalments to the VFL for the Swans licence. When the second instalment of $250 000 fell due, he didn't have it. Instead, he sought help from a company called Westeq, based in Perth, who agreed to help, effectively giving them ownership over half the club.

The VFL had gained a new co-owner and apparently they didn't even know.

MR RENT-A-KILL

By 1986, less than a year after Edelsten had purchased the Sydney Swans, the barbarians were at the gate. He was in serious trouble. The NSW Medical Tribunal were looking into claims he had overcharged patients, the Tax Office was chasing him and, even more concerning, the Stewart Royal Commission, which was looking into drug trafficking in Australia, had uncovered a tape of a conversation between him and Christopher Dale Flannery.

Flannery, also known as 'Mr Rent-A-Kill', was a notorious hitman. He was later played by Gary Sweet* in the ABC miniseries *Blue Murder*. Flannery associated with notorious corrupt cop Roger Rogerson, who would 'green light' certain criminals in return for a share of the profits.** Flannery was believed to be responsible for fourteen murders.

---

* Australian legislation requires Gary Sweet to be in every TV show.
** The 'green light' meant permission from corrupt police officers to carry out certain criminal activities without investigation or arrest.

Edelsten's troubles started when an amateur radio enthusiast managed to record telephone calls between Edelsten and his then wife, Leanne.

Leanne was twenty years younger than Edelsten, a model he had met and quickly married in 1985.* At one point, in 1986, Geoffrey tried to buy the Cronulla Sharks for her. The NSWRL, showing better judgement than the VFL, rejected the idea.

In the recorded conversations, Leanne and Geoffrey reportedly discussed Flannery and potentially having him assault a former patient.

Leanne asks, 'Bashing up people, is that all he [Flannery] does?'

To which Edelsten replies, 'No, he kills people. Nice young fella.'

With the tape coming to light during the Stewart Royal Commission, Edelsten began a legal battle to stop the transcript from being used by the NSW Medical Board during a hearing investigating complaints about him. In this he failed, with Mr Justice Lee ruling that the communications had been scanned and recorded in breach of the *Telecommunications (Interception) Act 1979*, but that they were nonetheless admissible in evidence.

By August 1986, Edelsten was summoned to appear in court, charged with perverting the course of justice and soliciting Flannery to assault a former patient.

The first of those charges arose from events that occurred in 1984. The accusation was that in concert with corrupt police, Edelsten had provided a medical certificate for Flannery that declared him unfit to stand trial for a murder. The alleged purpose of this was to help Flannery avoid going to trial with a certain judge, who the corrupt police believed would not be helpful to their cause.

Between these criminal charges and the medical board's

---

* Marrying a much younger model you've just met is the foundation of most good marriages.

investigation, Edelsten was forced out of the Swans by July 1986, less than twelve months after becoming chairman.

The trial itself wouldn't begin until 1990 but Edelsten filed for bankruptcy in 1987, was divorced by Leanne and in 1988 was struck off the NSW medical register for at least ten years.

The Flannery recording certainly didn't help his standing with the medical tribunal, who found he had been over-servicing patients (effectively charging them for things they didn't need) and involved in other professional misconduct since 1978.

The Medical Tribunal of New South Wales had the following to say about Edelsten:

> In the respondent's appearances before the Tribunal, he has misled and played with it, sought to qualify his earlier statements when their veracity or credibility has been questioned, distanced himself from decisions and procedures relating to his organisation when he has thought that they have been seen in an unfavourable light.
>
> He gave, at times, testimony so unhelpful as to be designed to conceal the true situation. He presented himself as a paragon of unblemished medical virtues and competencies. In striving towards those ends he has failed to paint a self-portrait of an honourable, if fallible, human.

The collapse was complete when, in 1990, he was found guilty of soliciting to assault and perverting the course of justice.

In his remarks, Justice Sharpe made the following findings:

- that the applicant urged Flannery to deal harshly with Evans in such a manner that he would not trouble him again; and

- that the applicant conspired with certain police officers and Flannery to give Flannery laser treatment in order to keep him out of the way for a few days so that he would not have to appear before a certain judge of the Supreme Court who they believed had a reputation not conducive to Flannery's chance [of] successfully defending his trial.

Edelsten was sentenced to a year in prison.

Since then Edelsten has taken issue with how the incident has been portrayed in the media. In a 2009 interview with the *Daily Telegraph* he disputes that he knew Flannery was a hitman:

> The media have hundreds of times summed up this situation by saying Edelsten hired Christopher Flannery, a well-known hitman, to bash a former patient.
>
> One, he wasn't hired. I was convicted of soliciting, and soliciting is the lowest form of petty crime because it means just even speaking to him about it. And Flannery was not known as a hitman until years later.
>
> But I did ask him one day, 'What do you do?', and this story I told to many people because it sounded so incredible.
>
> He said, 'I kill people for $50 000 and I bash them for $10 000', and I said, 'Gee, that sounds like a lot of money for a bashing.' And he said: 'Yeah, baseball bats are expensive.'*

I suppose Edelsten is right in pointing out he didn't hire Flannery, just sounded him out about it. It strikes me, however, that most

---

* I'm not sure this story helps Edelsten in the way he thinks it does.

people never find themselves in a position where they have to make this distinction.

Flannery famously went missing in 1985, before all this broke into the open. In 1997 a coroner ruled he was likely a victim of murder and that the corrupt cop Roger Rogerson had information about it.

Rogerson denies this, telling Channel Nine's *Sunday* program in 2004:

> Flannery was a complete pest. The guys up here in Sydney tried to settle him down. They tried to look after him as best they could, but he was, I believe, out of control. He didn't want to do as he was told, he was out of control, and having overstepped that line, well, I suppose they said he had to go but I can assure you I had nothing to do with it.

BACK HOME

Now unable to practise in New South Wales, Edelsten headed back to Victoria and began practising again. Medical tribunals later took a dim view of this, believing it showed he did not accept responsibility for his misconduct in NSW. In 1992 the Victorian Medical Board struck him off their register too.

Edelsten consistently attempted to be re-registered but was denied time and again. At one hearing he admitted he had lied to previous tribunals.

Despite being deregistered, Edelsten still launched a series of businesses in the medical area, including 'Gene E', a company offering paternity testing by mail. In 2005, he founded Allied Medical Group, which again ran 'superclinics', which he sold in 2011 for $28 million.

It was an amazing rebirth and helped fund the garish 2009 wedding to Brynne. But, like that marriage, the upturn in his fortunes wasn't to last. Edelsten's spending habits remained lavish, with the Allied money paying for a casino and a private jet, among other things. He eventually had to file for bankruptcy in the US in January 2014. He was being chased by more than thirty creditors in Australia, the US, the Dominican Republic and Singapore.

Moves were also made to have him declared bankrupt in Australia, and this happened in February 2015, with creditors receiving cents on the dollar. The Australian Tax Office revealed it was owed $14 million in outstanding taxes and penalties by Edelsten.

FORGIVEN NOT FORGOTTEN

Through all Edelsten's ups and downs, his original love, the Carlton Football Club, has remained the one constant.

When we talk forgiveness in sport we often think of our sporting heroes and how they can overcome any challenge. But the Cashed-Up Businessman can match anything the Wayward Champion can do.

Edelsten has been a big donor to Carlton over the years and the club has been more than willing to turn a blind eye to the whole going-to-jail thing. At one point he pledged $1 million to the club and in his US bankruptcy hearings, Carlton seemed to be the creditor he was worried about the most, reportedly telling the court: 'I'm absolutely obligated to pay. I made a donation in 2011 and it's a tax-deductible donation of $1 million to be paid over three years. $150 000 was due before the end of 2013 and I haven't been able to pay that.'

Despite the fact he had been struck from the medical register in two states, convicted for soliciting a hitman to assault someone and perverting the course of justice, in 2012 the Blues decided that he should be made a life member of the club.

Even after his second bankruptcy, where he left over thirty creditors out of pocket, Carlton welcomed him with open arms. In May 2015, Mick Malthouse coached his 715th game, setting a record for most games coached in the VFL/AFL. It was a big event for the club and, as the cameras focused on Mick in the coaches' box during the game, who was right behind him? None other than Geoffrey Edelsten.

But then, when it comes to the Cashed-Up Businessman, Carlton is perhaps the most forgiving sporting club in the land.

JOHN ELLIOTT

IN THE WEE SMALL HOURS OF THE MORNING

It was past 2 a.m. on Saturday 23 November 2002 and a seven-hour meeting of the AFL Commission had just finished. The media gathered to hear the outcome of this marathon hearing into accusations the Carlton Football Club had breached the AFL salary cap, the socialist mechanism that stops the richest clubs from buying up all the good players.

The AFL chairman, Ron Evans, entered the media conference, followed by then chief executive Wayne Jackson and then football operations chief Andrew Demetriou. The general mood of the three men was anger.

What was revealed was that under club president John Elliott – certainly no socialist – Carlton had spent $1 400 000 more on players than any other club in 2002. They hadn't just slightly gone over the salary cap, they had sped past with the top down and music blaring.

Worse still, this wasn't their first time. Carlton had been found guilty of salary-cap breaches in 1994, 1999 and 2001. That meant that any new punishment would trigger earlier suspended penalties. It was a right mess.

Evans said of the cheating: 'Carlton's latest salary-cap breaches were a deliberate, elaborate and sophisticated scheme to break the player payment rules. Carlton members and supporters ought to feel betrayed by the actions of their club.'

Wayne Jackson added that the Blues had been found guilty of 'a complex and deliberate scheme designed and implemented to hide payments and deceive the AFL'.

Then the hammer fell. It was announced the club would be fined $1 million and lose their first two picks in the national draft, which was happening in two days' time. Other draft picks were also lost due to the earlier salary-cap breaches.

Carlton lost the two gifted young players they'd been planning to draft: Brendon Goddard and Daniel Wells. The penalty was without precedent and even the veteran journalists in the room seemed shocked.

Carlton responded with a media conference of their own, but they were so angry with the size of the penalty they barred AFL officials from attending.

The new Carlton administration, led by president Ian Collins, who had not been at the club at the time of the cheating, was furious with the harshness of the decision. After all, the club was already financially destitute and in 2002, the season in question, had finished dead last despite the cheating.

'I think it is the lowest point in Carlton's history,' he told the assembled media. He was probably right, although since then the club has been attempting to surpass that record low on a regular basis.

The man who had overseen the breaches, John Elliott, was not there that night. He'd been moved on after twenty years as club president. Before the salary-cap cheating, he was known as the man who had brought Fosters beer to the world, an atrocity that was hard to forgive. Now he had set the Carlton Football Club back decades. So perhaps he wasn't all bad.

ECONOMIES OF SCALE

Elliott, like Skase and Bond, built his business career on the back of the easy credit washing around Australia during the eighties.

Born in 1941, Elliott studied business at Melbourne University before joining McKinsey & Company as a management consultant. There he identified an underperforming Tasmanian company, jam-maker Henry Jones IXL, as a potential target for a takeover. In 1972, he raised $30 million to do just that, and his new management team turned it into a profitable business.

Elliott recognised that Australian companies needed to get bigger if they wanted to compete with international firms, but he was not alone. In 1981, Alan Bond's nemesis, Robert Holmes à Court, made a hostile takeover bid for Elders GM, an enormous pastoral company. To stave off Holmes à Court, the Elders board turned to Elliott, creating a deal that saw Henry Jones IXL and Elders merge to become Elders IXL.

The new entity was instantly one of Australia's largest companies, with assets of more than $1 billion, a turnover in excess of $2.5 billion, and 500 subsidiaries in fourteen countries. In 1983, Elders IXL bought Carlton and United Breweries, making it a $7 billion company, the second largest in Australia and with huge agricultural, commodities, finance and brewing operations.

In the same year, Elliott became the president of the Carlton Football Club.

In 1986, he again fought off Holmes à Court, who was trying to take over BHP. In a $2 billion deal, Elders IXL purchased 20 per cent of BHP instead, giving Elliott a seat on the board.

These were dizzying heights. Elliott had built Elders IXL into the second biggest company in Australia, sat on the board of the biggest Australian company, was national president of the Liberal Party and, as president of a VFL club, he had even attained a position of real importance.

Yet from these heights the seeds of Elliott's downfall were sown.

ALL DOWNHILL FROM HERE

In 1989, Elliott was rich and powerful, with a personal fortune valued at $80 million. However, he had always resented the fact he'd built his companies working for other people, funded by their money. He wanted to be insanely rich, not just spectacularly rich.

Despite the 1987 share market crash sending a clear warning to all that the global economy was fragile, in 1989 Elliott launched a $2.5 billion management buyout of Elders through the private company Harlin Holdings.

It was a disaster.

Elliott just wanted to buy BHP's stake in Elders, but the National Companies and Securities Commission ordered Harlin to make a full takeover bid or nothing at all, to ensure all Elders shareholders got the same offer. To do this, Harlin had to take on huge debts – not a good thing to have once the recession of the early nineties bit, sending interest rates skyrocketing.

In 1990, Elders lost more than $1.3 billion. By 1992, Elliott left the newly branded Fosters Brewing Group, which was itself about to fall over with losses of $3.2 billion. At the same time, the debt-laden Harlin Holdings had the receivers called in.

A PYRRHIC VICTORY

As the Harlin Holdings deal was starting to unravel, word came that Elliott was also being investigated by the National Crime Authority (NCA), a precursor of the Australian Criminal Intelligence Commission.

In February 1990, ABC's *7.30 Report* revealed that the NCA was looking into Elliott's business deals, especially the 1986 deal that saw him defend BHP from Robert Holmes à Court's attempted take-over. Elliott claimed it was a political witch-hunt due to him being the federal president of the Liberal Party and indeed by October he was gone from that role under the pressure of the scandal.

The accusation and eventual charges were that he and others used $66.5 million in allegedly sham foreign-exchange transactions to complete the BHP deal.

It kicked off a long legal battle between Elliott and the NCA that was as expensive as it was brutal. Eventually, in 1996, Elliott was acquitted after Justice Frank Vincent of the Victorian Supreme Court ruled the NCA had acted beyond its powers. As a result, none of the evidence the NCA had gathered could be used and would never be presented to another court, no matter what it proved, as this would have constituted double jeopardy.[*]

It was a technical victory[**] but one Elliott was happy to take as resounding proof of his innocence and that it all had been an attempt to blacken his name.

Elliott was now determined to get vengeance against the NCA. Instead of walking away, he sued them for damages, which meant a new eight-year court battle that went all the way to the Federal Court. There, in 2001, his claim for $75 million in damages was dismissed, and instead the judge ordered him to pay costs to the tune of $5 million. This effectively turned his victory into a loss, a template Carlton have used ever since.

Elliott had wasted a decade fighting the NCA in an expensive legal action. But while the Liberal Party and the business community had cast him aside, the AFL was very forgiving. Elliott still had Carlton.

TIMES ARE CHANGING

As president of the Carlton Football Club, one can only assume Elliott's plan wasn't to set the club back decades, leaving it a shell

---

[*] I'm pretty sure that's why, if my understanding of the 1999 movie *Double Jeopardy* starring Ashley Judd and Tommy Lee Jones is correct.

[**] The Victorian Court of Appeal later rejected Justice Vincent's reasoning, demolishing as 'erroneous' his key ruling that the NCA had operated beyond its powers. This, however, didn't lead to an overturning of the decision.

of what it once was. But if that had been his plan, he couldn't have done a better job.

It's hard to believe now, but the Blues were once a powerhouse of the AFL, both on and off the field. They've won sixteen premierships in the VFL/AFL, but the most recent only in 1995. Sir Robert Menzies, Australia's longest-serving prime minister, was famously a supporter, having had a ramp built so he could drive right up into the grandstand at Princes Park and watch the team play from the comfort of his car.

But times were changing. The AFL brought in the draft and the salary cap, measures that limited the ability of wealthy clubs to buy the best players. The wider economics of the game were changing, too, with the AFL moving to 'rationalise' suburban grounds, effectively getting rid of them. Their preference was to use the MCG and the not-long-for-this-world Waverley Park, and they already had plans for a Docklands stadium.

As Carlton president from 1983, Elliott had overseen a period of great success, but it would be fair to say he read this changing landscape as badly as I read other people's non-verbal cues.

Once the salary cap was in place, Elliott oversaw an administration that continued on like the rules were merely guidelines. Further to this, when they were caught in 1994, 1999 and 2001, they didn't heed the warnings or come clean about everything. Rather than trying to tidy up this mess of their own making, they went out of their way not to help, with members of the board refusing to assist the AFL's investigation.

Elliott's other big mistake was trying to turn Carlton's Princes Park into the alternative to the MCG, ignoring the proposed Docklands stadium favoured by the AFL. He saw a future where other teams would play home games at Princes Park and pay the Blues a nice fee for the privilege. The problem was, no one else bought into his vision. The AFL had no interest, nor were the other clubs particularly eager to help Carlton out. But Elliott ignored them all and spent millions building new grandstands, including one called the 'John Elliott Stand'.

With AFL games in Melbourne all scheduled at Docklands Stadium and the MCG, no one was sitting in these new stands. Instead, they instantly became a white elephant, generating no revenue and costing the club a fortune.

In 2002, the club posted losses of $7.5 million, which rose to $11.1 million by 2004, mostly from devaluing these assets at Princes Park. Add to that the fines for the salary-cap cheating and Elliott left the club in ruins – a disaster financially and unable to effectively use the draft to rebuild for years.

TO FORGIVE IS DIVINE

Elliott's downfall continued after leaving Carlton in late 2002. At one stage, he didn't tell his wife he'd sold their Toorak mansion. Understandably, they got divorced soon after.*

He went bankrupt when his rice milling business, Water Wheel, failed. It was discovered the company had been trading while insolvent, meaning Elliott was banned from serving as a company director for four years. His bankruptcy was finally annulled after a deal was struck for him to pay 2.5 cents in every dollar of the $7.6 million owed.

You'd think that sending a club broke, ensuring it remained uncompetitive on the field for years, would mean you wouldn't be welcomed back. But this is sport. In 2007, new Carlton president Richard Pratt called on Elliott to chair a new coterie group to raise money for the club.

Now, it might seem odd to hand a coterie club (whose entire aim is raising money) to a man recently found to have allowed a

---

* It's a good tip for any relationship: don't sell the family home without telling your partner.

A FORGIVING BUNCH

While there's a strong argument that the Carlton Football Club might be the most forgiving club in the land, in recent times Essendon have given them some competition. James Hird and Mark 'Bomber' Thompson were key figures in the supplements saga that tore the club apart, yet they remained welcome at Essendon and at the club's 1993 premiership reunion.

Perhaps most amazing was that Thompson was welcome despite fronting the Melbourne Magistrates' Court the week before, after being hit with seven drug-related charges.

The AFL was pretty forgiving of Hird, too. Despite banning him from the game for twelve months they allowed him to present the Norm Smith Medal at the 2017 Grand Final.

company to trade while insolvent and who breached the salary cap multiple times, but this is Carlton. If Edelsten could be allowed to hang around, so could Elliott.

However, Elliott's return was short lived. Pratt himself was forced to step aside from the presidency in 2008, amid allegations he lied about his knowledge of price-fixing at Visy. This scandal saw his company fined $36 million for colluding with their main competitor in Australia's cardboard industry. Another example of a Cashed-Up Businessman causing problems, not solving them.

FALLING OUT. AGAIN.

Elliott's return to Carlton had ended quickly, and in 2009 he made the break-up permanent. He announced publicly that the Blues had given hush money to four or five women who'd come forward accusing players of raping them in the eighties and nineties.

He gave no further details, except to say the payments were made because the club didn't believe the women (what a shock). His comments led to a woman coming forward claiming to be a rape victim. 'Kate' told the *Herald Sun* that she was attacked by a player at Carlton's party after the 1999 grand final loss.

'If you know something, Mr Elliott, please come forward. If you are talking about me, please help me and do what is right,' Kate said.

Elliott responded, 'She said what? I have no idea and I'm not interested. The story has got totally out of hand. I'm really not interested at all.'

A fascinating response, given he was the one who'd brought it up in the first place.[*]

The incident meant Elliott's time at Carlton was now done for good. He was banned from attending official events. It was one thing to cheat the salary cap, or to send the club broke with white elephant projects, or to be found to have allowed a company to trade while insolvent – those things can be forgiven. But to bring up payments regarding rape accusations that could open up the club to a lot of awkward questions? Obviously that was a bridge too far.

CLIVE PALMER
HISTORY REPEATS

With the eighties providing the examples of Bond, Skase, Edelsten and Elliott, it would be easy to think administrators and clubs had learnt an important lesson about putting all your eggs in one basket, even if that basket was being held by a very rich person. It would be easy to think, but it would also be completely wrong.

When it comes to Australian sporting administrators, most seem to believe 'due diligence' is a movie starring Liam Neeson. And

---

[*] A week later Elliott would clarify his position, stating, 'I just want to make this short statement, and that is I have always found violence to women abhorrent, including sexual violence.' He did this on the most powerful platform known to humankind, community television. He had his own show on Melbourne's Channel 31 back then.

for rich people, owning a sporting franchise is right up there with owning a boat: it's a way of signalling that you're someone.

In 2009 the A-League* was riding high. Or at least they thought they were. They expanded into Queensland with two new teams, North Queensland Fury (based in Townsville) and Gold Coast United. Twenty-three years after Skase's shambolic Brisbane Bears launched on the Gold Coast, here was the A-League, trying to introduce soccer to people who were not particularly interested in sport and doing it by going into business with Clive Palmer.

Palmer was certainly rich, having made his money in mining, but he was also a man of unusual temperament. Aside from his foray into soccer, in 2012 he commissioned a full replica of the RMS *Titanic*, which was never built, and in 2013 he added 150 animatronic dinosaurs to his resort at Coolum. While these seemed eccentric but amusing distractions for a rich man, his three-year ownership of Gold Coast United would become Football Federation Australia's (FFA) biggest regret.

SOME SPEED BUMPS

In mid 2008, Clive Palmer secured the licence for the new Gold Coast team that was to enter the league the following year. The A-League was thrilled. The richest man in Queensland was backing their code. It was almost as if the FFA had never heard of the AFL's disastrous experiment with privatisation in the eighties, although maybe they had just failed to heed its lessons.

At the media conference announcing the new team and its owner, Palmer declared he would build a side capable of winning the title in its first season. It wasn't.

Things got off to a shaky start. Palmer was not thrilled by the low crowds in the early days. In response, he capped attendances

---

* The A-League had only been founded in 2004.

at home games to 5000, closing all but one grandstand. This would save him money on stadium rental and government transport levies.

The decision was not welcomed by Gold Coast fans or the A-League, which was trying to foster bigger crowds, not limit them. It didn't matter too much anyway – only 2616 people showed up to the next game.

Still, the A-League stepped in and ended the cap. Palmer was furious, seeing the FFA as a dictatorial organisation led by billionaire Frank Lowy. Palmer's move, though, had already alienated the fans. Crowds continued to dwindle.

Palmer was tipping in about $18 millio and expressed anger at the community for not supporting the team. By the next season, crowds were regularly below 2000 people and there were rumours of Palmer withdrawing financial support. While that didn't eventuate, it pointed to increasing tension between Gold Coast United and the FFA.

The FFA believed Palmer was failing to engage the local community and grow the game on the Gold Coast. This led to a series of bizarre events in the 2011/12 season, where one week Palmer insisted seventeen-year-old Mitch Cooper, who had never played a senior game, be named captain. When coach Miron Bleiberg called the move 'ceremonial', he was sacked.

Palmer then gave an interview where he said football was a 'hopeless' game and that he preferred rugby league. In the same interview, he labelled the A-League 'a joke' and said Gold Coast United was an 'insignificant' part of his sprawling business empire. In response, just 1141 people turned up to the next game.

Ten days later, now openly at war with the FFA, Palmer decided to protest by putting up signage at the next game and on the players' uniforms that said 'Freedom of Speech'. The FFA pointed out that this was not permitted under the licence agreement, but he did it anyway. This forced the normal shirt sponsor – Hyatt Regency – off the players' shirts. They were in a legal dispute with Palmer at the time.

So, all in all, things were travelling well.

The FFA was furious and used the breach as a trigger to terminate the licence in 2012, even though there were two more years left to run. Palmer, in response, claimed the 'Freedom of Speech' slogan was in support of refugees.

The FFA also pointed to the lack of community support for the club and blamed Palmer for the 'lack of community engagement and its inability to build a football culture around the club'.

Clive took being stripped of the licence well, tweeting: 'We intend to fight this ludicrous decision by incompetent FFA in the courts. Frank Lowy is an institution who now belongs in an institution.'

THE REBEL LEAGUE THAT WASN'T

Instead of actually fighting in the courts, Palmer launched a rebel organisation called Football Australia.

Palmer hired Archie Fraser as the CEO to lead this new organisation. Fraser was a former CEO of the St Kilda Football Club and CEO of the A-League, and he was perfect for the job; he had made bad decisions before.

At St Kilda, he moved the club away from its heartland of Moorabbin to the neighbouring suburb of Seaford, a move universally viewed as a total disaster and one that was reversed in 2018. Despite this, Fraser was hired by the FFA for the top job at the A-League, in another example of sporting administrators' reputation and employability not being linked to past performance or outcomes.

Joining Palmer's Football Australia may have been Fraser's most ill-conceived move, though, even worse than the Seaford one. At first it seemed this organisation was meant to be a rival to the FFA, with the media release stating, 'Mr Palmer said Football Australia aimed to replace Football Federation Australia, which he said was incompetent at both a domestic and international level.'

Yet a few minutes after that statement went out, Palmer explained at a media conference that the body was 'like the Lowy Institute to the broader economy, where Frank Lowy's done a great job to make people and politicians accountable for public policy'.

This made little sense for all involved, especially the praise for Lowy, who Clive was currently at loggerheads with. For his part, Fraser suddenly looked like a man who'd realised he had made a mistake of epic proportions. He attempted to spin things, claiming the plan all along was to be a pressure group, despite the media release sent out minutes before stating the opposite.

Fraser said, 'I would certainly extend my hand to the senior executives and the chairman of the FFA to actually embrace this and get involved, and put behind them the professional issues that they've had and stop playing the man, and start getting on with the job of making this game that we all love the number one sport in this country.'

The idea that the FFA, who had just booted Palmer out of the A-League, would have any interest in this was laughable, but it seemed likely he wouldn't be deterred. Palmer had explained, '[Football Australia] will publish papers, hold press conferences, lobby government and the FFA.' He promised it would tackle issues such as 'the role of women – we have a great national team that doesn't get enough resources'.

You'll be surprised to hear that it did none of these things. In fact, it did nothing. It didn't even go to the trouble of officially ending, it just faded away.

It was radio silence after that. Palmer turned his attention to starting his own political party, where he found just as much success as in his foray into football.

At the time of writing in 2018, Palmer is busy trying to relaunch his political career and fighting it out in the courts over his failed business, Queensland Nickel, which closed in 2016 owing debts of about $300 million to creditors and putting more than 800 people out of work.

NATHAN TINKLER
CROSS-CODE DESTRUCTION

While Clive Palmer may have done some damage to the A-League, he was small time compared to the work of Nathan Tinkler.

Tinkler's rise from poor mining electrician to Australia's youngest billionaire in about six years sucked in both the NRL and the A-League, as well as resulting in one of the biggest splurges on racehorses Australia has ever seen.

Once again, sporting administrators were dazzled by the huge sums of money being thrown around and didn't seem to consider at all that history could be repeating itself. You'll never guess what happened.

RISE

For the early part of his life Nathan Tinkler wasn't much of a success story. He had been an electrician in the Hunter Valley, working in the mines. Later he ran a mine machinery maintenance business, but he had little to show for it. He once lost the family home when he couldn't meet the mortgage payments.

This was all about to change, however, when in 2005 he had the idea to raise funds to purchase a coal deposit at the disused Middlemount Mine in Queensland. He was speculating that coal prices were about to go up significantly, based on the Chinese economy booming, and he timed his run perfectly – China soon switched to becoming a net coal importer. The price of coal shot up. Tinkler had raised $1 million to purchase the Middlemount coal deposit; just a year later he was able to sell his stake for $275 million.

Most of that money was on paper, in shares of the company that bought his stake, Macarthur Coal. That company was run by Ken Talbot, who became a mentor to Tinkler, and in 2008 they engineered the sale of Tinkler's stake in Macarthur Coal to Indian steelmaker ArcelorMittal for $442 million.

In two years, Tinkler had turned $1 million into $442 million. That would have been enough for most, but he wasn't done. His next big venture was another big coal play; this time he wanted the Maules Creek coal deposit in New South Wales, which was owned by Rio Tinto.

The deal was underway and in 2009 Tinkler had negotiated to buy it for $480 million. Considering he had received $442 million the year before, that shouldn't have been a problem, but the 2007 Global Financial Crisis, and the fact that Tinkler had spent a fortune on houses, cars, planes and racehorses, meant he couldn't come up with the $24 million deposit, only scraping together $9 million. Ken Talbot[*] offered to help, lending him the remaining $15 million.

Tinkler now had an even bigger coal deposit, as China's demand continued to push prices higher. Tinkler's company, Aston Resources, was floated on the stock exchange with a valuation of $1.2 billion. Later, Aston would merge to form the $5 billion Whitehaven Coal.

Just six years after buying Middlemount, Tinkler, now thirty-five, had become Australia's youngest billionaire.

---

[*] Ken Talbot was facing an uncertain future at the time, as he'd been committed to stand trial for payments to a former Queensland government minister, Gordon Nuttall. Nuttall was jailed, but in 2010 Talbot died in a plane crash in Congo, just two months before he was due to face trial.

OFF TO THE RACES

As a newly minted billionaire, Tinkler was keen to spend some money. He decided to put some of his hard-earned into horseracing. There aren't too many better investments than owning racehorses, are there?

To get some help, he did what any billionaire would do – he asked another billionaire for advice. Gerry Harvey, owner of retail chain Harvey Norman, told him to 'have a dabble' and test the waters by purchasing a handful of horses. Tinkler ignored this advice and instead went on a spending spree the likes of which the industry had never seen.

'Suddenly he's gone to the Inglis Magic Millions in New Zealand and spent $50 million in one hit – no one's ever done that,' Harvey said. 'He must have thought I was the world's greatest dickhead. Whatever I told him, he did the opposite.'

As well as buying horses like they weren't being made anymore, Tinkler purchased four properties in the Gold Coast hinterland for $21 million and combined them to form Patinack Farm. This was to become a world-class thoroughbred breeding and training facility and, to get it up and running, he spent an estimated $150 million in its first year.

His spending on horses never really slowed. At one point he went all-in by bidding $1.025 million on a yearling, All Too Hard. It was the half-brother of the legendary Black Caviar and had been sired by Patinack Farm's stallion, Casino Prince. Buying the horse was a huge coup for Tinkler as it won the Caulfield Guineas and two weeks later came second in the Cox Plate.

Tinkler had poured hundreds of millions of dollars into his horseracing operations, but he was at least seeing some return. He owned one of the country's most promising horses and arguably the best breeding and training operation in the country.

NEWCASTLE JETS

Not content with giving the horseracing industry a significant cash injection, Tinkler was eager for further sporting glory. His real love was League and in particular the Newcastle Knights, as he'd lived and worked in the Hunter Valley for years.

While owning the Knights was his dream, he knew he first had to win over the NRL and the members of that club. He began a charm offensive on the people of Newcastle. His first move was to rescue the A-League team the Newcastle Jets, whose owner Con Constantine had just lost the licence.*

Tinkler came in as a white knight, providing the financial stability the club desperately needed. He quickly moved to have the MLS's LA Galaxy play the Jets in Newcastle. The Galaxy featured none other than David Beckham. No one could quite believe that Tinkler had brought Beckham to Newcastle, even just for a visit.

Tinkler also organised three netball tests to be played in the town and saved the financially troubled Surfest.** Here was a billionaire single-handedly rescuing the town's sporting scene. To build on all this goodwill, he signed Socceroo Jason Culina as the Jets' marquee player. Tinkler's popularity in the Newcastle media and public was at an all-time high. He could do no wrong. It was time to make a move for the Knights.

NEWCASTLE KNIGHTS

When Tinkler became Newcastle's exciting new benefactor, the Knights were in bad shape, with debts of over $3 million. As the club was community owned, he made an offer the members couldn't refuse. As well as making a $100 million bid to buy the

---

* Constantine was a businessman whose financial empire was in dire straits. He was unable to pay player and staff wages, so the FFA stripped him of the licence. This stuff is more predictable than a Nicolas Cage movie.

** A surfing competition that's been won by the likes of Kelly Slater, Sally Fitzgibbons, Mark Occhilupo and shark nemesis Mick Fanning.

club, he announced he would pay off all the Knights' debts, provide a bank guarantee for $20 million and commit at least $10 million a year in sponsorship for the next ten years. Tinkler also said that if he defaulted on the bank guarantee, the members would be entitled to buy the club back for $1.

The Knights fans could hardly believe it. This would turn the club from a financial shambles into an NRL powerhouse. No one paused to question whether someone who had risen so quickly might not be the real deal. There were already rumours that Tinkler's racing empire was racking up massive debts, but it was hard to hear those over the sound of all this money pouring into their coffers.

In March 2011 a meeting of the club members voted to sell Tinkler the club with a 97 per cent majority. Club greats, the local media, the business community, all fell over themselves to approve the deal. It was an exciting night with optimism sky high.

Almost as soon as the deal was approved, the trouble began. Tinkler's $20 million bank guarantee had to be delivered by 31 May, but Tinkler asked that it be deferred until 30 June. But when that later deadline came, the bank guarantee was still not approved, placing everything in jeopardy. Tinkler's Hunter Sports Group, the business that owned both the Jets and Knights, claimed these were just normal issues in a complex deal.

Finally, on 5 August, the guarantee came through and the deal was finalised. The warning signs were there that Tinkler's wealth might not be as liquid as everyone thought, but Tinkler soon signed legendary coach Wayne Bennett, so no one cared that much. It seemed the Knights were on their way.

SOME EMERGING CONCERNS

Entering 2012, there were many problems besetting Tinkler. While most observers hadn't twigged yet, the signs were everywhere.

To begin with, the price of coal was no longer surging. The United States had begun 'fracking', an unconventional method of extracting natural gas from rock, and this turned the US from a net importer of energy into an exporter. Coal exports suddenly had international competition, which was a problem for Tinkler given his entire empire was built on high coal prices.

In April 2012, Tinkler became infuriated when he learnt that he had paid $5 million for the Jets A-League licence when other owners had paid far less, or nothing at all. The FFA argued that he had only paid $3.5 million, but Clive Palmer helpfully chipped in to say he'd only paid $500 000 for his Gold Coast licence. Tinkler threatened to return the licence and walk away, prompting FFA chairman Frank Lowy to meet with him and talk him off the ledge.*

Things got worse though when the *Newcastle Herald* began making inquiries about the white knight of Newcastle. The *Herald* had originally welcomed Tinkler with open arms, but rumours had been circulating about his business dealings. In an impressive about face, the newspaper admitted they had not done enough to scrutinise the businessman. They started to investigate him, providing some truly exceptional journalism.

The key piece ran in August 2012, with the headline 'Trail of debt: Hunter firms call on Tinkler to pay the bills'. The piece, written by Donna Page, detailed Tinkler's failure to pay businesses he owed money to. It was effectively pointing out that the emperor had no clothes. Suddenly, Tinkler's standing as a generous billionaire was shot. He was now seen as someone who was sending the community to the wall by not paying his bills, instead of supporting them as promised.

The source of Tinkler's cash-flow problems wasn't hard to pinpoint. News Limited revealed that court documents showed Tinkler

---

* By this stage, Lowy must have been wondering if dealing with all these other billionaires was really worth it.

was betting as much as $200000 on a single horserace. It was not unusual for him to drop $500000 in a month with betting agency Luxbet. Such were his losses that Luxbet sued him after he failed to pay $179200.

Betting these amounts while not paying small businesses what he owed them is perhaps the best insight into Tinkler's true character. At the same time, it was costing him over $500000 per week to keep Patinack Farm going. In fact, *BRW* estimated he was losing almost $2 million a day during 2012.

With extensive debt, cash flying out the door and the price of coal still dropping, Tinkler was in deep trouble. In response he did what all the best Cashed-Up Businessmen do: he kept spending money at a frightening pace.* Everything was heading down a familiar path.

IT ALL FALLS DOWN

By the end of 2012, with creditors circling and legal action all around him, Tinkler grew desperate for cash, which resulted in him having to sell assets, often at crazy prices. In December, he was forced to sell champion horse All Too Hard as part of a $25 million package deal with Vinery Stud, of which Gerry Harvey was a part owner.

This delayed the creditors briefly, but not for long, as it came to light that Tinkler owed Gerry Harvey up to $40 million for a loan. His inability to pay this led to a huge fire sale, with 560 horses from Patinack Farm being sold off in 2014.

Patinack Farm was over, with claims horses had no feed and were going hungry. In August 2015, Tinkler called in the administrators. There were just thirty-five horses and thirty-eight cattle remaining, and less than $4000 in the bank. That's not much to show for a $300 million investment.

---

* It seems that to get this rich you need to accept enormous risks and ignore the warnings most people heed. Bond, Skase, Elliott and Tinkler all shared an inability to adapt to changing conditions.

One of the reasons Tinkler was forced to sell up was that the Australian Tax Office had applied to have Hunter Sports Group, Newcastle Jets Pty Ltd and Newcastle Knights Pty Ltd all wound up over unpaid debts of approximately $2.7 million. The tax office said Hunter Sports Group owed $184 257, the Knights $1.4 million and the Jets $1.1 million.

The sale of his racehorses enabled Tinkler to kick the can down the road for a while, but his next major problem was that he needed to renew the bank guarantee he had committed to as part of buying the Knights. In 2014 Tinkler was in no position to renew it, triggering proceedings to remove the club from his ownership.

On 14 June 2014 the NRL formally took over the club, meaning the members were unable to exercise their $1 buyback. Instead they got a non-controlling stake in the club and were allowed to nominate a director to the board. Considering the club had been community owned for the past twenty-three years, it was a horrible outcome.

The Jets would be the next domino to fall. The *Newcastle Herald* was continuing its investigation into Tinkler's business activities and in 2015 Tinkler blew up at *Herald* journalist Robert Dillon after a Jets loss, calling the newspaper a 'cancer', accusing Dillon of 'spreading cancer', then telling him: 'I hope you get cancer and die.'*

The FFA was not impressed, but things were about to get much worse. A month later, it was revealed Jets players and staff hadn't been paid, and Tinkler was forced to place the Jets into voluntary administration. The club owed $1.5 million in wages and superannuation, $1.1 million to suppliers and $2.7 million to the tax office. A creditors' report said the club had $605.46 in the bank, $88 in office petty cash, some gym equipment, outdated merchandise and a 2009 Hyundai i30.

---

* An astounding overuse of cancer. Mix up your diseases if you're going on a similar tirade at a journalist.

As with Con Constantine, the FFA was forced to strip the Jets licence from a businessman who could no longer pay salaries. FFA CEO David Gallop said of Tinkler's Hunter Sports Group:

> HSG has behaved in a deplorable way towards the players and staff of the club in failing to meet basic obligations to pay wages.
>
> Anyone who takes control of a sporting club has an obligation to respect the people and the traditions of that club. HSG has failed miserably in this regard. Today's action to terminate the licence is the first step to restoring the proud traditions of football in northern NSW.

Funnily, the FFA had no comment to make on the fact that they seemed to regularly end up in this situation.

WASH UP

Tinkler was finally declared bankrupt in February 2016 after GE Commercial took him to court over a US$2.25 million debt for his private jet. It marked the end of a long unravelling of an empire that had hundreds of active and inactive companies in Australia, not to mention businesses located overseas. The ABC's *Four Corners* estimated that at one stage Tinkler was caught up in more than fifty different court actions.

In May 2017, Tinkler, the former CEO of Hunter Sports Group Troy Palmer, and Tinkler's sister Donna Dennis[*] were all disqualified by the Australian Securities and Investments Commission (ASIC) from managing companies. Liquidators were appointed to sixteen companies that the three had managed either together or alone.

---

[*] Having a family member involved in running your business is almost always a bad sign.

DO AS I SAY, NOT AS I DO

Brian Waldron was the architect of the Melbourne Storm salary-cap scandal, which saw the club keep two sets of books. Their cheating was so bad they had several premierships stripped retroactively.

Amazingly, afterwards Waldron still got work appearing on Melbourne sport radio station SEN. There he passed judgement on how clubs were being managed, like we'd all somehow forgotten he was one of the most corrupt administrators Australia has ever seen.

ASIC said Tinkler, Palmer and Dennis had all allowed companies to trade while insolvent, had failed to ensure the companies paid their taxes and allowed one of the companies to deliberately operate at a loss.

It was a stunning rise and fall, and another reminder that sporting administrators have frequently failed to manage the risks associated with allowing the Cashed-Up Businessman to get involved in their sports.

Gerry Harvey, the man who'd lent Tinkler money and offered him advice, told Sky Sports Radio that Tinkler's problems stemmed from him having a 'split personality'. 'There's something in his character where he has to rubbish everyone he knows.'

Harvey said that once on a Gold Coast golf course he diplomatically told Tinkler, in the most sensitive way: 'It's a shame because you're a schizo [. . .] Mate, you can be such a nice person, I've seen you talk to people, they all like you. But then the way you behave and what you say, they all hate you.'*

Tinkler currently lives in a $13.5 million oceanfront compound at Sapphire Beach, north of Coffs Harbour, the last asset that hasn't yet been called in by creditors.

But while Tinkler severely embarrassed the A-League and the NRL, he didn't cause the competitions themselves to almost go

---

* I imagine having Gerry Harvey do your performance review must be uplifting.

under. For Cashed-Up Businessmen who accomplished that, we must turn to the National Basketball League.

EDDY GROVES
SOMETHING ABOUT LEARNING (OR NOT)

What if I told you I knew a story about an NBL team that folded in catastrophic fashion? 'Doesn't that happen like, every five minutes or so?' you'd respond.

'Well that's true, but this one is relevant to this part of the book,' I argue, defensively.

'Go on then.'

Actually, it's a story about the collapse of *two* NBL teams in one year, plus another team that found itself in jeopardy.

In 2008, two entrepreneurs almost brought down the NBL competition, and caused the league to continue without teams in Sydney and Brisbane, two mildly important cities for a national league to have teams in.

The first was Brisbane's Edmund Stuart 'Eddy' Groves. Groves proved to be entrepreneurial early, running a significant milk delivery business when he was only nineteen.

In 1988, Groves was looking for a 'recession-proof' business and settled on a childcare centre in the Brisbane suburb of Ashgrove. This kicked off a business that grew steadily throughout the nineties. By 2001, ABC Learning had grown to forty-three centres and was ready to be listed on the stock market. This allowed it to begin rapid expansion, mainly through acquisitions, including a 2004 deal purchasing Peppercorn Childcare for $340 million, which gave the company 450 new centres.

By 2005, ABC Learning had 697 centres under its control and its share price was going through the roof, hitting a peak of $8.62 in 2006. Eddy Groves was valued at $300 million and ABC Learning turned its attention to expanding into the United States and Britain.

CONVERGENCE OF INTERESTS

Even before Groves had made the big time, he was living the high life, with flashy holidays and clothes, gambling at the casino, and partying. Like any self-respecting businessman on the up, the idea of owning a sports team appealed to him, and in 1999 he purchased the NBL's Brisbane Bullets.*

The Bullets were a foundation club when the NBL was formed in 1979. They'd won the championship in 1985 and 1987 and, during the golden age of the league in the late eighties and early nineties, the team featured Leroy Loggins, viewed by many as the second-best player (after Andrew Gaze) to ever play in the NBL.

It was a proud club that had reached the playoffs twenty-one times in its thirty-year history, and Groves quickly had the Bullets travelling in the right direction. He managed to turn the Bullets around financially, but the way he did it gives some insight into his somewhat unorthodox business practices.

By 2001 ABC Learning was a listed company, meaning Groves needed to manage it in accordance with shareholders' interests. Instead, he had more than ten ABC-affiliated companies sponsor the Bullets. Effectively this meant that a public company Groves was managing on behalf of shareholders was giving money directly to another company privately owned by Groves. ABC Learning paid the Bullets $200 000 in 2002 and 2003, $255 000 in 2004 and 2005, and $352 000 in 2006.

This sort of behaviour was also occurring within ABC Learning itself. In 2006, ABC paid a company called Austock $27 million in fees. Groves just happened to own part of Austock. ABC also paid Queensland Maintenance Services $74 million for maintenance work on its centres. That company's sole director was once listed as Groves' brother-in-law.

---

* Although purchasing an NBL team is usually a clear sign of financial illiteracy.

These sorts of arrangements should have raised red flags in the market, but ABC Learning was going well and Groves was seen as an excellent NBL owner. He was putting his money where his mouth was, even if some of it wasn't actually his money. In 2007, the Bullets won the NBL championship, seemingly proving Eddy could do no wrong.

Eddy's involvement with the league only increased, and in 2006 he purchased the Adelaide Dome, more often referred to as 'The Powerhouse', the home of the Adelaide 36ers.

STARTING TO LOOK CARELESS

Groves' rapid expansion of his business was built on a model we've seen before with other Cashed-Up Businessmen: accruing large amounts of debt to fund acquisitions.

By 2008, ABC Learning was operating 2300 centres in four countries. Yet the big institutional investors were growing concerned, not only with the performance of the business but some rather creative accounting decisions that, at best, seemed to confuse what the business's real revenue was. The company was also borrowing more and more money, going from a debt of $380 million to $1.8 billion during the 2007 financial year, as well as borrowing another $1 billion for capital raising.

By the end of 2008, the jig was up. ABC Learning collapsed under $1.6 billion of debt and was placed in receivership. Groves had expanded too aggressively and borrowed too much. He personally owed creditors more than $31 million and was declared bankrupt. It was like the eighties had never ended.

The bankruptcy proceedings were triggered by the Commonwealth Bank, over Grove's debt of $5 million on the loan he took out to purchase the Adelaide Dome.

UH-OH

Groves' financial woes left the NBL in an enormous mess. He was forced to hand back the Bullets licence. At first it seemed new owners would be found, then that plan fell over – but not before a conman tried to buy the team.

A man calling himself Geoffrey Cassidy approached the league, presenting himself as a high-flying businessman. That alone should have been enough to set off alarm bells.

Cassidy had previously tried to buy two yachts at the Gold Coast boat show, worth $7.8 million and $20 million. Boats International director John Rapmund reported a man had approached his Horizon Boats International stand. 'He said he couldn't use his credit card as he had put a $300 000 piano on it and it was "chockas".'

Rapmund noticed the man spelled Armidale as 'Armadale' on a form. 'I got one of the girls to ring the bank,' Rapmund said. 'They'd never heard of him.'

Sporting administrations may want to consider hiring John Rapmund to look over all potential new owners.

With no legitimate buyers in the market, the Bullets folded in 2008, just one season after winning the championship. But Groves' destruction wasn't over. In 2012, the Commonwealth Bank took possession of the Adelaide Dome, following Groves' failure to make repayments. With no other places to play, it made the Adelaide 36ers potentially unviable – it seemed Groves alone might knock off two teams in one season – but a deal was struck to allow them to keep playing there.

ASIC launched a seven-year investigation into ABC Learning but not much came of it. The former chief financial officer James Black received a suspended eighteen-month sentence after he pleaded guilty to making available false or misleading information. That's it. The wet lettuce leaf of white-collar crime justice had struck again.

Groves' current whereabouts are unknown.

He may have run his business into the ground, but at least it was an actual business. The same could not be said for Sydney Kings owner Tim Johnston's fuel technology company Firepower. As it turned out, the Bullets weren't the only NBL club to go under that year.

TIM JOHNSTON
SELLING A DREAM

Sometimes people want to feel good about themselves and get insanely rich at the same time. Sure, investing in a company that ruins the environment or exploits workers may be profitable, but isn't there something more?

Tim Johnston thought there was. In fact, he knew he could offer people something that would give them that warm fuzzy feeling of both making money and doing something good at the same time. It was a special pill that, when put in a car's fuel tank, would make the fuel last longer, reduce emissions, save the environment and, just for good measure, clean and maintain your engine.

Born in Brisbane in 1956, Johnston's first job out of school was for the petrol company Ampol. He then joined L'Oréal to sell shampoo – and sell he did. Johnston was a born salesman, able to extol the virtues of his products with a natural ease that won people over.

Around the same time Johnston had married Sandra Meeks, a Jehovah's Witness from New Zealand. He converted almost immediately, moved to Auckland and became enmeshed in the Jehovah's Witness church, going door to door. After all, it was still just sales.

It was in New Zealand that Johnson discovered an American woman by the name of Sandra Dedina who sold all sorts of fraudulent products, like anti-cancer pills and pills that improve your car's fuel. Spruiking something like that wasn't that big a leap from proselytising, as it was still just selling something based on faith rather that evidence.

There was just one problem: the New Zealand Automobile Association had tested the fuel pill and discovered it didn't work. It did nothing.

You'd think this would be an insurmountable problem when building a successful business, but you and I are not Tim Johnston, and we are wrong. You can build a very successful business on magic pills with no discernible benefit – just look at the wellness industry.

While the good folk in New Zealand clocked the fact that this was a bogus product, Johnston had already left, first heading to the US to source the pills directly from the supplier in California.* Johnston had figured out that Sandra Dedina was running a pyramid scheme and he decided he wanted to be at the top not the bottom, so he cut her out.

New Zealand was a bust, but his next target, Australia, proved a far easier mark. It turned out Australians were far less concerned with things like 'evidence' and 'science'. In fact, they would be excited about these little pills to the tune of $100 million.

But before that, Johnston needed some time to work out how to market something that didn't exist (and if it did, didn't work), but eventually he discovered the answer lay in sport and government. By the early 2000s, Johnston was finally getting some traction.

Now, this book's aim isn't to teach you how to run a successful sham business, but if I can teach you that along the way, what a great outcome.

---

* Who knew you still need a particular supplier for pills that don't work?

MAGIC BEANS

The first key plank in Firepower's success was to closely associate itself with the sporting world, and the easiest way to do that is to sponsor lots of it. Not only is your brand plastered everywhere and thereby given legitimacy, but as a sponsor you get invited to all the functions where you can mix with sportspeople, administrators, other businesspeople and government figures.

Firepower went big on sponsoring sport. As a spectator, you couldn't miss them. Based out of Perth, as much as a non-existent company can be based anywhere, they first sponsored the Western Force in Super Rugby before expanding to boxing, motorsport, the NBL's Sydney Kings and the NRL's South Sydney Rabbitohs.

The Rabbitohs deal immediately paid dividends when co-owner Russell Crowe appeared on *The Tonight Show with Jay Leno* and announced that Firepower was sponsoring the club.

Crowe even showed a Rabbitohs jersey with Firepower's name on it. Given it was an American show, the audience probably had no idea what Crowe was talking about, but this was a PR coup any company in the world would dream about.[*]

Spending on sport led to the second important plank in Firepower's success: government support. In late 2005, the chairman of the Western Force, Geoff Stooke, introduced his important sponsor to the then federal minister for science, Julie Bishop.

GOVERNMENT HELP

Bishop was not Firepower's first contact with government. A year earlier Austrade, the government body responsible for promoting Australia's trade around the world, had become very excited about Firepower. Suddenly the company was being touted as 'big in Russia'

---

[*] In fact, most people outside of NSW and Queensland probably had no idea what he was talking about.

despite it not selling any products. Austrade awarded the company $394 009 in export grants and put a case study on their website.

This cosy relationship with the federal government opened up Australia's embassies around the world and Johnston quickly used this to further prove his bona fides with potential investors.

And that is how the scam worked. Rather than spending investors' money on building the business, Johnston spent it on things like sporting sponsorships, which gave him greater legitimacy with potential new investors. After all, surely a company that could afford all this sponsorship must have some serious money behind it. Why not invest? Add to this the fact the Australian government were touting it as an international success story and who wouldn't want in? The promise of riches clouded everyone's judgement.

This was also how Johnston won over Julie Bishop. In the meeting that the chair of the Western Force helped facilitate, Johnston made noises about wanting to donate to the Liberal Party. This led to a fundraising dinner in Perth and two intimate dinners at the Lodge with then prime minister John Howard and other West Australian businesspeople, Bishop having put Johnston's name forward.

Like all those who saw dollar signs when they met Johnston, Bishop was left disappointed. 'It turns out he made no donations to the Liberal Party,' she said. 'He was going to be a big supporter and he didn't pay for his ticket to the [fundraising] dinner.'

Johnston told potential investors that these dinners at the Lodge came about because he was advising the government on climate change. He also hired a senior Austrade manager, John Finnin, to be his CEO, adding even more apparent legitimacy to his operation. It was a heady mix of sport and government, all giving an alluring appeal to a company that barely existed.

The final piece of the puzzle was getting money out of investors without having to show any returns. This proved to be alarmingly simple. Johnston told people they could get in early and buy shares ahead of the company's listing in London on the Alternative Investment Market. The shares were sold for between 5 cents and $1.33, with people believing they would be worth as much as $7 each when the company listed. The date for listing was late 2005, which became 2006, and then 2007.

All the way along, investors were handing over their money. AFL stars Wayne Carey and Mark Ricciuto invested $100000 and $175000 respectively, and AFL coach Neil Craig invested $30000, reflecting Johnston's focus on sport.

Those taken in by Johnston's government relationships included the Australian high commissioner to Pakistan, Zorica McCarthy, and the then head of the Australian Defence Force, Air Chief Marshal Angus Houston.

All up, ASIC alleged about 1400 investors bought shares in Firepower.

BUYING THE SYDNEY KINGS

In late 2006, Johnston decided to go from being a sponsor of the Sydney Kings to being the owner. He purchased the team for $2 million, delivering a 400 per cent profit to the Macquarie Bank consortium that had purchased it just five years before for $400000.

This didn't go unnoticed, and people started to pay more attention to the company. The *Sydney Morning Herald* started to examine Firepower's inner workings. When reporter Gerard Ryle* started pulling at the threads, it was alarming how easily everything unravelled, given the government and sporting organisations who had hooked up with Firepower.

Ryle discovered that both Austrade and the Rabbitohs had signed deals with companies that did not exist. They simply hadn't

---

* Gerard Ryle would go on to write *Firepower: The most spectacular fraud in Australian history*, the definitive book on the saga and well worth the read.

checked. 'This is what I found all the time; I would find a company that claimed to be part of this Firepower empire, do a simple company search and find that it didn't exist.'

The *Sydney Morning Herald* started raising questions about Firepower in January 2007, but still the money flowed into the company. In February 2007, Ross Graham, who had made his money in mining, kicked in $10 million, which kept Firepower going. By now many people dealing with the company were starting to get angry that they weren't getting paid. Graham, who had just invested, suddenly discovered Firepower owed money everywhere.

In August that year John Finnin, Firepower's CEO, was sacked after it was revealed he faced child sex charges. It turned out that Finnin had been investigated while still in his senior management role with Austrade. At the time he was recalled from Germany where he was based and told he was being investigated. No charges arose but he was allowed to quietly resign and move to Firepower, where Austrade still did business with him.

The Australian Federal Police continued to investigate Finnin and finally charged him. He later went to jail.

Firepower rolled on regardless, until May 2008, when Johnston failed to pay a month's wages at the Sydney Kings. The NBL told him to rectify the situation but when a month later he hadn't, they issued him a default notice.

It turned out the Kings had been trading while insolvent for more than two years. They owed the tax office $580 000 and CGU Insurance $130 000 for insurance premiums. That meant the players hadn't been insured all season.

The result was the NBL had lost a second team in the space of a year as a result of its owner going broke. Both the Kings and the Brisbane Bullets were gone. The league itself was left teetering on the brink of financial disaster, and soon it lost the Singapore Slingers and the South Melbourne Dragons.

THE MOST WANTED MAN IN AUSTRALIAN SPORT

Other sporting codes were also out of pocket. The Western Force had millions of dollars in funding that just never turned up, and four of their players were owed nearly $1 million for personal sponsorships. This resulted in the Force losing contracted players, most notably Matt Giteau.

Finally, in July 2008, ASIC took Firepower to the Federal Court and the company was put into liquidation, but Johnston had already fled to London after the Kings had collapsed.

Legal actions came from everywhere and Johnston did return to face court briefly, under threat of arrest. There he confessed that shareholders had purchased shares in an entity listed offshore that owned nothing. He then headed back to London.*

In July 2011, ASIC handed down a twenty-year ban on Johnston managing any company. The latest news was that he was attempting to restart the business overseas.

GETTING AWAY WITH IT

Perhaps the most depressing part of this story is the ending. In May 2012, the liquidator Bryan Hughes announced the investigation into Firepower was over because there was no money left to fund it. The creditors were simply unwilling to put more money into it.

Hughes said:

> I believe there is some money offshore, we can prove
> it in a commercial sense. It's very difficult to prove it
> to the requirements required by law to substantiate
> it but the trouble is we can track it so far [. . .] It's in
> third parties, it's in offshore jurisdictions, it's in other
> companies [. . .] It is just a shame I and so many

---

* Australia seems to let its wanted businessmen flee the country rather easily. Pretty poor for a country that was set up as a prison.

> other people have been left to carry the financial can
> when the $100 million invested [in Firepower] just
> went into his [Mr Johnston's] pocket or was com-
> pletely wasted.

The case highlighted the weakness of Australia's laws when it comes to prosecuting white-collar crime.*

BACK FROM THE DEAD

The NBL has recovered from the dark days of 2008. In the 2010/11 season the Sydney Kings returned, and the Brisbane Bullets came back in the 2016/17 season.

The league is booming again. It took a multimillionaire, Larry Kestelman, to buy the competition for $7 million in 2015 to sort it all out. Kestelman, a Ukrainian immigrant, made his money in property development and the internet provider Dodo, which he sold in 2013 for $203 million.

Like Frank Lowy before him in football, Kestelman actually has money, and it's allowed him to be a terrific benefactor to the league for some time. He's even done some proper governance things, like selling his share in Melbourne United to avoid a conflict of interest.

And this is the problem: occasionally, businesspeople like Kestelman and Frank Lowy can come in and make a positive impact in a sport, but the risk needs to be assessed realistically and then managed.

GOVERNMENTS, REGULATORS AND BANKS

If one thing is clear following all those stories of destruction, it's that sporting bodies should be incredibly careful when it comes to

---

* If a career as a criminal appeals to you, always go the white-collar route. The money is significantly better, the risk to your person lower and the punishments close to non-existent.

allowing a club's life or death to depend on the fortunes of a single individual, no matter how rich.

Yet this rather sensible premise is something we all seem to forget. Nathan Tinkler, for example, needed the members of the Newcastle Knights to vote themselves out as owners before he took over. And they did so with 97 per cent of the vote. But those innocent members are hardly alone. The veteran sports administrators of the NRL, AFL, NBL, FFA and ARU have all done business with Cashed-Up Businessmen – often more than one at a time.

In fairness to these bodies, they've also been failed by government, regulators and the banks, who have done little to curb the excesses of these groups and individuals. The sporting bodies and clubs could argue that it's impossible to do more due diligence when major financial institutions and the government are enabling these businessmen.

The Firepower scandal shows that it's possible for all kinds of regulatory bodies to do very little. A simple company search by a journalist unravelled Firepower, not the club about to sign a million-dollar sponsorship deal with the company or a league approving the owner to take over one of their teams.

Putting a single individual in charge of a club is an enormous risk, and those making that decision always need to do their own due diligence. It can't be outsourced.

Yet the risk will probably be taken again and again, and calamity will follow. When short-term financial problems present themselves, it's all too tempting to use someone else's money to make them go away. The risk is ignored in favour of a chance to deliver on the field – which is what people really want, after all. It's why Geoffrey Edelsten and John Elliott got to return to the Carlton Football Club: the promise of money injected into the club.

This desire for sporting success often clouds people's judgement; it turns rational people into emotional supporters. It happens to all of us. Sporting success means a lot to Australians.

Which brings us back to Alan Bond. The idea that delivering a single trophy – in sailing! – offsets the crime of fraudulently stripping a company of $1.2 billion tells you a lot about how much we forgive those who deliver us victory.

PART II

ANATOMY OF A SCANDAL

☙ SCANDAL 101 ❧

Now that we've covered the types of people who create sporting scandals, it's time to turn our attention to the scandals themselves. Sport scandals come in many shapes and sizes, from the footballer caught with cocaine down his undies to the ex-fast bowler shooting African wildlife.

At a glance, each embarrassing event seems unique, yet close examination reveals that they all fall along a predictable continuum. So what makes some scandals bigger than others? Why are some easier to manage? And why do some go on and on forever?

Once you've read this section, you'll be able to predict the size of a scandal the minute it begins, just like a media professional,[*] and then assess how well a club managed it. While the theory in this chapter is applied to sport, it's pretty much the same for every single scandal, whether it's a political crisis or something happening in the staffroom of your workplace.[**]

So next time Barry in Accounts Receivable steals Susan's can of

---

[*] Knowing how much trouble someone is in will allow you to really increase the amount you can charge them, too.

[**] You can probably also use it in relationships. How angry is my partner going to be about this?

Diet Coke, you'll be able to measure that against the time Robert Allenby got 'kidnapped', just like you've always dreamed.

AN ISSUE BECOMES A CRISIS BECOMES A SAGA

Scandals in sport have a frequency and similarity that is as predictable as the turning of the seasons. This isn't that surprising because sport provides the perfect conditions for a scandal: young men, money, alcohol, drugs, gambling and fame. Add to this the fact all professional athletes work in a relentless high-pressure environment and I'm often struck by the fact they don't get into more trouble than they do – and they get into quite a bit.

That isn't to say that athletes deserve a gold star just for going through their career behaving like a normal person, or that we should give a free pass to those who don't. But the outcomes are so predictable, despite the low bar, that it's surprising people are surprised.

Sporting scandals tend to fall into three categories of severity: issue, crisis or saga.

There are four factors that influence which category an incident is likely to fall into:

1. The number of people affected or interested
2. The size of the consequences
3. The existence of imagery
4. The timing and context

A scandal can transform from an issue into a crisis into a saga based on how long it goes on, its complexity and the number of arenas in which the story plays out.

1. HOW MANY PEOPLE ARE AFFECTED?

As a rule of thumb, people care most about issues that affect them.* A scandal tends to be bigger if more people are affected, although that can include being interested in something, like the team they support, as well as a direct impact.

Take the cost of petrol going up or mortgage rates rising. These topics receive a lot of interest because they affect lots of people. The media covers them at length because heaps of people are interested. It's a pure numbers game. The price of Aston Martins going up will never be front-page news.**

In sport the bigger clubs, of course, automatically amplify issues because they affect more people. Something involving Collingwood or the Brisbane Broncos is always going to be a bigger story than, say, something about the GWS Giants or the Gold Coast Titans. Likewise, a cricket controversy is going to get more coverage than a netball story, even if they're the exact same story. And of course it's true for big stars, too; Shane Warne doing something, even relatively minor, is going to get lots of attention while a first-year player for the Canberra Brumbies might only be covered in Canberra.***

DEFENDING THE GOOD BLOKES

[Former club champion] says it's important to remember that everyone associated with the sport is a 'great bloke'.

'There's future jobs and premierships on the line here, so remember everyone is a cracker of a bloke and if they've done several terrible things then it's because they're misunderstood.'

---

* I'd go a step further and say many people only care about issues that affect them.
** Even though it should be. The price of Aston Martins is outrageous and I'm now only buying a new one every second year.
*** If a scandal occurs in Super Rugby and no Australian is aware of it, did it really happen?

2. THE CONSEQUENCES

The second factor is the size of the consequences. If the price of petrol goes up by a cent overnight, it's not the same story as if it shoots up by a dollar.

A consequence alone can have a significant effect on the size of a story. Even though the same number of people are affected, a murder gets media coverage while a pickpocketing doesn't, because the impact is so much greater.

In sport, it works in a similar way. A player suspended for a week is one thing, but if it's for ten weeks, it's going to get a lot more attention.

Shane Warne testing positive for a banned substance was a huge story from the start because of the enormous consequences for him and for Australian cricket: the country's best player out of action for twelve months. By comparison, in America's NFL, a positive test for a banned substance can mean as few as four weeks out of the game. This means the same story becomes much bigger in cricket. Add to that the international popularity of cricket, and the fact Warne is one of its biggest stars, and you have a huge story.

3. THE EXISTENCE OF IMAGERY

Stories about mortgage rates going up don't have obvious visual material, but vision of a family being evicted from their home could ramp that same story up to the lead spot on the nightly news.

Good photos or video can make or break a story. Think of a video showing a car or person almost getting hit by a train – even if no one gets hurt, it can be compelling enough to make the news. Footage alone can be the story.

In a sporting context, when a story breaks, check to see if there are photos or video footage of the incident. If there is, the coverage will go up a fair notch. Because of smartphones and CCTV, these days footage surfaces of incidents that in the past were only rarely captured. In 2018 the AFL has had mobile phone footage of several crowd brawls spring up online, turning something that's always happened into a big story.

Basketball Australia certainly know the power of footage, after the wild brawl between the Boomers and the Philippines national basketball team went viral. It was a fight that would have been more at home in professional wrestling, and so the story was covered around the globe, including on ESPN in the United States.

Never before would they have been interested in a match between Australia and the Philippines. Twenty years ago, the game wouldn't even have been filmed. But in this age, it led news bulletins across the globe, because it was amazing footage of a brawl; none of these networks cared about the result of the game.

Many of the stories earlier in this book escaped a similar fate because of when they occurred. Young Griffo was never filmed turning up drunk to a fight and then rolling out of the ring when he couldn't be bothered anymore. If those fights had been televised, he'd probably have led the news every night.

The Melbourne Club's Frederick Standish probably couldn't have survived in an age of mobile phones with cameras either. These days it's much harder to sneak a prince of the realm into a brothel without anyone finding out. Trust me.

4. THE TIMING AND CONTEXT

As in life, timing is everything in crisis management.* Just the fact there's been a spate of a certain type of thing can cause a situation to escalate.

Take, for example, the series of umpire contact incidents that took place in the first half of the 2018 AFL season. Eight different

---

* Well, maybe not *everything*. A working heart is pretty important. Lungs too, now I think about it. Let's just say timing is really important, almost up there with functioning organs.

players got fined or suspended for making contact within the space of a couple of weeks.* Each incident on its own wouldn't be that big a deal, but the timing made it a much bigger story.

Meanwhile in the NRL, over a single weekend in 2017, Cronulla chairman Damian Keogh, Roosters centre Shaun Kenny-Dowall, New Zealand skipper Jesse Bromwich and Gold Coast's Kevin Proctor were all involved in incidents relating to cocaine.** Suddenly these were not individual stories – the NRL had a 'cocaine crisis' on its hands.

Other times, broader social issues and trends make a story bigger. Family violence was once barely covered by the media, let alone in sport – in fact, you could argue that it was covered up by police, the media and governments – but now it is a very real focus, even if a lot of the coverage it gets in sport is more talk than action.

Because of the national conversation, anything involving family violence and violence against women is going to attract more attention. Even if, as the Matthew Lodge issue showed, some sporting administrations are not exactly reading the mood that well.

APPLYING THE THEORY

Using these four factors we can make case studies of the sporting debacles we're served up on an almost daily basis. The following chart lets you map out a scandal when it starts, so you can figure out how worried you should be.

A big issue tends to combine all four factors: lots of people directly affected or invested, big consequences, plenty of good footage and playing into a broader context.

---

* It was like umpires were suddenly catnip to AFL players. If you ever want to hook up with an AFL player, wearing an umpiring uniform is probably your best bet.

** You couldn't make these things up. When Keogh was arrested by police during a random search at Bells Hotel in Woolloomooloo, the police officers had an ABC film crew following them for a documentary. His arrest was also caught on CCTV, with the footage sold to Channel Nine.

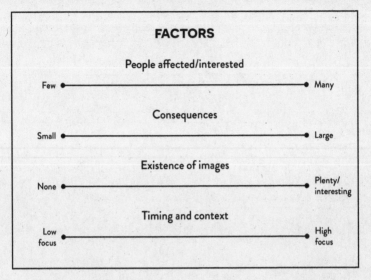

FACTORS

People affected/interested

Few ●————————————————————● Many

Consequences

Small ●————————————————————● Large

Existence of images

None ●————————————————————● Plenty/
interesting

Timing and context

Low
focus ●————————————————————● High
focus

Decide where an issue fits on each of these spectrums and you can measure how big it will get. The further to the right on this chart you mark each of the four factors, the more likely it is to escalate if it's not managed well.

ISSUES

If the incident is limited in its complexity and doesn't go on for too long, we'll refer to it as an issue. That's not to say it's not traumatic for those involved, or that they're minor events (although some are incredibly trivial), but rather that the attention they receive is relatively short-lived and they're not as difficult to manage.

For an entry level issue, let's look at St Kilda's Luke Dunstan. Dunstan turned in one of the weakest efforts in scandal history, which is a real shame coming from a club with such a rich tradition in controversy.

In 2016, Dunstan was out in the early hours of a Saturday morning after a night drinking. Police found him asleep in a public place and took him to the station, and he got an infringement notice for being intoxicated in public. He fully co-operated with police and St Kilda general manager of football performance Jamie Cox said, 'Luke notified the club immediately of the situation and is extremely remorseful.'

No one was hurt, it wasn't that big a deal anyway and Dunstan took full responsibility. If anything, he came out of it looking good. He hadn't done anything major and still went out of his way to handle it properly. If he hadn't been an AFL player, it wouldn't even have been rated as an issue; if I'd done it, it would just be called 'every single Saturday'.

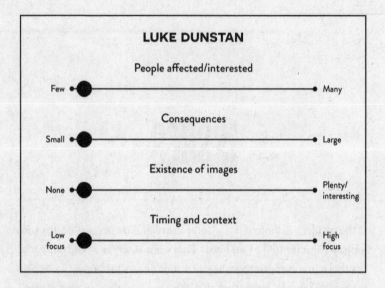

FAMILY ROAD TRIP

Obviously, Dunstan's effort was very poor, so let's look at an issue with a bit more to it. In December 2017, Parramatta Eels player Tony Williams drank about ten beers and numerous vodka shots at Parramatta's Albion Hotel. His wife then came to pick him up. The story should have ended there, but Williams – probably not in the best frame of mind – took the car keys and drove home with his wife and three children, aged four, one and three months.

Several members of the public notified the police – they saw him driving like someone who had just downed ten beers and a bunch of vodka shots. When the police pulled him over, he blew 0.122.* To put a cherry on top of the entire mess, he was on his P-plates.

Now, a drink-driving footballer would have to be the most basic of issues for a football club to manage. It's a serious offence, and

---

* This is a pretty high reading. To put it in context, a reading of 0.3 usually means you're unconscious and by 0.4 you're probably no longer alive. On the plus side, in that last scenario: no hangover.

anyone who has lost someone to a drink-driver would attest to the ongoing trauma it can cause, but it shouldn't be enormously complicated for a club to manage. No matter how much the club's leaders act shocked and disappointed, it's a familiar scenario.

Let's look at the four defining factors in Tony Williams' case.

Who cared about it? Well, fans of the club, especially as it would make it harder to win games while he was suspended. The NRL media were interested, and the broader media cared a bit, especially in Sydney. Fans of other NRL clubs didn't care very much; they were really only interested if he'd miss the game against their club. After that, interest dropped away pretty fast. It wasn't even news outside New South Wales, except maybe in Queensland.

In terms of consequences, Williams didn't injure anyone with his reckless actions. A player drink-driving, even with his entire young family in the car, is less of a story if by some miracle no one is hurt.

Luckily for Williams there wasn't any video footage of him swerving all over the road, making it less of a TV or social media

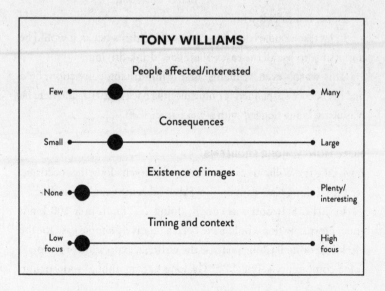

story, and there was no focus on drink-driving in the wider culture at the time.

An issue of this size is the lowest form of complexity in terms of a scandal. For those running the club, it's an annoying day at the office. Even though Williams put his family and the wider community at risk, the story was forgotten by the next media cycle.

Addressing something like this involves making a statement condemning the player's actions, perhaps the CEO fronting the media saying how their trust has been broken and will need to be rebuilt, the announcement of some sort of education program or community work, and a suspension.

DID YOU KNOW?

Scientists believe if two Good Blokes came into dispute with each other, the universe could end.

In Williams' case, he received a two-match suspension and was ordered to do a safe driving course. The court suspended his licence for a year, fined him $1000 and gave him a twelve-month good behaviour bond.

Done. Issue dealt with.

In fact, so regularly do these types of incidents occur, it would be impossible to list all the cases of athletes drink-driving.

This wasn't even Williams' first drink-driving conviction; he'd had his licence suspended for nine months back in 2010, and here he was again being flogged with a wet lettuce leaf.

MORE MONEY, MORE PROBLEMS

If we take the Williams case and move it a notch along the spectrum, we get Geelong Cats captain Joel Selwood being caught speeding.

In 2017, Selwood was caught doing 127 km/h in a 100 km/h zone. Normally this would have been a relatively simple case for the Geelong Football Club: a slap on the wrist, an expression of remorse, some community service. But Geelong had an annual sponsorship of approximately $250 000 from the Victorian Transport Accident Commission (TAC). One of the TAC's major objectives is to reduce road trauma – the captain of a sponsored club tearing down the road was hardly what the marketing manager would have called 'brand synergy'.

Adding to this, Selwood's was the seventh driving incident the Geelong Football Club had been involved in over the past decade. The penultimate straw had been Selwood's teammate Billie Smedts taking a selfie while driving in 2013.* The TAC had warned the club back then that another incident would see the sponsorship deal torn up.

The TAC was true to their word following Selwood's indiscretion, making this a little more complicated than a standard issue. It probably fell short of becoming a crisis because Geelong was the

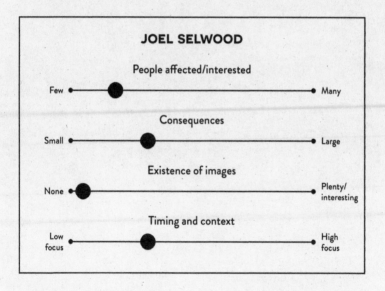

* While this wasn't the cleverest idea, it wasn't even Smedts' worst. In 2013, he and teammate Josh Caddy thought it would be funny to scare a teammate by pretending to break into his house while wearing balaclavas. The only problem? They got the wrong house and were arrested by police at gunpoint.

third AFL club to lose their TAC sponsorship. Richmond and Collingwood had lost their TAC sponsorship in 2005 and 2008 respectively, in similar circumstances. By the time it happened to Geelong, people had become so used to it happening they barely blinked.

Much like Tony Williams' drink-driving, we've become conditioned to these things happening, and everyone involved reacts accordingly. This is when timing and context work in a club's favour. It falls into the 'boys will be boys' category.*

---

* 'Boys will be boys' is one of the worst phrases ever. Whenever I encounter it I always replace it with 'horrible people will be horrible people' and suddenly the sentence makes absolute sense.

CRISES

When the complexity of an issue increases to the point where it takes more than a few days to manage, and numerous groups with conflicting expectations get involved, an issue will morph into a crisis.* For that to happen, you need a bit of novelty, or the size of the act needs to be substantial enough that it stands out above similar cases.

It also needs to play out beyond just the club and the sport itself. Crises tend to involve different public and private arenas. The more arenas, the bigger the crisis. These include the media (local, state, national and social media), politics (local, state, federal), regulatory (government and industry bodies), legal (police investigation, court cases, mediation), community (discussions, campaigns, protests), financial (sponsors, members), workplaces (workplace disputes, investigations, sackings, enterprise bargaining agreements) and private negotiations.

Wayne Carey's Miami holiday, for example, played out in the media, in the legal arena, in the workplace (he lost his media jobs) and in the community.

---

* The term 'crisis' gets used so often these days it's almost lost all meaning. The other day I couldn't find the remote and I thought to myself, *THIS is a crisis*. It probably was actually a crisis, as Michael Slater and Ian Healy were commentating together.

The Williams drink-driving case played out in state media, his workplace and the legal arena. By comparison, Selwood's story added the financial arena to the mix. That wasn't a bad attempt at raising the profile of an issue to crisis level, but to see how to get that over the line we need to turn to a group that can really do the job properly: the Australian cricket team. If you want to know what case study will be used in PR courses across the country for decades, to instruct people in what not to do in a crisis, it will be this one.

THE DAY CRICKET DIED

In South Africa in March 2018, just after lunch on the third day of the third test, the Australian cricket team killed the soul of the game by rubbing a small piece of sandpaper against a cricket ball in front of four million cameras.

Who knew the soul of cricket was so sensitive? But it was.

Ball tampering* is an age-old art, long employed by cricketers the world over. Roughing up one side of a cricket ball while keeping the other smooth causes greater drag on one side, resulting in the ball moving more in the air when bowled and making it much harder for the batsman to hit.**

Numerous techniques are used. Shining one side as much as possible on your uniform, for example, is common practice. But using a foreign object*** like sandpaper is seen as blatant cheating. It was already a monumentally idiotic thing for the Australians to do, but doing it while being filmed added a whole new layer of stupid to proceedings.

---

* 'Ball tampering' will never not be a funny term. The fact that this crisis occurred in the same week as Stormy Daniels' *60 Minutes* interview about her encounters with Donald Trump made it even more perfect, giving us two ball-tampering stories in the one week.
** For most cricketers, this is the closest they'll come to learning a scientific theory.
*** 'Foreign object' is never a good term to hear someone say, whether in a WWE wrestling ring, at border security or a doctor's office.

The aims of cheating are pretty simple: do not get caught, and win. The Aussies managed to do neither.

Australians had never cheated like this before (well, not so blatantly). It caused an existential crisis back home.

Some events in history just stay with you. The moon landing, the assassination of JFK, the dismissal of 1975 and now a 25-year-old rubbing sandpaper on a leather ball. Every Australian remembers where they were when they heard we'd cheated at cricket. It was a Sunday morning in Australia and we all felt a deep sense of shame – not that unusual for a Sunday morning, but this time it wasn't because of something we'd done, which just confused things further.

I was certainly shaken. I'd always thought 9/11 would be the biggest event of my lifetime, but judging by the Australian media's reaction to the ball-tampering incident, I was wrong. Unlike a regular issue to be managed, this involved many interested parties – such as the entire cricketing world – who loved nothing more than watching the Aussies come a cropper after years of arrogance and aggressiveness. It drew international media interest and was trending on social media in numerous countries.

Even Malcolm Turnbull, a man not known for his interest in or knowledge of sport,* felt the need to get involved: 'I've spoken with David Peever, the chairman of Cricket Australia, a few moments ago and I've expressed to him very clearly and unequivocally my disappointment and my concern about the events in South Africa.'

The fact that our prime minister rang the head of Cricket Australia to express outrage, and then told everyone about it, showed he could read the mood of the country. He knew it was important to be seen to be doing something.

Cricket Australia didn't read the mood of the country quite as well.

---

* Turnbull once said the Roosters were his favourite AFL side, even though they played in the NRL. Amazingly, he was allowed to stay on as prime minister.

An issue often becomes a crisis when there's not a clear under-standing of what has occurred. While an investigation is taking place, all sorts of wild speculation is thrown around. That means you need to move quickly to show you're taking events seriously.

In the case of the ball-tampering crisis, Cricket Australia moved about as quickly as a confused, geriatric sloth and took no interim steps to reduce the mounting speculation. In other words, they mismanaged the entire thing to within an inch of its life.

POURING PETROL ON A FIRE

During the third test between South Africa and Australia, the cam-eras of the South African broadcaster SuperSport were following every single move of the ball. You're probably thinking, *This isn't that surprising. Isn't the idea of a sport broadcast to show the actual sport?* Well, you'd be right, even if Channel Seven's tennis coverage has forgotten that in recent years.

But this was something else. The network decided they would have a camera on the ball even when it wasn't in play. This wasn't normal; often after a delivery, as the ball makes its way back from the wicketkeeper to a few fielders and finally to the bowler, the TV cameras focus on something else entirely.* But SuperSport had been told by several sources that the Australians were cheating by tampering with the ball, so they were watching the Aussies like hawks.

On the third day, they found what they were looking for. The relatively junior player Cameron Bancroft was filmed rubbing what appeared to be a piece of yellow paper against the ball. This was shown to viewers at home, but also on the big screens around the ground.

---

* South African networks usually use this break in play to find the most scantily clad women in the crowd and linger on them for a creepily long time; Australian networks use it to promote terrible reality TV shows.

The South African commentators couldn't believe their luck. It was clear to them and anyone else with a brain that the Aussies were cheating. They had just been caught red-handed. The young player was then filmed stuffing the object down his pants.[*]

When the umpires confronted Bancroft, he showed them another cloth for cleaning his sunglasses, and captain Steve Smith defended him. The umpires deemed the ball was not damaged in any way and decided to let play go on. But this was short relief. Everyone watching knew this ruse was not going to stand up once the players got off the field and were shown the vision.

DO NO HARM

In managing a crisis, your first objective is to not make things worse. You might not be able to erase the original mistake, but a spin doctor should follow the same principle as a real doctor, *primum non nocere*: first, to do no harm.

At the very least, react to the situation in a way that makes people feel the person or organisation in question understands the gravity of events and is taking them seriously.[**] Cricket Australia did not do this. Despite knowing what was coming, they did nothing.

Shortly after coming off the ground, Steve Smith and Cameron Bancroft went in front of the media. Just the two of them, not the coach or anyone else who might offer support, and without any real preparation or strategy. They were allowed to just throw themselves to a media pack who had seen everything.

Given the events of the afternoon, this should never have happened. It was obvious no one at Cricket Australia understood the significance of what the Australians had just been caught doing.

---

[*]   Stuffing a mysterious object down your pants certainly means no good will come of things, especially if it's caught on camera, unless of course it's in private between consenting adults.

[**] Even if you aren't taking something seriously, you should at least feign that you are. If you can fake sincerity, you can do anything.

Smith admitted to the attempt to tamper with the ball. He could hardly do otherwise, given the incriminating footage that was being broadcast everywhere. When he was asked whose idea it was, he said: 'It was the leadership group. I'm not naming names but the leadership group were talking about it and Bangers [Bancroft] was there at the time and we spoke about it and thought it was a possible way to get an advantage.'

He also said later in the press conference, 'I'm embarrassed. I know the boys in the shed are embarrassed. I feel for Cam [Bancroft] as well. It's not what we want to see in the game.'

Smith had thrown the whole leadership team under the bus. From his comments, it didn't sound like many of 'the boys in the shed' were unaware of the plan.

The media conference was a disaster and set up problems that ran for weeks to come. It made later attempts by Cricket Australia to claim that only three people knew about the plan seem like an attempt at a cover-up, even if the claim was true.*

Given he had just confessed to cheating as part of a plan devised by the leadership group, Smith was asked if he'd stand down as captain. He said, 'No, I won't be considering stepping down. I still think I'm the right person for the job. Obviously today was a big mistake on my behalf and on the leadership group's behalf as well but I take responsibility as the captain – I need to take control of the ship.'

That statement was a major problem. Once again, it showed that Smith and Cricket Australia didn't get the magnitude of what had just happened. The person who has just run the ship aground is probably not the best person to take control.

The team had just been caught on camera cheating and Smith

---

* The question of how many people were in on the plan is a bit like the JFK assassination conspiracy. Of course, the Cricket Australia ball-tampering scandal is a more significant historical event.

had just admitted it was a premeditated plan he'd been a part of. He wasn't going to survive that.

Smith was in an untenable situation, but no one had explained that to him or given him the time to come to that conclusion himself. In the rush to get him in front of the media, no one had considered the implications of Smith answering questions like this. He shouldn't have been put in that position.

Another complicating factor was that the decision about the captaincy was not Smith's to make, that was for Cricket Australia to handle. Now that Smith was on the record saying he thought he should stay on, any attempt to remove him would make it clear it was not a mutual decision.

Perhaps even worse was the media conference's impact on Cameron Bancroft. He was inexperienced at this level and, in front of the media, had only his captain to help him. But in the very first exchange with a journalist, who asked for an explanation of the footage and what had happened since, Smith gestured to Bancroft and said, 'Do you wanna explain?'

No help from his captain, then. Smith had the option to explain things first, but instead threw the question to a teammate with nowhere near his level of media experience.

It fell on Bancroft to give the first explanation of what happened, and he panicked. He lied about the foreign object, saying it was some tape with some 'granules from the rough patches on the wicket'. This was not true. It was sandpaper, which suggested this was a slightly more thought-out plan than those involved were initially claiming.

Bancroft later admitted, 'Yes, I lied about the sandpaper and I panicked in that situation, and I'm very sorry.' Cricket Australia should have prevented him from even being in that situation – they had time to cancel the media conference.

After the end of play but before the media conference, the key players had to front the match officials. At this point they were charged with attempting to change the condition of the ball. This was the moment for Cricket Australia to take control and change who would speak to the media. Instead of sending his two players out there, coach Darren Lehmann should have addressed the media and announced he was concerned by the events, that they would be fully investigated, and that he would not comment any further until he had answers.

The media would have been annoyed, but they already had the incriminating footage and more than enough to report on.

This isn't just the benefit of hindsight. Communication professionals in all industries manage issues every day by putting some thought into potential reactions and outcomes, and how best to minimise further problems. Cricket Australia has a significant media unit whose job is to do exactly this, but it seems they were asleep at the wheel.

DOUBLING DOWN

Those first public comments were a clear admission that the team had set out to cheat, and insinuated the entire leadership group knew about it – possibly the whole team – but that the captain, despite all this, would not be stepping down. They also included an outright lie about what had been used to rough up the ball.

As Australia woke up on a Sunday morning to all this news, the CEO of Cricket Australia, James Sutherland, was about to make things worse. In a hastily arranged media conference, he announced an investigation, with Cricket Australia's head of integrity, Iain Roy, and team performance manager, Pat Howard,* heading to South Africa. Notably, Sutherland wasn't going himself.

---

* Pat Howard had been a Rugby Union player who represented Australia twenty times. He was the high-performance manager for the Australian Rugby Union in 2007. In 2011, he was appointed General Manager, Team Performance at Cricket Australia. Obviously the 'high' part of his title was dropped during the move based on his record at the ARU.

Sutherland refused to say the players had cheated, which was surprising, considering his captain had already confessed to that a few hours earlier. Also, footage of the cheating was being broadcast every half-hour on cable news in multiple countries.[*]

It was a bizarre position to take, to say the least. It showed Cricket Australia was completely misreading the situation and Sutherland came across as anything but a straight shooter. The idea that this could possibly *not* be cheating was farcical. The horse had bolted, yet Sutherland was not just trying to close the gate behind it but insisting to everyone that the horse was still inside.

The reaction to this second media conference was bewilderment. Cricket Australia was trying to batten down the hatches and ride out the storm, but it was too late for that.[**] Smith had said he wouldn't stand down as captain and Sutherland hadn't countered that position. In fact, Sutherland had made no decision at all except to send some people to South Africa to look into what happened.

The Australian Sports Commission (ASC), the federal authority for distributing government funds for sports and providing strategic direction to the government, was not impressed. They released a media statement:

> Given the admission by Australian captain Steve
> Smith, the ASC calls for him to be stood down imme-
> diately by Cricket Australia, along with any other
> members of the team leadership group or coaching
> staff who had prior awareness of, or involvement in,
> the plan to tamper with the ball.

---

[*] People often do this when speaking to the media: they avoid using certain words because they believe it'll stop everyone from thinking about them. Instead it just makes everyone think that person either has no idea what they're talking about or they're trying to mislead the public.

[**] The ship had actually sunk, which is also why Steve Smith couldn't 'take control of the ship'.

For a government body to be calling for the captain of the Australian cricket team to stand down is definitely a crisis. It's the equivalent of calling for the president of the United States to be impeached. Actually, it's more serious than that; calls to impeach the US president occur every day.

The ASC's view reflected that of the cricketing public and media: how could a national captain who just confessed to a premeditated plan to cheat remain in place? Even temporarily standing him down would have meant something.

By late Sunday afternoon, Cricket Australia was starting to suspect they'd made a mistake. The negative feedback to Sutherland's performance was intense. They had to do something.

They issued another statement, this time announcing that Steve Smith would stand down as captain and Dave Warner as vice-captain while the investigation continued. How this hadn't happened at the Sutherland media conference was beyond everyone. It was the only option Cricket Australia had but it took public, media and government pressure for them to do it.

SYSTEMIC FAILURE

We've already learnt that taking personal responsibility for your actions is not something a sporting hero should ever do. It's better to claim 'systemic failure'. This is when people argue the system was corrupt, not the people acting within it; everyone is sort of guilty, so therefore no one is.

This has often been trotted out during NRL clubs' repeated salary-cap breaches, as well as in the Essendon supplements saga. The most famous use of this defence was following the collapse of the United States banking system in 2007. Apparently, no one was guilty there.

Don't be fooled though, 'systemic failure' is just a modern variant of the Nuremberg defence: 'I was only following orders.'

If this had been their first statement, not their third, things may have progressed very differently. Instead, Cricket Australia had wasted a whole day. The only thing they'd achieved was giving people a sense that they had no idea what they were doing. Luckily for them, the next day was even worse.

THIS IS SERIOUS

It's the status quo for cricket fans to be upset with cricket's administrators. Cricket Australia certainly doesn't worry about something as trivial as the opinions of the people who are the lifeblood of the sport. On the Monday after the incident, however, with the events splashed all over the media, a group of people valued by Cricket Australia were very upset: the sponsors of Cricket Australia and the sponsors of individual players.

They had watched the last thirty-six hours unfold with horror. Cricket Australia's ham-fisted response had certainly not calmed them and now the media were putting the pressure on the sponsors. Sanitarium, Qantas, Lion, Commonwealth Bank, KFC, Accenture, Magellan Financial Group and Bupa all put out statements condemning the events in South Africa.

Worse than that, some were saying they were considering pulling sponsorships. Sanitarium, who sponsored Steve Smith, said: 'Like the rest of Australia, we're incredibly disappointed. The actions taken by the team in South Africa are not aligned with our own – Sanitarium does not condone cheating in sport.'

This was obviously breaking point: the makers of Weet-Bix were unhappy. Although you'd have to say some good did come out of this: we now knew that Sanitarium was not in favour of cheating in sport. I'd often stared at a box of Weet-Bix and thought, *I wonder where these guys stand on cheating in sport?*

Cricket Australia now finally seemed to understand they were in trouble. It turned out all they needed was a dollar figure attached.

James Sutherland decided he needed to travel to South Africa himself, and he left that night.

The crisis was now playing out in the workplace, the international media, the community, the political, the regulatory and the financial arenas. But just because Cricket Australia understood the size of the crisis, that didn't mean they'd manage it well.

HAMMER FALL

As Sutherland flew to South Africa, rumours swirled in the media that coach Darren Lehmann had offered to resign and that players Mitchell Starc, Josh Hazlewood and Nathan Lyon – part of the leadership group – were deeply unhappy to have been accused of having knowledge of the plot.

Upon landing, Sutherland was briefed before calling a media conference to reveal the outcomes of the investigation and announce sanctions. By the time Cricket Australia were ready to deliver the findings it was Wednesday, and the media and public had started to focus on the culture that allowed such a series of actions to occur. The media conference was another chance for Cricket Australia to set the record straight, to show they were taking the situation seriously and that they were addressing these broader cultural issues.

Sutherland presented the outcomes of the investigation first. It was an interesting series of findings.

Vice-captain David Warner was identified by Sutherland as the mastermind of the plot. Never before had anyone used the words 'mastermind' and 'David Warner' in the same sentence. Warner was accused of forming the plan and instructing the younger player, Bancroft, to carry it out, going so far as to show him how to use the sandpaper to tamper with the ball. (Sutherland also confirmed that Bancroft used sandpaper, not yellow tape, and that he had lied about this at the media conference.)

Cricket Australia's criticism of Warner continued, stating that Warner had failed to 'voluntarily report his knowledge of the plan after the match', while Smith and Bancroft had admitted their involvement. This was corporate speak for 'he lied to us and we're furious'.

Smith, it turned out, was not directly involved in the execution of the plan but he did have prior knowledge of it and didn't do enough to stop it going ahead. Sutherland also said Smith had tried to conceal Bancroft's actions from the umpires once he was exposed, and from match officials after the day's play. Further to this, Smith was accused of making misleading statements in the media conference after the match, mainly that the entire leadership group knew about the plan and had sanctioned it.

Reading between the lines, it appeared Warner had come up with the plan and got Bancroft to do it. Smith had heard them talking about it and didn't want any part of it, but also did nothing to stop it. Warner and Smith's relationship had already deteriorated before the ball-tampering incident to the point where they barely spoke.

When Bancroft was caught on camera, Smith tried to protect the younger player by trying to conceal what had gone on from the umpires and match officials. When confronted by Cricket Australia, however, Bancroft and Smith had come clean. Warner only admitted his role after Bancroft and Smith had confessed.

As a result of these findings, Cricket Australia announced twelve-month bans for Smith and Warner and a nine-month ban for Bancroft. They also announced Warner would never hold a leadership position again.* Cricket Australia knew they had to offer up a sacrifice to the angry cricket community to save their own skin, so Warner, Smith and Bancroft were handed huge suspensions.

---

* Once again shutting the gate well and truly after the horse had bolted.

Despite the severity of the sentences, Sutherland still refused to say the players cheated, a ridiculous position.

The biggest question everyone had was: who else knew of the plan? On this Sutherland was clear: 'No other players or support staff had prior knowledge, this includes Darren Lehmann who despite inaccurate media reports has not resigned. He will continue to coach the team under his current contract.'

ABC cricket broadcaster Jim Maxwell later summed up a lot of people's view, saying he wasn't convinced that no one else knew what was going on, or that it was the first time they'd tried to cheat in this manner. 'As I understand it, this was the third time they'd tried this little trick of sandpapering one side of the ball,' he said.

Cricket Australia effectively threw the three suspended players on a sacrificial pyre and hoped that would appease the angry masses and, more importantly in their view, the sponsors. The problem was that many felt Cricket Australia's investigation was trying to cover up broader involvement across the team by shafting just three players.

Even if their version of events is true, Cricket Australia wasn't exactly trusted, having coddled their players for years. This kind of protection went right back, at least to the time they tried to deal with the Mark Waugh and Shane Warne bookmaking incidents in secret.

SEEDS OF DISASTER

Dealing with any crisis requires addressing the root cause of the problem, otherwise people can sense that you're just papering over the cracks. Sutherland's media conference in South Africa and the results of the investigation were doing just that. Coming four days after the events on the field, the cricketing public had started to focus on the culture that led three players to think cheating in this way was somehow acceptable.

In this regard, Cricket Australia's bumbling response and refusal to actually label the players' actions as cheating didn't help. At the heart of the issue was the governing body's acceptance of poor player behaviour over a long period of time. Given they had just identified David Warner as the chief villain in all this, the question was: how was he allowed to become vice-captain in the first place?

There was a time when the idea of David Warner being vice-captain of Australia would have been laughable.* Warner was universally seen as one of the biggest hotheads to have ever played the game. He frequently got in verbal arguments with opponents on the field and with journalists off it, and in 2013, he punched English batsman Joe Root on the chin in a bar in Birmingham at two in the morning.** At the time, Sutherland had described Warner's actions as 'despicable'.

Following this, Warner tried to tone down his behaviour but, in January 2015, he got in an ugly verbal spat with India's Rohit Sharma and appeared to tell him to 'speak English'. Despite this incident, in August that year Warner was made vice-captain of the team, at the same time Steve Smith was named captain.

The decision was controversial. Sutherland himself had seemed less than enthusiastic. A week before the announcement, he said of Warner possibly being appointed to the position, 'I don't think that's necessarily an obvious next step.'***

There was a broader view in Cricket Australia, however, that appointing Warner to the vice-captaincy was a way to keep him 'in the tent', so to speak – to have him toe the company line. It was also

---

* That time was right up until he was named vice-captain.
** No one should ever be in a bar in Birmingham at two in the morning. In fact, try to avoid Birmingham altogether.
*** This was code for 'That would be a crazy decision on so many levels I can't even fully comprehend it would be considered by any person on earth, outside David Warner.'

believed that the alternative – not appointing him – would leave him as a loose cannon outside the leadership group.*

Warner would show them he could be a loose cannon inside or outside the tent.

Sutherland appeared to be the only dissenting voice to the appointment. When asked about Sutherland's view, Warner said, 'That's James' opinion. He's our boss and I have to respect what he says. But the board obviously approved me being vice-captain and I thank them for their support, trust and faith in myself to be under Steve and help Steve as much as I can with my knowledge of the game.'

It was to be a terrible decision, made on the basis of appeasement. But it had been ticked off by the nine-member board, the coach and the then chairman of selectors, Rod Marsh, who said, 'David has matured and developed into an important senior figure in the Australian team. He has come a long way.'

He hadn't.

Compounding the mistake was that Cricket Australia had just appointed one of the youngest ever captains in Smith and, instead of supporting him with a vice-captain with lots of leadership experience, they handed that position to someone whose temperament was hardly suited to the role.

This, again, is not a view formulated with the benefit of hindsight. Warner's appointment caused raised eyebrows throughout the cricketing world. In the 2018 test series in South Africa, Warner played a key role in turning the test before the ball-tampering incident into one of the most antagonistic ever played.

The Durban test was a tense affair. Both sides verbally sparred with each other on the field. Warner, as a leader of the Australian

---

* Trying to make a loose cannon change their ways by giving them what they want is a tactic parents learn doesn't work with small children. The fact it keeps happening in the corporate world is bizarre.

team, was not exactly keeping a cool head, at one stage unleashing a verbal attack on Aiden Markram.

On day four, during the tea break, things boiled over again. Warner got into a clash in a stairwell with South Africa's Quinton de Kock. Warner had to be restrained and later said the confrontation was the result of a verbal attack on his family. The whole thing was caught on CCTV. There wasn't a lot of sympathy for Warner; he was seen to live by the sword all too often.

After the incident, tensions were even higher between the two teams. Warner wasn't suspended for his actions and was cleared to play the next test – a fateful decision by Cricket Australia and another failure to address the team's poor culture.

By this stage Smith, as captain, was not on good terms with Warner. The young captain couldn't control him. In a test series that had suddenly turned highly antagonistic, instead of having a calm confidant to support him, Smith had Warner, one of the chief antagonists and a man who wouldn't take orders from anyone.

As Smith met with match officials and South Africa's captain Faf du Plessis, Warner was stewing over the incident with de Kock. In the third test, he took this anger and directed it towards a win-at-all cost approach in the form of ball-tampering.

Cricket Australia was the clear author of this situation. They had recent evidence Warner was not up to the position they'd put him in, and they could see Smith was not able to manage him. So ultimately blaming only the three players involved in the ball-tampering incident was ridiculous and everyone but Cricket Australia knew it. If David Warner had not been vice-captain, or if a more experienced captain had been in place, none of this would happened.

The incident ruined Australia's cricket reputation and destroyed the career of Steve Smith, the most promising Australian batsman since Don Bradman. Any suggestion that those who had made the decisions that fostered this culture were immune to the fallout was astounding in its brazenness.

The symptom had been addressed, but not the cause. The crisis was not dealt with.

A COSTLY EXERCISE

With Cricket Australia's investigation now completed, the reactions came quick and fast, and they were not positive.

The first to react were the sponsors. Almost immediately, electronics company LG pulled its sponsorship arrangement with Warner. ASICS cut its ties with Warner and Bancroft as well.

On top of that, Warner had his $2.4 million contract with Indian Premier League (IPL) side Sunrisers Hyderabad ended. Smith was also booted from the IPL, losing his $2.4 million contract with the Rajasthan Royals as well as his personal sponsorships with Sanitarium and the Commonwealth Bank. Smith and Warner both stood to miss about $4–5 million in earnings and sponsorships during their twelve months out of the game.

Cricket Australia was next. Magellan Financial Group, just one year into a three-year deal as major sponsor of Australia's domestic test matches, pulled their $20 million deal with the governing body. Magellan's chief executive Hamish Douglass said:

> A conspiracy by the leadership of the Australian Men's Test Cricket Team which broke the rules with a clear intention to gain an unfair advantage during the third Test in South Africa goes to the heart of integrity.
>
> Regrettably, these events are so inconsistent with our values that we are left with no option but to terminate our ongoing partnership with Cricket Australia.

You know you're in trouble when the finance industry is shocked by your lack of integrity.

While sponsors were fleeing like someone who'd accidentally wandered into an Adam Sandler movie, some decided to stay, with Qantas and Lion, the brewer of XXXX Gold, believing Cricket Australia had done enough in response. They were probably the only ones in the world who thought that.

NOT OVER YET

When Steve Smith and Cameron Bancroft returned to Australia, both fronted emotional media conferences where they expressed their remorse. Perhaps what was most noticeable was who wasn't there: neither Cricket Australia nor the Australian Cricketers' Association were alongside the players. This was no different to when Bancroft and Smith had fronted that first ill-fated media conference in South Africa. The three men who'd been suspended had well and truly been cut adrift. The message was clear: this was an act of rogue agents, not Cricket Australia.

The problem for Cricket Australia was that Christina Matthews, the chief executive of WA cricket, did sit next to Bancroft at his media conference. Matthews is a former Australian wicketkeeper who's played more test matches for Australia than any other woman. She laid it out very clearly for the assembled media.

'A culture is everybody's responsibility so if we talk about Australian cricket – it's my responsibility, it's David Peever's [Cricket Australia's chair] responsibility, it's John Warn [NSW cricket chairman] in NSW's responsibility.

'As the leaders and the CEOs of all of those organisations it's our job to set the standard and to bring our staff and our players on that journey.'

Matthews had nailed them all. They could run but they couldn't hide. Cricket Australia had not only failed to curb the worst excesses of Australian cricketers for over a generation, they were now attempting to dodge the responsibility for it.

Further to this, their explanation of events left a lot of questions unanswered. If the Australians had never cheated before, how did the SuperSport network know to film the ball all the time? Was that just blind luck? And why was Warner instructing Bancroft in how to doctor the ball? If this was the first time ever, how did he know how to do it?

Where was the sandpaper from? Who had procured it? Sandpaper being at the game seemed to suggest a degree of planning. Did Warner bring it or did someone else give it to him?

And was it really possible that a plan to create extra swing on the ball could be executed without the bowlers having some knowledge of it? Wouldn't they notice the changed condition of the ball?

How could someone remain coach of the team when something like this had occurred, even if they had no knowledge? Did the coach not command enough respect? Wasn't this a reflection of lack of discipline within the team?

Cricket Australia had spent almost a week trying to limit the damage yet all these questions remained. The defence they'd spent a week building wouldn't last twenty-four hours.

GETTING WORSE

The day after Cricket Australia had publicly exonerated him, Darren Lehmann quit as coach. 'The feeling is that Australian cricket needs to move forward, and this is the right thing to do. I'm ultimately responsible for the culture of the team and I've been thinking about my position for a while. Despite telling media yesterday that I'm not resigning, after viewing Steve and Cameron's hurting, it's only fair that I make this decision.'

The announcement meant the crisis continued to drag on. Loose ends that should have been tied up days before continued to unravel. It now seemed Lehmann had either been quietly pushed or he'd realised what Cricket Australia had not, that he couldn't possibly remain in the job.

Had Cricket Australia and Lehmann come to an agreement behind the scenes where they would exonerate him if he subsequently resigned? No one really knew. Like their handling of the investigation, it made Cricket Australia appear indecisive, or to be operating in a secretive manner.

Even worse for them, on the back of Christina Matthews' comments, Lehmann had also raised the issue of culture, taking responsibility for his part in it. There seemed no danger that Cricket Australia would do the same.

WARNER SPEAKS. SORT OF.

The one person who could answer some of the lingering questions was David Warner, who so far had not spoken to the media at all. Almost a full week after the soul of cricket died, Warner finally fronted the press.

It started off well enough. Like Smith and Bancroft, Warner said he was sorry for his actions and appeared genuinely remorseful. Then the questions began. It quickly became clear the media didn't believe Cricket Australia's version of events at all. Warner was asked who else knew of the plot.

'I am here today to accept my responsibility for my part and my involvement in what happened in Cape Town. It's inexcusable. I'm deeply sorry. As I said, I'll do everything I can to earn the respect back of the Australian public.'

'You haven't answered the question,' responded the journalist.

There was no response and the media was told to move on. The next question was whether the plan was his idea.

'As I said, I'm here to take full responsibility for the part that I played in this. It's extremely regrettable. I'm very sorry. And I really just want to move on from this.'

He was then asked if it was the first time he'd been involved in ball tampering.

'As I said before I'm here to accept my responsibility for the part that I played in day three of the Newlands Cape Town Test.'

The last question was whether he was a scapegoat.

'As I said before I'm here to speak about myself and take responsibility for the part that I played in this.'

Not exactly a forthcoming explanation of what went on. It left the media furious and the public even more disenchanted, both with the cheating itself and the response of the parties involved.

It didn't help that the person managing Warner's public relations, Roxy Jacenko, was highly visible at the conference. When you're spinning as much as Warner was, it doesn't look good to have your high-profile spin doctor filmed for all to see.

Why front the media if you're not going to answer any questions? In that case Warner should have just put out a statement. It was another case of managing the situation poorly.

So vociferous was the reaction to his media conference, Warner took to Twitter later that day to defend himself, tweeting: 'I know there are unanswered questions and lots of them. I completely understand. In time I will do my best to answer them all. But there is a formal CA process to follow.'

I believe that formal process must be very rigorous indeed, because at the time of writing Warner hasn't done anything more to answer any questions.

On 3 April 2018, more than a week after the third test, the Australian Cricketers' Association awoke from their slumber and launched a half-hearted defence of the players they represent. They raised the very reasonable point that Bancroft and Smith should never have been rushed into that first media conference. But coming more than a week after those events, it just seemed odd.

WITCH-HUNT

A fortnight on and the pressure on Cricket Australia had not subsided. The attempts to minimise the crisis and to ring-fence the rest of the organisation from the three players directly involved had been met with incredulity. Like any true crisis, the incident itself was the result of an environment that had been created over years. Rarely does a crisis spring fully formed out of nowhere.

Cricket Australia chairman David Peever had been an invisible man during the biggest crisis Australian cricket had faced in at least a decade. But with pressure coming from the media, fans, government, sponsors and other international cricketing associations, on 6 April he was forced to finally front the media.

Peever's media conference was his attempt to draw a line under events and end the pressure being put on the organisation. He announced a 'root and branch' review into the culture of the Australian cricket team.* This was a step in the right direction, but he then spent the rest of the conference undoing any goodwill it might have garnered.

First he ruled that CEO James Sutherland was safe, an odd statement given the review hadn't even started yet. Sutherland had been in the role seventeen years, so you'd think he was a significant contributor to the organisation's culture.

He then went on to praise Sutherland's handling of the entire mess, saying he'd done an 'outstanding' job. This had the media and the public scratching their heads, because of, you know, facts.

Peever then doubled down on Cricket Australia's bunker

---

* 'Root and branch' is something people say when the investigation or review has a narrow focus and little authority. The less powerful an investigation is, the more you talk it up as being a big deal.

mentality, calling the very reasonable questions people were asking an attempt to start a 'witch-hunt'.

> I think we're all going to come under the microscope in terms of what is occurring back in the organisation that might have contributed to this.
>
> But I can tell you this, circumstances like this are not the time for witch-hunts.
>
> I know people in these circumstances call for everybody to be sacked. Clearly, that isn't going to solve any problems.

Rubbishing anyone who was asking sensible questions was an aggressive move and only confirmed people's worst fears about Cricket Australia's culture. It was also insulting to cricket fans, who had been severely let down by the organisation they supported both financially and emotionally.

Cricket Australia is tax-exempt because it's a community organisation. It can't just label any public scrutiny a witch-hunt; it has a duty to all Australians to account for its behaviour and decision-making.* But Peever announced the governing body would release no further details or confirmation about what had actually occurred.

'The integrity review made its findings, made its recommendations, sanctions were offered, have been accepted. There's been a lot [of detail released] in terms of the advice that was provided from the investigation itself.

'I don't anticipate there will be more release of information. We're moving forward from here. The announcement of the review today is all about moving forward.'

Peever wanted everything to go away. His comments reflected

---

* It could of course avoid that scrutiny, but I don't see them rushing to start paying tax any time soon.

the view of many powerful people: that if they say something it must be true.

Even the culture review, which was to be led by ex-players, was met with scepticism.

Ric Charlesworth* said of the review: 'A joke. As if they're going to rat on their mates.'

Peever's media conference had sent a very clear message: he had the polar opposite view to Christina Matthews. This wasn't about accepting responsibility, this was about protecting the organisation and using power to avoid accountability.

UNFINISHED BUSINESS

Cricket Australia and Peever had a billion reasons why they wanted the issue to be wrapped up.

For starters, the timing of the crisis was terrible – they were in the middle of negotiating a new TV rights deal. This, more than anything else, was why they wouldn't and couldn't sack Sutherland. Fostering a culture that resulted in players cheating is one thing, but jeopardising a billion-dollar deal is another. Cricket Australia decided to hang on with the executive team it had, rather than risk harming those negotiations.

Just over a week after Peever's media conference, Cricket Australia announced a new six-year TV deal with Channel Seven and Fox Sports worth $1.182 billion. Seven and Fox banked on the fact that Australians would forgive Cricket Australia and the Australian cricket team. If history is any guide, it was a fairly safe bet.

In early May, Cricket Australia announced Justin Langer as the new coach of the team. Langer, in perhaps a sign the culture of the team wasn't going to change that much, said of Smith, Warner and Bancroft:

---

* Charlesworth played first-class cricket for Western Australia and represented Australia in men's hockey. He also coached both the men's and women's national hockey teams.

When I think about Cameron Bancroft and Steve Smith, besides Mike Hussey, they love the game more than anyone I know.

They are cricket tragics and they're great kids. That's why it's such a surprise they made the mistake that they did.

Davey Warner's the same, he's a really good young bloke. He made a mistake.

The idea that a premeditated plan is a 'mistake' suggests Langer is not that far removed from what's gone before. A mistake is when you forget to pick up milk on the way home. But then Langer's position is no different to that of any previous Australian cricket coach: he only keeps his job if he wins. These are good players, and he knows he has to keep the door open for them to return.

Langer did have some views on changing the culture. His former teammate Adam Gilchrist said, 'Actually, I've heard him say he wants his players to be good enough blokes that he would consider allowing them to marry his daughters.' It's a strange way to select a cricket team and I'm not sure it necessarily addresses any of the issues the team faces. Will some sort of dowry now be required to play for Australia? Do women still need their father's permission to marry, or did we cross into the twenty-first century at some point?

With the TV deal done and a new coach installed, Cricket Australia felt far enough removed from events to quietly restructure the organisation. In late May they made their head of integrity, Iain Roy, redundant. Having just gone through the ball-tampering crisis, deciding you no longer need a head of integrity is a strange move.*

---

* A bit like responding to a robbery by removing all the locks.

This was followed by Sutherland announcing in June that he'd step down as CEO, giving twelve months' notice. David Peever praised Sutherland, saying, 'The game has never been in a stronger position.' This was an opinion that didn't quite seem based on facts; the public and the media's trust in those running the game was at an all-time low.

> **DID YOU KNOW?**
>
> Sport is one of the few industries where a 25-year-old is referred to as 'a young kid'.

Peever also said Sutherland's resignation had nothing to do with the ball-tampering crisis. Unfortunately, that part was almost certainly true. Peever had shown no interest in accountability for the incident beyond suspending the three players and there was no reason to think that would change now.

WASH-UP

With Sutherland leaving, the head of integrity gone and a new coach in place, Cricket Australia wanted to think the crisis was over. Yet the unanswered questions and managing the potential return of the suspended players, together with the treatment of fans and the media, left a lingering sense that it wasn't all over.

It's inevitable that at some point further details of what actually occurred will come out. That could happen in years or just weeks, as retired players write tell-all books.

Assessing how things played out, from the moment Bancroft was filmed rubbing sandpaper on the ball, it was always going to be a crisis. It was probably also certain that sponsors would leave; a crisis like this is often a welcome excuse to get out of a sponsorship deal early. And it was inevitable the players involved would cop heavy bans.

The slow reaction from Cricket Australia, though, made the situation worse. Their at times aggressive response to reasonable

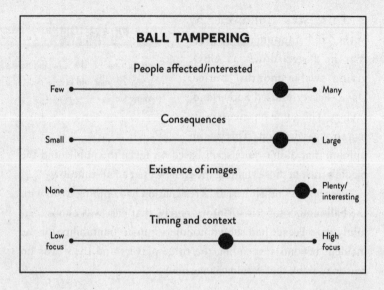

questions, and their refusal to accept any real responsibility for the culture, meant the crisis went on longer. In fact, it has never come to a clear end.

Peever, Sutherland and Lehmann have all damaged their reputations, partly because they have so clearly tried to restrict the fallout to just three players. They should have read the tea-leaves sooner.

This issue was always going to play out in many arenas, and it ticked all four factors for a big crisis. It affected a lot of people, it had big consequences, it had amazing footage and, coming off the back of the heated second test, it had inflammatory timing and context.

SAGAS

Very occasionally, a crisis will develop into a saga. In a saga the scandal goes on far longer than a crisis and it plays out in every possible arena. It's usually so complex that it has numerous sub-issues and sub-crises within it.

Sagas are also incredibly rare. The Super League war certainly qualifies as a saga, as does Kerry Packer's World Series launch.

Perhaps the scarcity of sagas indicates that PR professionals have learnt a thing or two about how to handle issues and crises. And yet somehow the Essendon Football Club's supplements saga dominated the sporting media for six years.

WHATEVER IT TAKES

The supplements scandal at Essendon is the best example of an issue that became a crisis and then a saga. It began in 2012 and it's still going today. Recounting the entire chain of events would take a whole book but, simply put, it started as a workplace issue and ended up going on so long there are primary-school children who have never known life without it.

An injection program undertaken by the Essendon Football Club in late 2011/early 2012 was later determined to have involved banned substances.* In 2016, thirty-four players were found guilty of having used the banned peptide Thymosin beta-4 and were suspended for two years.

By January 2012, questions were being asked by Dr Bruce Reid, the club doctor, about the injection program, which was occurring under the sport scientist Stephen Dank. At this stage, it still wasn't that different from many issues that have to be managed now and then. A swift reaction – a tightening of procedures or a shutdown of the program – would have seen it contained to being an issue, even if it had become public.

There are issues of a similar scale playing out in organisations around Australia every day. Most get sorted quickly and go no further; some become the issues, crises and sagas that play out in public. This was initially nothing more than a workplace issue, but it wasn't dealt with. It continued until 5 February 2013, when Essendon

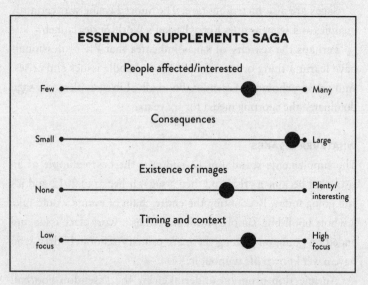

* The Court of Arbitration for Sport determined this and the Federal Supreme Court of Switzerland upheld it. Before people write to me with their views about how nothing has ever been proved – I get your position.

self-reported that illicit substances may have been administered during the supplements program.

At this stage, the issue exploded out of the workplace and into several arenas. It entered the regulatory arena with the Australian Sports Anti-Doping Authority (ASADA) announcing a joint investigation with the AFL. It was also in the media and political arenas, with widespread interest being generated. From there, it only spread.

BETTER GET A LAWYER, SON

In August 2013, Essendon coach James Hird challenged the charges levelled at him by the AFL in the Supreme Court of Victoria, pushing the issue into the legal arena too.

From an issue-management point of view, this was a disaster for Essendon and the AFL. Managing an issue requires control of the arena in which it's playing out. The AFL can control its workplace to a certain extent: it sets the policies and the procedures clubs must follow, and the penalties for not doing so.

The same goes for private negotiations. Often an issue is sorted out privately, with both parties left satisfied. That's why most organisations prefer dealing with something by negotiating it internally. A pay-off, or a deal where everyone is happy, keeps the issue in a private arena.

Often an issue only become a crisis or a saga because a group or individual reaches the stage where they can't progress things privately. Take for example the #MeToo movement. Attempts to deal with many of these cases in workplaces, through private negotiations or even in court had met dead ends. As a result they spilled out into the media, online and community arenas.

When people say something like 'this shouldn't be a trial by media' they're often missing the point that if the case had been taken seriously in the workplace or the legal system, there would be no need for a public movement like #MeToo.

In this way, Essendon failed to contain the issue. When the club first became aware of it they still had control, and could have managed it within their workplace.

If sorting out an issue privately can't be done, keeping it in an arena you control is the next best thing. The AFL Tribunal is an example of this. But the political arena, the legal arena, the regulatory arena and the media arena are out of an organisation's control. You might be able to influence them, but you don't run them.

An issue or a crisis is hard enough to handle if it plays out in one arena you don't control, but in a saga, it's often in all of them. This is a disaster scenario. Court proceedings, regulator investigations and findings, political inquiries and media reports all feed on one another and often kick off more problems in other arenas.

For example, in this case the AFL tried to deal with the issue in their own backyard by announcing disciplinary charges for Essendon and James Hird. But when Hird contested these in court, they lost control. Dr Bruce Reid also successfully challenged his charges and suspension in the Supreme Court of Victoria. These court cases, in turn, generated more media coverage and heightened tensions.

Essendon tried a similar approach to the AFL, looking to regain some control over proceedings by launching an internal inquiry headed by former Telstra CEO Ziggy Switkowski.* Crucially, an investigation like that buys time. You can say you won't be making any further comments while the investigation is occurring.

Often that's the only reason an investigation, a committee hearing or a legal appeal is announced – to provide a shield from awkward questions. Wait for enough time to pass and when the public's or media's interest has cooled, quietly put out the findings or drop the appeal. This is a very effective tactic in managing most

---

* Getting a person named Ziggy to conduct a drug investigation is one of my favourite things ever.

crises. If you're lucky, another big crisis will spring up and you can dump the findings out while everyone's looking the other way.

But when related issues are popping up across multiple arenas like spot fires, this is harder to do. You can tell the media you won't be making further comment while a workplace investigation is underway, but not a Supreme Court judge.

This state of affairs means no one group has control of events. Even ASADA, the regulator, found this out the hard way. ASADA issued show cause notices to the thirty-four Essendon players in June 2014,* only to have the legality of their joint investigation with the AFL challenged in the Federal Court by Hird.

A FORGIVING MAN

Lawyer Julian Burnside QC may be the most forgiving man ever. Not only did he stand up for Alan Bond, saying people who wanted to paint him as a villain would change their mind if they had a coffee with him, he also represented James Hird during the Essendon supplements saga.

When Hird received a twelve-month ban for bringing the game into disrepute and conduct unbecoming, Burnside said of Hird accepting the sentence, 'I reckon what he did ... was nothing short of heroic.'

This delayed ASADA's process, as they now had to defend their investigation in court. It took until the end of September 2014 for the court to declare ASADA's investigation legal, and then another month for ASADA to reissue the show cause notices after an almost five-month delay and more than eighteen months after Essendon first self-reported.

CRISES WITHIN CRISES

Other crises continued within the saga. WorkSafe Victoria began investigating and ended up convicting the club for breaching Victoria's *Occupational Health and Safety Act 2004* by failing to

---

* This called on the players to 'show cause' for why they shouldn't be suspended. It's a fairly common process in cases like this.

provide the players with a workplace free of health risks. The penalty was $200000, enough to hurt a club already groaning under lawyers' fees.

Another attempt to get the issue back under AFL control saw the AFL Tribunal hear the case in 2015. The tribunal was quick to clear the thirty-four Essendon players, declaring them all not guilty of using a banned substance.

This verdict suited Essendon and the AFL down to the ground. The players had been cleared and wouldn't be suspended. Finally, it seemed, everyone could move on.

But the AFL didn't have control of events, and the World Anti-Doping Agency (WADA) announced it would appeal the AFL's decision in the Court of Arbitration for Sport (CAS). The CAS upheld WADA's appeal, finding the players guilty, only to have the players challenge it in the Federal Supreme Court of Switzerland,* which in the end did not uphold the players' appeal.

It was now October 2016 – more than four years since the injection program had begun – and the players had exhausted their options. The backdated two-year ban, which had effectively ruled the players who were still active out of the 2016 season, would stand.

But even this wasn't the end of the saga. In July 2018, a hearing in the (Australian) Supreme Court examined whether several statements by AFL CEO Gillon McLachlan about the AFL's joint investigation with ASADA were misleading or deceptive. The case was resolved when the two parties reached a settlement.**

---

* This is perhaps the best example of how losing control of an issue can see it grow into a crisis and then into a saga, with no one able to predict where it will end. An injecting program occurring in a footy club in Melbourne had wound up in the Federal Supreme Court of Switzerland.

** Personally, I believe the Essendon saga will never end. Following the inevitable nuclear Armageddon, only cockroaches and the Essendon saga will survive.

THE
DOWNRIGHT ODD

While issues, crises and sagas all present challenges for sporting clubs and bodies, the majority are alarmingly predictable. Even the use of performance-enhancing drugs is hardly surprising.

For unfortunately common events, like alcohol related incidents including drink-driving, violence and sexual assaults, there exists an extensive playbook on how to manage them. Illicit drugs are similar. It's not too difficult to deal with because most people are not too surprised that in a big group of young men under immense pressure and with lots of disposable income, some of them might turn to excessive drinking or drugs.

Salary-cap cheating is now so well rehearsed, especially in the NRL, you barely need to read any of the statements. They're all just versions of what the last club that got caught cheating said.

Occasionally, though, an issue will come out of left field that can only be described as downright odd. Unlike salary-cap cheating, drugs, alcohol, gambling, racism or sexism, these issues are so strange they barely need to be managed, as those in charge could never have been expected to anticipate them.

HE DID WHAT?

During a game in 2001, Wests Tigers player John Hopoate on three occasions inserted his finger into an opponent's anus in an attempt to put them off their game.

Watching the League community wrestle with this issue was probably one of the greatest moments of my life. It certainly produced some of the funniest quotes you'll ever read.

To start with, Hopoate himself tried to play down the issue. He claimed he was only giving wedgies to the North Queensland Cowboys players, Glenn Morrison, Peter Jones and Paul Bowman. He said this was common in the game: 'You get wedgies all the time and jabbed in the stork.* I'm a great believer that what happens on the field should stay on the field.'

I bet he's a great believer in what happens on the field stays on the field; I would be too, if I was doing that.

Peter Jones wasn't buying it: 'It wasn't a wedgie. That's when your pants are pulled up your arse. I think I know the difference between a wedgie and someone sticking their finger up my bum.'**

I tend to agree. I think most people would know the difference between the two, even if you'd never experienced either before.

Hopoate's coach Terry Lamb tried to defend his player, claiming such incidents occur up to ten times a game. That seems like a lot.***

Writer and former Wallaby Peter FitzSimons didn't agree this behaviour was common: 'It's disgusting. This is the absolute bottom of the barrel. There's an unwritten code [. . .] At the very top of the barrel you have got the king hits, fisticuffs, I hit you, you hit me. A little bit lower down you have got kicking, lower down still

---

* I can only assume that by 'stork', dear reader, he means what you and I think he means, but I can't be completely sure and I don't want to ask in case it's something worse.
** Is this the greatest quote in the history of sport? Yes.
*** It is a lot. An NRL season, including finals, is 201 matches. That means in a single season it would be occurring 2010 times. It also means during a game it's happening on average every eight minutes. I doubt they'd have time to fit any footy in.

you have got eye-gouging, testicle-pulling, that sort of thing. This, nobody has ever heard of it.'

Good to know where testicle-pulling fits in on the scale of on-field sins.

Before deciding to suspend Hopoate for twelve matches, NRL commissioner Jim Hall told the hearing: 'In forty-five years of involvement with Rugby League I've never come across a more disgusting allegation.' Considering all the things that have happened in League over those forty-five years, that's really saying something.

TWICE IS A TREND

Since the Hopoate incident, League has had more strange cases.

In November 2010, Joel Monaghan quit the NRL after a photo came out of him simulating sex with a dog during Mad Monday celebrations.[*] You'd think that would be an issue not likely to reoccur but, in 2016, video emerged of Sydney Roosters co-captain Mitchell Pearce doing the same thing. That's arguably a trend. And to the best of our knowledge, these are just the instances of this behaviour caught on film.

They say you can't legislate against stupidity, and these incidents seem to prove that. You can't blame the NRL for not having policies in place that specifically prohibit this behaviour. How could you even think of them?

Take for example when, in June 2014, the Sharks' Todd Carney was photographed urinating in his own mouth. I'm not sure how someone comes to be doing that, let alone someone else saying, 'Hang on, let me take a pic.' I don't think we should judge the NRL for not having a policy proscribing that practice.[**]

---

[*] Yes, you did read that sentence correctly.
[**] Apparently this is called a 'bubbler'. It worries me when things like this have a name. You don't name things that only happen once.

Carney was run out of the NRL as a result. After all, it wasn't like he'd done something forgivable like assaulting a family in New York.*

This was also another case of a story becoming bigger because of the existence of a photo. The picture spread like wildfire on social media and gave television producers nightmares over what to blur out and what to leave in.

WE DID START THE FIRE

The NRL is not alone in having odd cases to deal with. The AFL and its Mad Monday celebrations are another centre of excellence for bizarre behaviour.

In 2013, St Kilda players were celebrating the end of their season and hired a dwarf as entertainment.** During the event, the entertainer, Blake Johnston, was set on fire by Saints player Clint Jones.

'There was just smoke coming off me. I was on fire,' said Johnston.

When Johnston complained to Leigh Montagna, the player who had hired him, and asked him to replace his burnt clothes, Montagna responded:

> If you actually followed your job description and said
> you would entertain us, I'd be happy to. But to sit on
> a seat and drink water for two hours and still want
> your money does not constitute work in my book.
> I am sorry if you felt your clothes were affected, but I
> also feel ripped off that I paid you money to entertain
> and you did not make any effort to try and entertain.***

---

* See Matthew Lodge's story on page 7.
** Yes, 2013, and it was still a thing.
*** Whenever I'm performing live, this lingers with me. The pressure to entertain everyone is immense given I now know what could happen if I don't.

This was not exactly the best way to handle things. An apology here might have ended the matter, but instead it ended up in the media, a further example of not heading off an issue while it's within an arena you control.

This forced the club to front the press and put on the record that they did not support setting people on fire, regardless of their stature. While some people laugh about them having to do that, they're the only club that's made their position clear. We're in the dark as to where the rest of Australia's sporting clubs stand on this issue. Perhaps they're all pro people arson? We just don't know.

Clint Jones, the player responsible, apologised in a statement, saying: 'I am embarrassed if this has caused angst and certainly had no intention to cause any harm to anyone, including the St Kilda Football Club and its members.'

I think if you try to light someone on fire with a cigarette lighter, you can't really claim you 'had no intention to cause any harm'.

Mr Johnston said the incident upset him so much that it forced him to cancel his next gig, as a gorilla chasing a strip-teasing banana in a Fitzroy burlesque show. A tragedy on every level.

SKIMMING THE SURFACE

A saga like the Essendon one is beyond the control of any one person or organisation. That's why, unlike in an issue or a crisis, it's almost impossible to manage.

That said, a poorly managed crisis can turn into a saga. Cricket Australia seems to have narrowly missed the ball-tampering crisis becoming a saga. If Smith, Warner or Bancroft had appealed their suspensions, either with Cricket Australia or in court, that could have spun events out of their control. But because they accepted Cricket Australia's findings, the governing body didn't lose control of determining the consequences.

By comparison, the Essendon saga is an example of how a club and a sporting body can't always keep an issue under their own control. Unlike a crisis, the Essendon saga contained multiple issues that, even on their own, would have been difficult to manage. Normally the WorkSafe investigation and fine would have been a crisis in its own right, but within this saga it was a footnote.

Other events, like claims that Essendon tried to engage Mick Gatto to sort things out – denied strongly by the Bombers – would usually have been a big issue to manage, but Essendon didn't even have time to deal with it. They denied the claims and everyone quickly moved on to the next spot fire.

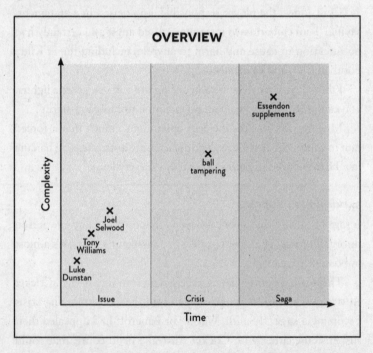

In giving an overview of what constitutes an issue, a crisis or a saga, I have only skimmed the surface. Yet now, within moments of hearing about the latest scandal, you can probably have an educated guess about how bad things are going to get.

In researching this section, finding examples to illustrate each point was easy; the problem was only being able to fit a small percentage of the examples in one book.

More alarming is that of the incidents I researched – not just the ones I mentioned – so few were career ending for the people involved. Some of them deserved a second chance, but many should have never been able to re-enter high-paying, high-profile jobs. They certainly would have lost their job in almost any other workplace.

But sportspeople have rare skills and many people have an interest in forgiving them, so a carefully orchestrated dance occurs after every issue, crisis or saga. It's a dance like the movements of the planets around the sun, everything following a clearly defined path. This dance is controlled by two forces as powerful as gravity: the power of redemption, and the desire to win.

PART III

THE PATH TO REDEMPTION

FORGIVING
ᕦᕤ AND FORGETTING ᕡᕣ

Within minutes of a Wayward Champion entering a scandal, the gravitational pull of forgiveness will start to tug on them. Often subtly at first, then with increasing power.

Even as Steve Smith and Cameron Bancroft confessed to ball tampering just after the end of play, forgiveness was already a presence in the room (unlike anyone from Cricket Australia). As Australians reacted in disbelief, questions started to pop into their heads. What if these two players were suspended? What effect would that have on Australia's chances of winning? Would this mean we could even lose to England?

Forgiveness is a gravity field that pulls everything towards the most powerful force in the Australian sporting universe: winning.

Australians love winning. We love it almost as much as we hate losing, to paraphrase basketball great Larry Bird. We love the players who we think are going to win us things and we especially love people who have won things for us in the past.

That's because the great sporting moments bring us so much happiness. We remember John Aloisi slotting home that penalty against Uruguay in 2005, taking us to the World Cup for the first time since 1974, or Cathy Freeman crossing the line first at the 2000 Olympics, ending racism in Australia forever. Or perhaps our greatest sporting moment: Brendan Fevola defying the odds and winning *I'm a Celebrity . . . Get Me Out of Here!*

Winning makes us love people – at worst it makes us mildly fond of them. Did anyone like Lleyton Hewitt at the start? No! Do they like him now? A bit. Sometimes. Well, we're fine with him. Because he won 'us' the US Open and Wimbledon. He made us happy.[*]

The ability to win triumphs over the tendency to repeatedly stuff up. It explains how Shane Warne has been forgiven countless times[**] and the contrast between how Alan Bond and Christopher Skase are remembered.

Winning is the centre of everything. Clubs, players, fans – no one can resist its pull. Life isn't that complex; sports clubs are set up to win, corporations to make money, political parties to get votes. Sure, they'd all like to do good things along the way, but that's a secondary concern.

If you understand what an individual's or organisations's purpose is, you'll rarely be surprised by what they do. Sporting clubs and the industry that surrounds them all follow the same basic rule; the clubs want to win and the governing bodies want their sport to grow. What they say is window dressing. Don't believe it.

Do they care about sending a clear message that violence against women is bad? Sure! Happy to wear a white ribbon, but they're not going to do anything that hinders their ability to win. A player assaults someone in public? That's a shame, but they're kind of essential to us making finals, so let's make sure their suspension ends relatively quickly.

The path to forgiveness is well trodden, but it's not always as simple to travel as it seems. While the ability to win is important,

---

[*]   Most people now say they like Lleyton because he is an insightful commentator, but they always say it with surprise in their voice, which makes it less of a compliment.

[**] Scientists predict that even at the current rate, Warne will take until the year 2356 to use up all his goodwill.

there are other forces that affect whether a Wayward Champion makes it back.

HAVE POTENTIAL AND MEET IT

The number one influence is how good a player you are, or if you're retired, how good you were back in the day. Being insanely good at sport means redemption is always within your grasp. NRL great Andrew Johns falls into this category, as does the AFL's Wayne Carey.

Nick Kyrgios is in a similar vein. His tennis talent is so great that people are never quite ready to write him off, despite the on- and off-court tantrums, the giving up in the middle of matches and just behaving like a delinquent teenager at a shopping centre food court most of the time.

Take some of these headlines after Kyrgios made it through to the fourth round of the 2018 Australian Open (where he lost):

> Has Nick Kyrgios finally grown up?
> Fans heap praise on former bad boy Nick Kyrgios
> Nick Kyrgios a role model? You'd better believe it.

Both journalists and fans were desperate to celebrate him making it through a few matches without behaving like a goose. People were falling over themselves to tell you how he'd changed.* He hadn't, though. In June 2018, the BBC had to apologise to viewers after Kyrgios was caught on camera using a water bottle to simulate a sex act at the Queen's Club Championships.

Why are people so determined to find proof he's changed? Because he's so talented. He's Australia's best hope of winning a

---

* In one match at the Open he kept turning to his player's box and yelling 'stand up!'. He often did it even though everyone in his box was already standing. You could see the nervous glances among the people in the box: 'We can't really stand up any more than we currently are.'

grand slam. If he does ever win the Australian Open, all will be for-given so quickly even Jesus would say, 'Well let's hold on a minute.'

It's all about potential.[*] Kyrgios may never fulfil his, but if you make the most of your talent and become a great, nothing you do can stop you being praised and honoured.

DIVINE FORGIVENESS

Gary Ablett Snr is one of the greatest AFL players of all time. To watch him play was to feel electricity run through your body. He was extraordinary, he could do things no one else has done before or since.

Ablett was one of the AFL's biggest stars in the eighties and early nineties. In the 1989 grand final, despite his side losing, he kicked a record nine goals. I remember many occasions where I was watching him play in person and he did something that made me disbelieve my own eyes.[**] Footy fans called him 'God' for his super-natural ability.

Only four players have kicked more goals than Ablett, all legends of the game – Tony Lockett, Gordon Coventry, Jason Dunstall and Doug Wade. But they were all key forwards, while Ablett only played some of his career up front.

In 2000, Ablett checked into room 1265 at Melbourne's Park Hyatt hotel with Alisha Horan. She was a twenty-year-old infatu-ated fan. Ablett was thirty-eight.

They partied for the next three days, taking a variety of drugs and drinking heavily. On the third day, Horan found Ablett about to snort a quarter of a gram of heroin. Ablett explains what happened next:

---

[*] Not fulfilling your potential is perhaps the cardinal sin of sport. Mark Philippoussis is a great example of this – all the talent in the world, but never realised. No one cares about him anymore, he's just a footnote in Australia's sporting history and in this book.

[**] I felt the same watching Warne and Carey live too. I saw Tony Lockett and Jason Dunstall, too, but Ablett was more exciting.

Basically, she caught me with it. She asked what it
was. I didn't really want her knowing that it was what
it was. And I told her it was cocaine. And she wanted
some.

I only gave her a very tiny amount.

Ablett passed out not long after this. When he woke, he found
Horan unconscious. He rang an ambulance but then fled. This
meant when the ambulance arrived, he wasn't there to tell them
what she'd taken.

Horan never regained consciousness. She passed away two days
later.

Initially Ablett refused to assist police with their questions, citing
legal advice. Not a helpful stance. Ablett claimed he'd 'received
pressure from certain avenues not to give all the facts'.

He said that, just before the inquest into Alisha's death, he got a
message via legal representation:

The family [of Alisha Horan] didn't wish me to give
evidence to protect their daughter.

They just basically wanted to protect her reputation. Obviously . . . since the incident . . . things
surfaced. And I think that the parents did discover
things they never knew and, not wanting to cause the
family any more grief, I, even though I wasn't really
comfortable with it, I chose to respect the family's
wishes.

Alisha's father, Alan Horan, refuted this: 'It's a load of rubbish.
Ablett's just done this to protect his arse.'

Ablett eventually gave a partial confession to police, but only
after the inquiry was over.

In March 2001, coroner Noreen Toohey restated submissions from a barrister for Ms Horan's family that alleged Ablett had failed to 'protect their young daughter when she was in trouble'.

This was clearly a matter for the law, and yet the football community had a problem. Just as the coroner was handing down her findings in 2001, Ablett became eligible for the AFL Hall of Fame. It would look terrible if they honoured Ablett's on-field greatness within months of a coroner being highly critical of his role in the death of a young girl.

The AFL's Hall of Fame charter states the selection committee 'may consider individual record, ability, integrity, sportsmanship and character'. That pesky character bit has caused a few problems over the years. The debate still rages over whether you can decouple the player on the field from the person off it. The same debate occurs with artists and their art, especially in light of the recent revelations that almost every man in Hollywood is awful.

Some argue that these men are just footballers, that we shouldn't pretend it's about anything more than that, and that awards like this just honour what they did on the field. Others argue that players are community figures and that the tolerance or condemnation of their behaviour sends a huge message about what's acceptable in society.

But it's hard to argue they're just footballers. The Hall of Fame event is televised and some of the most powerful people in Australia show up wearing tuxedos and ball gowns. People care about this a lot more than other professions; the awards for Australia's greatest heart surgeon aren't televised.

That's always been sport's problem. Clubs want the power and influence that come with being huge cultural institutions, but when the associated social responsibilities are raised, they plead that they're just a sporting institution and that their influence is overstated.

It's hard to follow that line of thought when every politician wants to be seen to be at the NRL grand final, media outlets are willing to spend billions of dollars for the TV rights and players are given lucrative sponsorships for products that have nothing to do with sport. You can't tell TV stations that they should give you billions of dollars then claim you have no cultural power.

DEFENDING THE GOOD BLOKES

[Prominent media identity] says [player's name] is a 'good bloke'.

'I'm not saying this just because he's got a lot of dirt on me and I played footy with his dad. Although that's mainly why I'm saying this.'

With all that at stake, when you're as good as Ablett was, the sporting community can't help but try to forgive you. In Ablett's case the AFL waited until 2005 before inducting him into the Hall of Fame – four years after Horan died.[*]

On the night he was inducted the then chairman of the AFL Commission, Ron Evans, said:

> By any definition, Gary Ablett is a football genius, a football genius who has always been a troubled soul. The very best outcome to tonight's induction would be that it encourages Gary to reclaim his place in the football world, and by doing so, confront and deal with some of the issues in his life. Gary Ablett, in doing so, would put his demons to rest.

There is so much wrong with this quote I almost don't know where to start. 'Troubled soul' certainly stands out, as does 'reclaim his

---

[*] I was impressed they managed to restrain themselves that long.

place in the football world', like him losing it was not the direct result of his own actions.

Perhaps the most troubling thing is simply the general tone of sympathy for Ablett, a man heavily involved in the death of a woman and who refused to co-operate with police afterwards. I had to re-read the coroner's findings to remind myself that Ablett wasn't the one who died.

The key here is that if Ablett had been a fringe player, he wouldn't even be remembered today. The AFL and the media would have erased any memory of him so quickly it would be like he never existed.

THE OTHER SIDE OF THE COIN

In 2016, a young man called Colin Sylvia used stolen credit card details to buy 'deluxe service' sessions with a prostitute at the Daily Planet brothel. He also used the stolen details to transfer $4060 into a betting account. Then, in 2017, he climbed into a vacant apartment to spy on his ex-girlfriend and film her as she slept.

Colin Sylvia played 157 games with Melbourne and six with the Fremantle Dockers, before being forced into retirement in 2015. After footy, his life seemed to go off the rails.

Sylvia's crimes made the news, but it all blew over pretty quickly. Unlike Ablett, there have been no calls for him 'to reclaim his place in the football world' or 'put his demons to rest'. Sylvia was not one of the greatest players of all time and has not troubled the Hall of Fame selection committee. He was not a big enough body in the sporting solar system to attract the gravitational pull of forgiveness.

Without us wanting to remember him, there is nothing to draw him back into the fold. He left fans without any special memories to cherish. If anyone remembers him, it's with a sense of frustration.

The reason people keep trying to figure out when we can forgive Gary Ablett Snr is that, deep down, we don't want to let go of our memories of him playing, even if the man himself doesn't deserve our adulation. It's about us, not the player. We want to enjoy those memories guilt free.

HAVE A MEDIA CAREER

When Cricket Australia portrayed David Warner as the chief villain in the ball-tampering crisis, it seemed his career was over, at least in terms of playing for Australia. There was talk that his teammates didn't want to play with him again, and the public certainly weren't desperate for his return.

But within three months, and despite being suspended, Warner appeared as part of Channel Nine's commentary team. Now, some would say having to spend time with Nine's commentary team should be considered part of the punishment,* but not everyone saw it that way.

Respected sports broadcaster Gerard Whateley was one of many who came out against the decision: 'It feels too soon for me. I'm not anti for it in the long term, but I actually don't think people are ready for that.'

Whateley was certainly right about it being too soon. People were outraged. But he had articulated a common position when a Wayward Champion has disgraced themselves: when will it be alright for them to return? The idea that perhaps they shouldn't return at all never seems to be considered.

What the Warner case highlights is the willingness of the sporting media to forgive our Wayward Champions. It also highlights the breathtaking speed with which it often happens. Even if we

---

* Channel Nine have since lost the broadcast rights to the cricket, meaning we'll no longer hear their commentary. This outcome was welcomed by the United Nations Human Rights Council.

accept Whateley's underlying premise that time heals and that there's a 'right time' for a disgraced player to make a comeback, the media's belief seems to be that the right time is as soon as possible.

HOW LONG? NOT LONG.

The case of Matthew Johns, former League player and brother of NRL 'Immortal' Andrew Johns, raises some interesting questions about timing.

While Matthew didn't rise to the level of his brother, he was a very good player in his own right. He won the 1995 League World Cup with Australia and won an NRL premiership with the Newcastle Knights in 1997 (before Nathan Tinkler got his hands on them).

But in 2009, ABC's *Four Corners* ran a story, 'Code of Silence', about events in Christchurch in 2002 when members of the Cronulla Sharks were involved in a group sex session with a nineteen-year-old. The woman involved said up to twelve players and staff entered the room over a two-hour period, with six of them having sex with her.

New Zealand police investigated the incident, but no charges were laid. However the woman said the experience left her traumatised: 'I thought I was worthless and I thought I was nothing. And I think I was in shock. I didn't scream and they used a lot of . . . mental power over me and – and belittled me and made me feel really small like I was just a little old woman.'

Matthew Johns was the most high-profile player involved. After his retirement in 2002 he'd built a career in the media. At the time of the events in New Zealand, Johns was married and thirty.

When the news of his involvement broke ahead of the *Four Corners* story, Johns issued an emotional apology, in which he didn't apologise to the woman in New Zealand but instead to his wife and children. He reiterated that the woman had consented to the events.*

He delivered this apology on Channel Nine's *The Footy Show*, where he was a co-host. It was immediately followed by a 'comedy' skit in which he played 'Elton Johns', the fictional sibling of the Johns brothers. In the not exactly subtle skit, 'Elton' is rushed to hospital for being gay. Hilarious, right? It featured Andrew saying, 'I'm so ashamed of him.'

It was an unorthodox transition following a 'heartfelt apology'. Former League player Ian Roberts, who had announced he was gay in 1995, the first rugby player in the world to do so, said after the skit: 'Those blokes at *The Footy Show* – and you can quote me on this – are absolute f— morons [. . .] People like the Johns brothers need to be held accountable for their actions and their effect on others.'

Roberts would have been disappointed with what transpired afterwards. While Channel Nine stood down Matthew Johns following the airing of the *Four Corners* story, he was hardly held accountable. Not six months later, Nine CEO David Gyngell was begging for him to return to their NRL coverage. Johns declined that offer.

Not long afterwards, Channel Seven announced Johns would host *The Matty Johns Show*, a new 'family friendly' program to begin in March 2010. Now, you can't tell me someone at Channel Seven didn't wonder if hiring someone who had just been caught up in a group sex scandal, in which he cheated on his wife, was the best choice for a 'family friendly' show. Apparently it wasn't a deal-breaker.

---

* This kicked off a lot of interesting debate, with media commentators writing columns either criticising group sex as morally wrong or defending it, so long as it's consensual. Personally, I have so little experience with even just two people involved, I feel under-qualified to present a strong view, except to say it sounds complicated.

GREAT EXCUSES IN HISTORY: ANDREW JOHNS

After London police caught him with ecstasy in his pocket, Andrew Johns' management put out a statement that said 'he recalled an unknown person pushing a tablet into his jeans at a crowded entertainment venue last Sunday'. He later confessed to taking the drug throughout his playing career.

If you wrote this stuff as satire, people would tell you it's too unbelievable to publish.

While Matthew Johns was hardly a superstar like his brother, he was popular in the media. His rapid return to our screens showed that, if you want forgiveness and weren't one of the true stars of the sport, so long as you're a 'personality' who can bring in ratings the media doesn't care too much about your history.

In 2011, Triple M hired him to co-host the Sydney breakfast show and in 2012 Johns was announced as the face of Fox Sport's NRL coverage. At the time of writing in 2018, he still holds both positions.

When it comes to forgiveness, the media gives our old friends in the racing industry a run for their money.

THE DEAD ELEPHANT IN THE ROOM

If someone who was a champion player is seen as a workable media talent, that person will always have a high-paying job. Another who fits this mould is Glenn McGrath, who was announced as part of Channel Seven's new cricket commentary team in 2018.

McGrath famously shot an elephant while on a safari in 2008. In 2015 photos emerged of him sitting in front of an elephant he'd just shot, gun in hand and with a broad smile on his face. There were other photos of him with other African animals he'd killed for fun, but the one with the elephant really caught people's attention – remember, there's little that magnifies a scandal as much as good footage.

McGrath took a common route in explaining his actions. He said he was going through a difficult time in 2008; his wife, Jane, had passed away that year after a long battle with cancer. I'm not even slightly downplaying that McGrath had been through a lot, but lots of people negotiate difficult times without shooting an elephant.

McGrath's excuse that this was out of character didn't ring true either – he'd been a keen shooter for years. A 2006 issue of the Sporting Shooters' Association of Australia magazine had a story about McGrath and fellow former players Brett Lee and Jason Gillespie going on a hunting trip in the NSW bush.

McGrath told the magazine:

> I'm keen to get into trophy hunting, no animal in particular, but a big safari in Africa would be great [. . .] It's not about the quantity of trophies; although quality is important, it's not everything. Just being out there in that environment would be amazing.

While McGrath has apologised for decluttering Africa of its wildlife, surely shooting an elephant goes to the heart of someone's character. What sort of person wants to shoot an elephant for fun? Most of us get through life without shooting a single one. It's not like you can accidentally shoot one, especially in Australia.* Shooting an elephant actually requires a rather enormous amount of planning and travel – you have to really want to do it. There's plenty of time to have second thoughts.

---

* It would take an extraordinary series of events. You'd have to be at the zoo, for starters. Then a gun would have to be there, too. Perhaps you get into a confrontation with an armed robber and in the ensuing scramble, as you wrest control of the gun from the assailant, the gun goes off, tragically killing an elephant in a nearby enclosure. Even coming up with a hypothetical situation about an elephant getting shot makes me sad for the hypothetical elephant. I may be overthinking this.

Thanks to McGrath, one of the greatest bowlers to ever play the game, we can now add 'shooting an elephant' to the list of things that won't stop you being hired as a sports commentator in Australia.

WE'VE ALL DONE THAT

Here is a list of some of the things sporting legends and commentators can do and still work in the media. See if you can guess who's done what – play along with your colleagues during lunch!

1. While drunk at an airport, approach a woman you don't know and ask for a kiss. When they refuse and say they are married with kids ask, 'Did you have a caesarean birth?'
2. Refer to someone as a 'black c—' during a training session
3. Dress up in blackface on national TV. To be fair, that was last century. That is, 1999 – but technically still last century.
4. On television, grope a mannequin in lingerie with a photo of the female journalist you're criticising stuck to it
5. On air, liken a Malaysian man to a monkey and refer to him being 'not long out of the forest'
6. Be suspended for taking a prohibited substance
7. Take money from a bookie
8. Plead guilty to indecent assault after grabbing a woman's breast in the street
9. Provide character evidence for gangster Jason Moran
10. Strike your girlfriend in the face with a wine glass
11. Assault police
12. Call someone a 'big poofter' on live TV
13. Joke about drowning a female journalist in an ice bath while others do 'bombs' on her while she's being held under
14. Suggest an Indigenous Australian could be used to promote a musical about an ape

15. Be caught up in a group sex scandal
16. Shoot an elephant*

It's a fair list, and there'd be few other industries that could match it. If someone gave you the job of pulling together a group of people who've done all those things, you'd struggle. It would be like the worst university orientation-week scavenger hunt ever run. Finding someone who'd shot an elephant and someone who wore black-face would drive you mad – until you remembered the mature-age student in your group, Jeff, had done both (and at the same time).

Yet the Australian sports media ticked off that entire list without blinking.

Some argue that these great players provide insights into the game others can't. The only flaw in that argument is we've all heard these people provide 'special comments' and stating the bleeding obvious is not a skill in short supply. Every meeting I've ever been in has involved at least three or four people proficient in explaining at length what everyone already understands.

Are we to assume that there are no alternative insightful sports-people or commentators out there who have lived relatively scandal free? More likely it's the famous boys' club that has ruled the sports landscape for all these years.

HAVE POWER

While it's interesting what the media will forgive, who isn't for-given is just as illuminating. In a segment on Triple M radio in June 2018, former AFL players Barry Hall and Nathan Brown, broadcaster Mark Howard and journalist Damian Barrett were

---

* So you can see how you went against Barry in Accounts Receivable, here are the answers: 1. Andrew Johns; 2. Andrew Johns; 3. Sam Newman; 4. Sam Newman; 5. Sam Newman; 6. Shane Warne; 7. Shane Warne, Mark Waugh; 8. Wayne Carey; 9. Wayne Carey; 10. Wayne Carey; 11. Wayne Carey; 12. Brian Taylor; 13. Eddie McGuire, James Brayshaw, Danny Frawley; 14. Eddie McGuire; 15. Matty Johns; 16. Glen McGrath

chatting with former St Kilda player Leigh Montagna about an upcoming match.

Montagna was expecting his first child, and he brought up his wife's imminent labour. Why this was a topic of conversation for a footy pre-game show is beyond me, but there he was, explaining she had to have a medical procedure known as a 'membrane sweep'.

To my knowledge, none of the co-hosts had any medical expertise. This didn't seem to deter Montagna, who obviously also hadn't heard of the term 'overshare': 'The obstetrician just has a little feel and makes sure that she's starting to dilate and puts a couple of fingers up and checks. It's a procedure they do before birth.'

At this stage there was laughter from the co-hosts.

Then Hall, obviously enjoying the innuendo that was causing all the laughter, thought he'd join in and said: 'Joey was a bit disturbed because the doctor was a good-looking rooster about forty years of age and then he did the sweep with his fingers and licked his fingers afterwards. That's disturbing stuff.'

This was met with even more laughter from his co-hosts. *Now this is comedy*, Hall probably thought.

I'm still unsure how anyone arrives at thinking what he said, let alone saying it out loud. To do it on radio requires you to miss several checkpoints where a working brain would normally step in and halt proceedings.

Perhaps the biggest checkpoint that had been sailed past was that Hall had been allowed on air in the first place. It's amazing how many indiscretions Hall had been forgiven for, allowing him to appear in the media:

- In 1997, Hall punched an opponent, Sam McFarlane, in the jaw, breaking it in three places. It took the next three days to wire McFarlane's jaw back into place. McFarlane only played two more games before leaving the league. Hall was suspended for five matches.

- In 1998, Hall was tackled by Steven Febey. Hall dropped his knees into Febey's head. He then stood up and slung another opponent into the ground. At this point he got into a disagreement with his own teammates and had to be restrained by trainers. He was suspended for four matches.
- In 2002, he clawed the face of Port Adelaide ruckman Matthew Primus and was suspended for five matches.
- In the 2005 preliminary final, Hall punched St Kilda's Matt Maguire in the stomach. Only a technicality saw him get off and play in the following week's grand final.
- In 2008, he knocked out West Coast Eagles player Brent Staker with a coward's punch that rolled Staker's eyes into the back of his head. It could have killed him. Years later, Barry did an interview with Staker about how much this incident still upset him. Poor Barry. He got seven weeks.
- In 2010, while tying his shoelace, Hall was pushed over by North Melbourne's Scott Thompson. Not the brightest decision by Thompson. Hall got Thompson in a headlock that lasted about fifteen seconds – long enough to make everyone wonder if they were about to witness a murder.
- To cap it all off, in 2017, playing in the Queensland AFL in his last ever game of footy, Hall punched two opponents. The first was unprovoked and the second was in response to an opponent yelling at him for punching the first bloke.

Hall was inducted into the AFL Hall of Fame in 2017, the same year as he was still clocking blokes.

His on-field performances deserved it. A prolific goalkicker, he led his club's goalkicking tally eleven times. He played for St Kilda,

I'M A CELEBRITY ... GET ME OUT OF HERE!

When you've behaved badly, and especially if you've sustained that behaviour over a long period of time, the best way to clean up your reputation is not to change your behaviour but to go on *I'm a Celebrity ... Get Me Out of Here!*

Barry Hall's return to favour was certainly helped by being the runner-up in the 2015 season. Hall got a chance to show his sensitive side – the side where he isn't sucker punching blokes.

Following his lead, Brendan Fevola and Shane Warne both went into the jungle in 2016. Warne was voted off by the public just before the final and appeared shocked but Fevola went on to win the whole thing, leading to a renaissance in his media career.

Not a bad recovery after a history where he assaulted a barman in Ireland; received a black eye and was kicked out of Crown Casino at 3 a.m.; urinated on a nightclub window; took a nude photo of model Lara Bingle that found its way into the public domain; appeared in public dressed in a woman's nightie and brandished a sex toy; and went on a drunken rampage at the 2009 Brownlow Medal after-party, including launching tirades at fellow players.

This is not an exhaustive list. But such is the power of reality TV, it washed all that away. As the winner, Fevola got to nominate a charity for the prize money. His choice? The Shane Warne Foundation, which had awkwardly closed down while he was in the jungle.

I'm a Celebrity ... Get Me Out of Here! can't fix everyone, however. In 2018, both Bernard Tomic and Anthony Mundine went into the jungle, only to quit. Neither changed anyone's opinion of them.

Sydney and the Western Bulldogs, and captained the Swans to the 2005 premiership, their first since 1933.

Because of this – and despite his history of violence – after his playing career ended, Hall did a fair bit of media for Fox Footy and Triple M, as well as interviews about how he'd changed.

But the birth comment regarding Montagna's wife saw Hall sacked from Triple M within about forty minutes, before his shift was even over.

I'm not saying Hall shouldn't have been sacked – I'm saying he shouldn't have been hired in the first place. Triple M and much of the sports media have fostered an idiotic, blokey culture for years. The whole model is built on controversy never being far away. Both the AFL and NRL footy shows have taken this same approach, as did Channel Nine's cricket coverage. Triple M's swift action to remove Hall would be more impressive if he wasn't just one part of that culture – and a fringe part at that.

No one was surprised by this latest controversy. They may have been surprised by the specifics of what Hall said (how could you not be?), but not by the fact that a conversation on Triple M had gone off the rails.*

THE BOYS' CLUB FULL OF MIDDLE-AGED MEN

Triple M built and protected this adolescent boys' culture, and now they were pretending to be shocked and offended by it. Consider what's been said before on the station.

In 2013, Eddie McGuire, host of the Melbourne breakfast program and president of the Collingwood Football Club, was promoting the musical *King Kong*.** In the conversation that followed, McGuire suggested Indigenous footballer Adam Goodes could be used to promote it. Goodes had been copping racial abuse while playing, which had begun with a young spectator calling him an ape. McGuire asked his co-hosts if they thought the musical should 'get Adam Goodes down for it'.

Luke Darcy said, 'No, I wouldn't have thought so. Absolutely not.'

---

* This wasn't even the first time Triple M has had issues discussing childbirth. In 2015, Triple M Adelaide had Andrew Jarman discussing ways to induce labour with former Port Adelaide captain Domenic Cassisi, whose wife was nine months pregnant. Jarman helpfully suggested the best way of inducing labour was 'just f— the guts out of 'em with your big c—'. Apparently this wasn't meant to go to air. Jarman was given a few days off.

** My shock was twofold: what McGuire went on to say, and the fact Triple M was promoting a musical.

But McGuire continued, explaining, 'You know with the ape thing, the whole thing, I'm just saying the pumping him up and mucking around and all that sort of stuff.'

Following the immediate outrage, McGuire apologised on-air during the same show. Unlike Hall, McGuire is a powerful figure in football and the face of Triple M, so the station did not punish him for these blatantly racist remarks. Then AFL chief executive Andrew Demetriou said the league would not be punishing him either, saying, 'He's punishing himself this morning, I've got no doubt.'

In 2016, Triple M was part of the coverage for the Queen's Birthday blockbuster at the MCG, where the Big Freeze 2 was held before the game to raise funds for FightMND (Motor Neurone Disease). The event involves various celebrities going down a slide into an ice bath.

Eddie McGuire, James Brayshaw (then also North Melbourne Football Club president), Danny Frawley, Wayne Carey and Damian Barrett were speaking before the game. The following exchange occurred about journalist Caroline Wilson.

> **Eddie McGuire:** In fact, I reckon we should start the campaign for a one-person slide next year. Caroline Wilson. And I'll put in ten grand straight away – make it twenty. [laughter] And if she stays under, fifty. [laughter]
>
> What do you reckon, guys? Who else is up there? I know you're in, JB?
>
> **James Brayshaw:** No, yep. Straight in.
>
> **Danny Frawley:** I'll be in amongst it, Ed.
>
> **EM:** Is Duck there?
>
> **Wayne Carey:** Yes, I'm here, mate.
>
> **EM:** Duck's in. Danny's in – already spoken up.
>
> **DF:** Yeah, I'm in, Ed.
>
> **EM:** I could do an auction here today.

DF: I'll actually jump in and make sure she doesn't – I'll hold her under, Ed.

EM: I reckon we could charge ten thousand for everyone to stand around the outside and bomb her.

Damian Barrett: I'm on Caro's side now, Ed. I'm on Caro's side these days, Ed.

[indecipherable]

EM: She'll burn you like everyone else, mate. She's like the black widow. She just sucks you in and gets you and you start talking to her and then bang! She gets you.

JB: If you ran that auction from down there, I reckon you'd start grabbing some bids out of the seats too. There'd be money piling in everywhere.

EM: It'll be magnificent. I think we should do that next year. It's all good for footy.

JB: Bloody oath.

Listening to the audio, it's clear that those speaking, except for Barrett, really disliked Wilson, a tough journalist but no more so than many others. This was no gentle mocking; the malicious edge to it all is palpable.

The comments led to an outpouring of disgust from the public. Even a few men were upset by them!

McGuire apologised several times, mainly because his first few attempts weren't really apologies and only made the situation worse.

On 3AW, speaking to Neil Mitchell, McGuire said, 'I'm so sorry that those comments have resonated that way.' A classic of the non-apology genre, insinuating that the problem is with the receiver of the message not the message itself.

Regarding criticism that this conversation had been part of a culture that enables violence against women, McGuire tackled the philosophical question of when someone is a genderless entity rather than a woman, telling Mitchell, 'No one spoke of Caroline in the context of her being a woman, it was Caroline the media performer, who skewers people left, right and centre.'

Try this one at home: 'I wasn't criticising you as a person but as the dishwasher who didn't wash the dishes.'

It would have been so much easier to just say, 'I'm sorry.'

Once again Triple M did very little. McGuire's not Barry Hall – he pulls in ratings and sponsors, and as a result he has power.

The AFL also did nothing, except to say they were disappointed. Considering the incident involved two current club presidents, a radio station that covers their games and a person who'd been in trouble before, this was amazing. All that inclusion talk the AFL regularly serves up had run smack-bang into the boys' club that surrounds the game. The AFL's lip service about equality didn't stand a chance.

Why? Because the AFL is part of it. Taking on the boys' club is as unnatural to them as cutting off your own arm would be. The AFL knows these guys behaved appallingly, but they are all 'mates' who occupy important positions.

McGuire has a major platform from which he could attack the AFL. He owns a media company that makes AFL-related programs, he's the president of Collingwood, one of the most powerful sporting clubs in Australia, and he sits on several committees within the AFL.

This is the famous boys' club that has run sport since Frederick Standish was sitting in the Melbourne Club, drinking heavily and considering a new race called the 'Melbourne Cup'.

McGuire is as ingrained in the centres of power as Standish was in his day. Standish survived numerous parliamentary inquiries and McGuire has seen off repeated calls for him to be sacked. Eddie, like Standish, has charm when he wants to use it. He is well liked by a lot of people and has made it his business to be liked by the right people. If you have power, you can hold on.*

The forgiveness often on offer is jarring when you consider Adam Goodes himself was booed mercilessly in the later stages of his career, supposedly because he occasionally 'staged for free kicks'. It was a big reason he left the sport and remains estranged from it to this day.

Goodes has devoted a lot of his life to advancing equality for Indigenous Australians, for which he was named Australian of the Year in 2014. When he was being booed out of the game, unfortunately I don't think he would have had to wonder too long why he wasn't getting the same forgiveness as our Wayward Champions. I'm a simple man but perhaps there was something more to the booing than free kicks.

Sport is such a small and tightly knit community, most people don't want to upset anyone in it too much because they know they'll never get a job again.**

People who work in sport – be they athletes, media personalities or administrators – rarely criticise others publicly, especially any past appalling behaviour. They know they'll bump into those individuals in the media, at meetings and social gatherings and it will be heaps awkward. They know that to criticise media performers like McGuire or media outlets will mean never being invited back on their shows.

In private, they all gossip like crazy, and say all the same things footy fans say about players and administrators.

The AFL and most players know incidents like those described above hurt the game, but this is entrenched power. The talk of change is mainly just talk.

---

* Like Frederick Standish before him, McGuire is well connected in business, government and other centres of power. While Standish was corrupt and McGuire isn't, he may still want to avoid being put in charge of hunting down a notorious gang.

** This is advice I keep forgetting to follow. After reading a copy of this book, my agent said, 'This is the longest career suicide note I've ever read. Couldn't you be more like Rosanne Barr and do it in a single tweet?'

Following the Hall incident, Damian Barrett said, 'I would like to say – and it may sound really hollow – but we [Triple M] have fixed ourselves up, and we had until the madness of that conversation that went off the cliff last Friday night.'

Unfortunately, it did sound hollow, a bit like Hall's claims to have changed from his violent past. You can say all the right things, but if your actions keep proving the opposite, eventually people stop believing you.

Hall claimed to have changed but kept belting people along the way. Triple M said they'd fixed themselves up, but on-air incidents keep happening. They're both just lucky that, in the sports world, power means never having to say you're sorry.

COMMIT YOUR SINS AGAINST WOMEN

Sadly, in the sports world the crime you'll have the best chance of being forgiven for is one committed against a woman.

The NRL has sent a very strong message about respecting women, except it's the opposite of the one they're claiming to send. Actions always speak louder than words. At the time of writing, in mid 2018, the NRL has five active players who have either pleaded guilty or been found guilty of a family violence offence.

It was six, but one of the players, Kenny Edwards, just got released by Parramatta after fleeing from police following a random roadside check and not telling the club for three weeks. He had previously pleaded guilty to common assault against his former partner, receiving a six-month good behaviour bond.

Matt Lodge is one of the five. We touched on him at the start of this descent into the world of sporting scandals, but he's just the poster boy for a very big problem. Having five players running around who have either pleaded guilty or been found guilty of a family violence offence is a bit of a concern.

Don't worry though, NRL CEO Todd Greenberg is on the case.

In 2017 he said: 'When it comes to this fundamental issue of violence against women we're going to get very, very strong and I can't send a stronger message than to say that.'

Except you can: you could do something.

Greenberg said this before Matt Lodge was let back into the league, so when he said 'we're going to get very, very strong' on the issue of violence against women, he didn't mean right away, or in 2018. Presumably he meant at some undefined point in the future.

Again, try that out in your own life and see how you go.

'Boss, I'm going to get very, very strong on the issue of doing some work and I can't send a stronger message than to say that. Now, I'm off to lunch.'

'It's 9.30.'

The other guilty players currently in the league include one of the best players in the game, Greg Inglis, who pushed his partner onto the bed with an open hand after she had 'got into [his] face'. He missed two games for that but came back in time for the finals.

Another is Kirisome Auva'a. In 2014, he pleaded guilty to seriously assaulting his ex-girlfriend. He showed up at her house and when she told him he could sleep on the couch he pushed her to the ground, then swung her into the garage door. She was left with bruises and cuts. For good measure he punched holes in the walls of the house.

The court gave him a two-year good behaviour bond without conviction and made him pay $3000 into the court fund.

When Auva'a was charged, the NRL suspended him 'indefinitely', which is what you say when you have no idea how long a suspension will be, but you want it to initially seem harsh. NRL CEO Dave Smith said at the time: 'Let me make it clear [. . .] we abhor violence against women and it will not be tolerated in our game. Everyone needs to understand if you are violent against women there is no place for you in Rugby League.'

Strong words and an impressive response, which made it

interesting when, nine months later, Auva'a was back in the NRL playing for Parramatta. It seems there is a place in League for violence against women.

Come to think of it, there seem to be quite a few places for it. There's also Zane Tetevano of the Sydney Roosters, who was sentenced to eighteen months' imprisonment with a non-parole period of nine months for assaulting his girlfriend. In a series of attacks, he punched and kicked his then partner, including at one stage grabbing her singlet and using it to throw her across the room. He also smashed her phone and damaged her car.

Police obtained an apprehended violence order on the victim's behalf in January 2014. Tetevano and his girlfriend later asked for it to be revoked, which it was, but he then started beating her again, leaving her with bruising.

Despite being sentenced and sent off to jail, in October 2016 the Sydney Roosters signed him up. He's still playing today.

Rounding out the list is Addin Fonua-Blake, who in 2015 pleaded guilty to kicking his partner in an argument. He received a twelve-month suspended jail sentence, a fine of $1000 and was ordered to undergo counselling. A youth team player at the time, he was dumped by the Dragons in response, but in 2016 he was signed by the Manly Sea Eagles, where he remains.

It's quite the list. To put it into some context, in the AFL there is not a single player currently on a club list who has a domestic violence conviction. No Rugby Australia players have been found guilty of family violence since the code went professional in 1996. But in the NRL, it seems forgiveness comes easy if your crime is against a woman.

HAVE THE RIGHT MATES

We've already learnt that the path to redemption can be real trouble if you were not a superstar of the game, or if you have little power and don't have a media career. What could possibly stop you, then, if you were a great on the field and have a flourishing media career? You have to be AFL premiership player Jason Akermanis.

Akermanis played at the Brisbane Lions and the Western Bulldogs, winning the Brownlow Medal in 2001 and playing in three premierships. To the fans, he was an incredibly entertaining player: fast, skilful and with a lot of flair about him.

He was also outspoken, making him the perfect media performer. Before long he was regularly appearing on Channel Nine's *The Footy Show*, writing a column in the *Herald Sun* and appearing on radio. He often ran headlong into controversy. In one famous case he wrote a column saying he believed homosexual players should stay in the closet as the football world wasn't ready for an openly gay player.

In 2012, in his debut segment on the Sunshine Coast's Mix 92.7 FM, he told listeners that the public outpouring of sympathy and grief at the passing of footballer Jim Stynes was 'overkill' and that Stynes 'was a nasty man in his day'.

These sorts of controversies can be overcome – they're nothing compared to what some of the other players in this book have said and done – but Aker is pretty much universally disliked by his ex-teammates, peers and a lot of powerful people in the game.

In response to his Stynes comments, former Melbourne captain Brad Green tweeted, 'Show some respect', and Richmond great Matthew Richardson tweeted, 'I think Aker may have finally done his dash. #low'.*

After years of putting people offside, there would be no protection from the boys' club for Akermanis. The radio station dropped him immediately.

In his playing days at the Brisbane Lions, Akermanis fell out with coach Leigh Matthews after criticising him publicly and ahead

---

* Matthew Richardson is one of the most beloved people in the AFL and not often critical of others. This tweet, therefore, was the equivalent of a death sentence.

of the 2003 grand final leaking to the media that teammate Nigel Lappin had broken ribs.

A teammate at Brisbane, Justin Leppitsch said of Akermanis: 'I'd say, "Jason, you can't do that. That affects the team. You can't talk poorly about your teammates. You can't talk poorly about Leigh. You can't tell the world Nigel Lappin has broken ribs going into a grand final."'

He was run out of Brisbane and went to the Western Bulldogs, where they probably hated him more. Not that it's a competition.

When Akermanis released his autobiography, *Open Season*, Peter Gordon, at the time a former chairman of the Bulldogs who has since returned to the role, wrote a book review for *The Age* that went like this:

> Western Bulldogs chief executive Campbell Rose asked me to look at the Jason Akermanis' book and give some legal advice to various people around the club who had been the subject of sportsmen's night abuse, courtesy of Akermanis. I had the dubious privilege of reading it over the weekend, an unpleasant task more than rewarded by the team's gutsy fight-back win on Saturday night.
>
> I'm going to tell them all not to bother ... either reading it or responding to it. The book is just a tantrum in paperback. It's a grown man sitting in a giant cot and clanging his keyboard against the sides demanding attention.
>
> The book is called *Open Season*. It's immediately clear why. Like a crazed Dick Cheney, Aka wanders through its pages taking pot shots at anything that moves ... even if what moves turns out to be an old friend.

That's quite the review. The sports community is a tight-knit group – it's okay if you don't get along with a couple of other people, but to be hated by everyone is a sure-fire way to place yourself outside the gravitational pull of forgiveness.

As always, the reverse is also true: being mates with lots of people is a great way to ensure you're forgiven.

DO AS WE SAY, NOT AS WE DO

When the AFL moved on two senior executives in July 2017, it sent shockwaves through the industry. Football operations manager Simon Lethlean* and general manager of commercial operations Richard Simkiss resigned after inappropriate relationships with female staff.

I would have thought sleeping with younger staff was one of the perks of working at AFL House, now it was suddenly frowned upon.

What perplexed a lot of people was that the relationships were consensual. Both men were married, but the argument went that cheating on your partner was a personal issue, not a work matter.

Many footy fans flooded the talkback airwaves, defending the two men. It's strange what issue people decide is the hill they're going to die on.** Footy fans usually think AFL executives are idiots who are ruining the game while drawing massive salaries, but suddenly they were rushing to the barricades to defend their right to sleep with junior staff.

'What do we want?' 'The right for AFL staff to have consensual sexual relations with junior staff!' 'When do we want it?' 'Now!'

The point people were missing was that the AFL wasn't interested in the fact that the men were having affairs. It was about people in power putting themselves in positions where it could be deemed they were abusing that power.

---

* Lethlean was the second in charge of the AFL.
** A lot of the public commentary was that many people had met their partner and fallen in love at work. While this is true, this is not what had happened in either of these cases.

This was actually a huge step for the AFL; they'd acted on what had previously been mere words. Their workplace would not be a place where senior staff could abuse their power, whether it was sexual in nature or not. The message was being sent: where there is a massive power imbalance in the workplace, consent becomes irrelevant.

This is actually a position that all workplaces will increasingly adopt. They won't want to take the risk of an executive sleeping with a junior staff member, because the chance is very high that staff member will turn around and say they only consented at the time because they felt they couldn't say no.

The danger of these things taking a bad turn is very high. The staff member involved with Simkiss apparently could not face reporting for work as a result of the relationship, regardless of it having been consensual.

Organisations want to send a message that even making advances on junior staff is a problem, as they are likely to be unwanted. In the past this has created environments like those the #MeToo movement is now exposing. Employers want an environment where staff can come to work and not be hit on by bosses.

For a day or two the AFL took a lot of heat for their decision, but they were also praised by some for being progressive on this issue. They had actually taken a leadership role, not just talked about being leaders.

Then they undid it all straight away.

AFL CEO Gillon McLachlan, who had engineered the two men's resignations, was also a friend of both, especially Lethlean. In the days that followed he said on radio: 'I know our industry is forgiving and these are people who have made mistakes but they are high-quality people and unbelievably good executives, so as long as their behaviours and accountabilities continue to be as strong as they have been, I feel confident they will get another chance.'

It sure is a forgiving industry. Soon Lethlean was in the running

NINE LIVES

What has more lives than a cat? A sporting administrator.

Take for example the miraculous career of Ian Robson, who was CEO at Essendon when the largest doping program in Australian sporting history occurred there.

Essendon's own report revealed that during Robson's time the club was 'a disturbing picture of a pharmacologically experimental environment never adequately controlled or challenged or documented within the club during the period under review'.

According to Robson, he takes 'full accountability' for this, while also stating he had no idea it was occurring. Robson also denies ever seeing a letter written by the club doctor Bruce Reid voicing his concerns about the injections program. Former football manager Paul Hamilton says he remembers Reid voicing those concerns in a meeting and that he relayed these to Robson.

Despite all this, Robson wasn't sacked. He resigned in May 2013 and in July 2013 became the new CEO of the A-League team Melbourne Victory. A rather astounding appointment. Then in 2017, Robson decided to move on from the Melbourne Victory and was appointed CEO of Rowing Australia.

Asked about his time at Essendon, which saw thirty-four players suspended and many careers ruined, Robson said: 'I'm not a regrets kind of guy. You reflect, you learn, you move on. Regrets, to me, always have a heavy connotation to carrying baggage. I try not to do that.'

Indeed.

for vacant roles at Hawthorn, Carlton, Collingwood and Essendon. McLachlan was letting clubs know that both men would be welcomed in clubland. This was an odd position to take, seemingly implying that the standards at headquarters were higher than what was expected of clubs.

A lot of the clubs saw this as ridiculous. Hawthorn ruled Lethlean out immediately. After all, what sort of message would it send to the women who worked at the club?

Carlton was very interested, with Blues president Mark LoGiudice publicly stating, 'I would hope Simon Lethlean will be part of this process.' Awkwardly, though, they had the Australian sex discrimination commissioner, Kate Jenkins, on their board and on the selection panel for the job. Lethlean missed out.

Luckily for him, St Kilda stepped in and offered him the role of general manager of football, less than six months after the AFL had moved him on. When St Kilda CEO Matthew Finnis was asked if in appointing him the club had considered the reason Lethlean had left the AFL, he said: 'Of course it was [considered]. The reality of the situation and the opportunity was that we would not have been in a position to secure Simon if it hadn't have been for the circumstances he left the AFL.'

Basically, Finnis was saying, 'Look! I got this jacket for 80 per cent off just because it's got this giant stain on it!'

It was an odd appointment as St Kilda had just spent a decade trying to change the perception that they had a terrible culture, especially regarding women. This was the club that, in the early 2000s, was involved in the dwarf burning incident,* had a long-running scandal involving player Stephen Milne that resulted in him pleading guilty to a charge of indecent assault, and the so-called St Kilda schoolgirl scandal.

That was all swept away as St Kilda saw a chance to grab a senior executive who might help them win. Besides, they had the blessing of the head of the AFL.

Simkiss was hired as group business director at Crocmedia, owner of sports radio station SEN and producer of a lot of the AFL's media content.

Again, it was made clear that if you were friends with the right people, you were safe. The boys' club was still very much alive. For now.

---

* Page 224, if you want to refresh your memory.

ARE GOOD BLOKES AN ENDANGERED SPECIES?

As we've seen, the path back to forgiveness is clear, but not always equally accessible. The complication we are seeing is that the world outside sport – always a pesky distraction – is changing. The power structures in sport are being challenged. The younger generation has all these crazy new ideas about equality.

Which brings us to a critical question: are Good Blokes an endangered species?

Humans live such short lives, it's easy to miss how things change over periods longer than our own lifetimes. Thought patterns that seem entrenched, industry standards that appear unassailable – suddenly, one day, they're gone.

In a relatively small period of time the old order is cast aside and a new order is in place. The divine right of kings, serfdom, VHS, all these things seemed permanent and inviolable, only to be rapidly cast aside by democracy, capitalism, LaserDisc. These things now seem normal to us* but in a few hundred years (or maybe a decade if our relationships with our phones are any indication) being ruled by robots and kept as their pets will seem normal to us.

---

* Okay, not LaserDiscs. They had a shorter shelf life than an *Australian Idol* contestant's 'career'.

For so long, male dominance, acceptance of players' bad behaviour and the exclusion of minorities seemed to be the way of things in the world of sport. It was just boys being boys in a landscape filled with 'characters'.* Our Wayward Champions, Colourful Racing Identities and Cashed-Up Businessmen had free rein.

In the past few decades, though, the climate has begun to change, and increasingly at a pace that many people feel concerned about – especially those people in positions of power.

It's a lot like a scene in the movie *Pleasantville,* where in the fifties a small town in the US Midwest is confronted with modern problems like racism and sexism. The men who run the town are confused by these changes and get together to discuss what to do. There's a sense of them being under siege as the mayor, Big Bob, addresses the group: 'Well – we'll be safe for now – thank goodness we're in a bowling alley.'

This is how a lot of the administrators of sport, the people running the sports media and many ex-players appear to be reacting. They seem genuinely confused that the way things were supposed to work forever is now getting them in trouble. Things used to be so simple.

They are surrounded by forces they don't understand and occasionally they lash out at these forces. The old brigade is under siege.

POLITICAL CORRECTNESS: DESTROYER OF WORLDS

Perhaps the biggest threat to the dominance of the Wayward Champion is the rise of 'political correctness'. It's often said as an insult, with the implication that political correctness is an attempt to minimise free speech or curtail debate. But at its heart, it's a desire

---

* Claiming that a more equal society would kill off the 'characters' is always the first line defence for those resisting social change. It's a narrow view of what a character is. In sport, the quickest way to become a 'character' is to behave so poorly that in normal circumstances no one would ever talk to you again.

to avoid actions or expressions that exclude or marginalise groups that are disadvantaged or discriminated against. That's a pretty reasonable aim.

This move towards being more considerate of marginalised groups doesn't stop you saying what you like, it just means you may not get a response you like.*

But political correctness is a problem for a lot of those former champions now working in the media and those who run sports. They think no one really believes in it, that it's been forced on them by 'elites'. It's a strange position, given how most of the time someone's complaining about it, they're doing so on radio and TV programs. They seem to be able to argue they're being silenced from very big platforms.

Mainly, they find this push for a more thoughtful attitude towards marginalised and disadvantaged groups confusing and annoying. What they really don't get is why many, especially younger people, actually believe this stuff. They haven't been 'brainwashed', they just don't find jokes aimed at groups like women, LGBTQI+ people or ethnic minorities funny.

Take for example the incident where Eddie McGuire and others 'joked' about drowning Caroline Wilson. In response the Richmond Football Club players boycotted Triple M. A bunch of twenty-somethings were sending a message to the older generation that the world had changed.

Sam Newman, one of the headline acts of Channel Nine's *The Footy Show*, is perhaps the most prominent example of being left behind by this societal shift. Once, Newman – a former Geelong Football Club champion – could get away with wearing blackface

---

* I've no doubt that some attempts to be inclusive and not offend anyone go too far. The thing is, when I hear people complain about 'political correctness' it's never about something trivial, it's usually because they've said something racist or homophobic. Funny that.

on air, demeaning women and making racist jokes. In fact, his irreverence to everything and everyone made him immensely popular, a huge star who rated through the roof.

Now Newman finds himself on a show with dwindling ratings and current players like Geelong's Patrick Dangerfield questioning his standing: 'From my point of view, I just think he's irrelevant.'

Richmond's Alex Rance summed up what has happened to Newman:

> It's definitely a persona he puts on and puts out there and I think it's what made him so humorous and loveable in the early days[,] his lack of political correctness if you will, but now I think there's been a couple of things he's said which have been cracked down upon and maybe he feels the tide's changing a bit and he can't be himself as much as he was before.

As a result, Newman has railed against political correctness in the media fairly regularly. It's very similar to recent claims by comic Kevin 'Bloody' Wilson, who said political correctness is ruining his act. 'I can't go on TV anymore as it's so bloody PC . . . or do the Sydney Comedy Festival.'

In response, comedian Nazeem Hussain said:

> Old school comedians get upset and blame political correctness because they can't pick on minorities. The audience doesn't buy that homophobic, racist and sexist stuff anymore. It's lazy comedy, they should find new jokes and get a laugh.

Social values change and you either change with them or get left behind. Triple M's scandals fall into this category too. The same shtick that worked so well in the nineties is now getting the station into trouble fairly regularly. There's still an audience for it, but it comes with problems, such as advertisers not wanting to be attached to their blokey culture. In recent times, Triple M has made noises about changing its approach to be more reflective of modern views, but it seems they've found it hard to implement using people who hold those modern views.

The NRL's stance on family violence is another example of the changing times. League administrators never had to worry about women being belted by their partners in the past. It was seen as a private matter, and the police and governments thought this too. Then it all changed. While victims should always be afforded privacy, it's now everyone's business if you're a perpetrator.

The NRL went along with this rhetoric in their marketing and positioning, because saying things is ridiculously easy. Then they realised it would mean having to do actual hard work, just like Sam Newman updating his twentieth-century act, and they baulked.

Now they come across as confused about the world, lashing out at it, wondering why people are angry with them and then feeling forced to offer apologies they don't understand.

COVER-UP UNITS

Once upon a time, sporting bodies put all their efforts and resources into doing deals with police, giving journalists exclusive interviews and stories if they didn't report on certain other stories, paying off women who'd been sexually assaulted and anything else to make sure some news just never got out.

But in recent years, as sponsors have demanded a better culture to limit the risk of damaging their brands, the codes have been forced to resource proper integrity units. Integrity units are essential if you want some of that sweet, sweet gambling money our sporting administrators are so keen to get their hands on. Those annoying law enforcement agencies want to know where that money is going.

The main advantage of a sporting body having an integrity unit is that whenever something bad happens they're able to say they have one. 'We've referred it to our integrity unit. We are doing things! We can't answer any more questions while they investigate, even though they work for us.'

But integrity units present a huge problem for our Wayward Champions. Once upon a time, being one of the game's stars meant you were the apex predator – now you're the hunted.

The AFL's integrity unit, for example, can:

- take possession of 'all documents, records, articles or things in the possession or control of a person relevant to any inquiry or investigation'
- access any premises 'occupied by or in control of a club'
- sanction any person contravening AFL rules 'in any manner they in their absolute discretion think fit'
- stand down 'any person subject to an inquiry or investigation from participating in or in connection with the AFL competition'.

That's enormous power. It's scary stuff.

The NRL is also beefing up its unit. In 2017 they pledged to give it $35 million over the next five years and increase its powers.

These units are now well staffed, often by ex-police, which is why you see a lot of men in short-sleeved shirts with moustaches.* A former homicide squad senior detective now heads up the AFL's integrity unit; I hope they can cope with the stress of now having to conduct very serious, high-pressure investigations.

---

* I may just be thinking of *NYPD Blue*.

THE FUN POLICE

Drugs in sport are probably as old as sport itself.[*] In the good old days, you could snort a line of cocaine, drink ten bourbons and cokes and then play a game the next day – or even the same day – but now you run the risk of getting drug tested. Bloody fun police.

INEVITABLE APOLOGIES

'I now understand a Nazi uniform is not appropriate for Mad Monday celebrations.'

'I offer an unreserved apology to all BHP shareholders.'

'Obviously that sort of violence has no place at a polo match.'

Different sports have different drug policies but, in general, players are now tested for both performance-enhancing and illegal recreational drugs, with various penalties attached to each.

While some ex-players such as the NRL's Andrew Johns and AFL's Dane Swan have admitted to taking recreational drugs during their playing days, the Wayward Champion will find it increasingly difficult to maintain a career doing that. Testing is getting better and more regular.

The days of a drunk Young Griffo being rushed from a bar straight into the ring are sadly over. In the future there may just be fewer Wayward Champions, because they'll get caught long before they become a champion.

THE INTERWEBS

Like all new technologies, the rise of social media has its benefits and its terrible excesses.[**] On the negative side, it's often a Wild West of vindictiveness, trolling and abuse. It's probably turning us all into horrible narcissists who can never know true happiness.

---

[*]   Ancient Greek athletes were known to eat raw animal testicles before competing. I'm fairly convinced this was a practical joke that got out of hand.

[**] Actually, email has no positives, it's just the worst.

269

Social media has also given a voice to sporting fans that never existed previously. I'm not talking about the vitriol that comes after a loss, that's always been given expression, I'm talking about more constructive feedback.

In the past, the media had the power to forgive someone like Wayne Carey or Matthew Johns and, if they did, that was the end of it. They're hardly going to do stories about how people are outraged the individual in question is back on TV.

On social media, however, no such restrictions apply. Carey has been slammed, Channel Nine's cricket coverage criticised for its all-male, out-of-touch approach and the NRL's acceptance of Matt Lodge has been ridiculed.

It's highlighted an important distinction: who is actually doing the forgiving?

Increasingly, we are seeing that the media and the sports industry might accept someone back but the public – long thought to blindly forgive any sporting hero – are not that forgiving at all.

THE DEATH OF PRIVACY

It seems implausible that fifteen years ago, if you saw something crazy or newsworthy happen, you didn't have a camera on you to film it. This is something I'm constantly thankful for, looking back on my teenage years, my awkward improv-theatre decades and not to mention those three days in clown school.

Now everyone has a personal TV station in their pocket. They can film, edit and broadcast a high-definition video to the world in minutes. This is rarely used for good, but it sure has delivered some great footage of drunk athletes. As discussed in Part II, Anatomy of a Scandal, terrific photos and vision make a story so much bigger.

The chance is high that any bad behaviour, be it small or large, will be caught on camera. This raises all sorts of questions about privacy. Take for example NRL's Mitchell Pearce, who was caught on video by friends at an Australia Day party, pretending to have sex with a dog.

We've all been there. Well, okay, not all of us. Yes, you're right – almost none of us. But nonetheless, this occurred in a private house. In the past it may have been a rumour that did the rounds, but it wouldn't have been seen on every TV channel and remained on the internet for all time.[*]

Effectively, there is no privacy anymore. Athletes are now required to maintain a far higher standard. They can't trust that whatever they do won't end up plastered across every media outlet within hours. This is not all bad – terrible behaviour isn't to be encouraged – but a lot of athletes behave no worse than the average twenty-year-old. Players being filmed while drunk or taking drugs and then having the images splashed across social media and front pages is perhaps setting the standard a bit too high, considering hardly anyone else is scrutinised that closely.

Privacy debate aside, the smartphone is one of the biggest threats to our Wayward Champions' longevity.

DID YOU KNOW WOMEN CAN PLAY SPORT?

In recent years, we've discovered women like to play sport too. Who knew?

For most of Australia's history, men thought women couldn't play any sport, let alone contact sports like rugby or football. Men thought that if women went above a light jog, they'd die.

Then – and this is just my working hypothesis – attitudes began to change when instead of being at the pub for the birth of a child, men were allowed to see their partner during labour. I reckon

---

[*] Perhaps my favourite bit of that story is that some media outlets decided to blur out the dog's face. Can you imagine the discussion among the producers? What did they think was going to happen? The dog is at the park and another dog says, 'Hey aren't you that dog in the Mitchell Pearce video?'

they took one look and thought, *Yeah, she could probably tackle someone.*

So, men said, 'Alright, you can play AFL and NRL,' and women said, 'Great.'

Then the men said, 'Can we please stop coming into the birthing suite now?'

Women's sport has reached new heights with the start of AFL Women's and Women's Rugby League, a new netball TV deal and greater broadcasting of women's cricket. Many local football clubs are now experiencing a huge influx of girls and women wanting to play. This is reinvigorating many clubs and competitions, bringing in playing fees and boosting engagement with the local community.

For the big leagues, it not only makes them feel socially progressive, it's creating new content they can sell to sponsors and broadcasters. It also creates more interest in the codes overall. Many have become newly interested in cricket, AFL and NRL through the women's leagues but then started to enjoy other levels of the sport as well.

All these positives mean sporting administrators have a much bigger incentive to be female friendly. Or at least to stop being 'female hostile'.* The NRL is certainly feeling this pressure – it's hard to claim to be a welcoming place for women when you're also welcoming back Matt Lodge.

The AFL has different problems. While their record on family violence is better than the NRL's, their media coverage is still dominated by men and, as we've seen, regularly strays into hostility towards women.**

---

* Women have such strange needs. They want to be treated with respect and have equal opportunities and rights in the workplace. Calm down ladies, these are crazy demands.
** Women are also sensitive about people joking about drowning them. It's all terribly confusing.

But these are probably short-term problems. Generational change and the pressure to attract women or lose them to other codes will mean the end of unconditional forgiveness so long as you're in the boys' club.

CAN WOMEN BE GOOD BLOKES?

There is an alternative view. Female sports stars could find equality by themselves being forgiven for behaving terribly.

Dawn Fraser has for some time showed that women can be Good Blokes. She has had to apologise for comments such as 'I'm sick and tired of the immigrants that are coming into my country', and telling Nick Kyrgios and Bernard Tomic to 'go back to where their fathers or their parents came from [. . .] if they act like that'.

Until recently, though, there have been far fewer chances for women to behave like entitled brats. Could this all be about to change with the rise of women's sports?

Michelle Payne famously won the Melbourne Cup in 2015 on Prince of Penzance and then in 2017 she tested positive for a banned substance, proving she is a trailblazer in more ways than one.

Unfortunately, while this was a good start, she took full responsibility: 'The onus is 100 per cent with me . . . I regret not seeking more guidance. I wasn't thorough, and that is completely my fault. My sincere apologies to everyone.'

That's just not how it's done. Clearly women's sport still has a long way to go. We've learnt from the examples of Shane Warne and Eddie McGuire that as a Wayward Champion it's best practice to never take full responsibility when apologising. Always provide some excuses as to how you're not fully accountable for your actions, no matter how implausible.

So far, I've also been left unimpressed by female footy teams on end-of-season trips. They seem to have avoided controversy entirely. Not even some minor antics have been revealed in the media. Let's hope that as their fame and salaries increase, we can finally have equality with both female and male athletes behaving appallingly.

IS IT REALLY THE END?

It's tempting to see all these new challenges to the Good Blokes of the world as an indication that their time is finite, that they are as doomed as the dinosaurs. But even some dinosaurs survived – they are the birds you see all around you. They adapted to their changing environment and thrived.

It's likely we'll always forgive many of our sporting stars, it's just forgiveness will sometimes take longer. Some acts will move into the unforgivable category, as seems to be the case with family violence, albeit a slow transition.

Younger athletes are already evolving to fit into this world. Many came out strongly in support of marriage equality in the non-binding, expensive and unnecessary postal survey.

But don't discount the entrenched power structure that's still in place and has been since the time of Frederick Standish. Change is slow, as shown by the NRL's handling of family violence, cricket's mishandling of the ball-tampering crisis, the AFL's blokey media culture and John Coates remaining in charge of the Australian Olympic Committee despite an independent review finding a dysfunctional culture marked by favouritism, unfairness and fear within the organisation.

But while it seems like the old power structure is still exerting a firm grip on things, it's quite possible that these examples are like remote islands whose inhabitants don't realise the war is over. They're still fighting, spouting 'political correctness gone mad' rhetoric, despite having already lost the culture war.

There's some evidence to support this. Channel Nine recently tried to reboot their *AFL Footy Show*, retaining Sam Newman and getting Eddie McGuire back as host, and doubling down on the humour it rose to success with in the nineties. It has bombed.

It comes as no surprise that a sporting media and administrative landscape populated by Good Blokes has been highly sympathetic to other Good Blokes. But a closed shop can't stay closed forever,* and while small, the signs of change are there.

Channel Seven has recently announced their new cricket commentary team and, lo and behold, they've actually allowed women into the commentary box, something Channel Nine resisted like the plague when they had the broadcast rights.

In recent times the NRL have been ahead of the AFL when it's come to women being involved in their television coverage. Yvonne Sampson has hosted Nine's *Friday Night* Rugby League broadcast and, in 2016, she became the first woman to anchor the network's State of Origin coverage.

While the environment is changing, we need to consider whether it was ever what we thought it was. Have the Australian public always been so forgiving of their sporting stars?

In a lot of cases, the rather forgiving views in the public record are those of people who know those involved. They're ex-teammates or associates, such as when *Australia II* skipper John Bertrand and Bob Hawke praised Alan Bond.

Other times it's people who are working in the media or industry, so have a vested interest in toeing a company line. If your boss tells you to work with someone and you want to keep your job, you're hardly going to say, 'I think hiring this person is a disgrace.'

But these are not necessarily the views of the general public. My experience of sports fans is they have a far more nuanced view of their sporting heroes, but winning is a powerful force to overcome. We still love it.

---

* Unless of course you're the pharmacy guild, in which case it's pretty much all gravy forever.

HOPE FOR THE FUTURE

The growth of women's Australian Rules offers some hope for the future that women footballers will behave as poorly as their male counterparts. In 2018, an under-18 girls game between the Essendon Doutta Stars and Tullamarine had to be called off after an all-in brawl.

The president of the Tullamarine Football Club, Peter Labbad, said of the incident: 'There was some push and shove with the girls, it was pretty brutal, more brutal than some of our senior men's games. You're talking about girls slapping each other.'

He said the language from both sides was 'really poor' and commended the umpires for calling off the game.

We loved Shane Warne's 'ball of the century'. We loved the strength and elusiveness of Andrew Johns. We loved Wayne Carey's ability to singlehandedly change a game. We even want to love Nick Kyrgios, but it's proving very difficult.

This is the eternal problem. Can we keep the memories and ignore the person? Deep down I think we know it's difficult to justify that.

Even the old-boys' club is finding it harder and harder to turn a blind eye to appalling behaviour just because someone is 'a good bloke'. Violence, sexual harassment and assault, homophobia and racism, these are things society will no longer accept. Our sporting heroes are caught in broad social trends beyond any of our control.

We now have two powerful forces butting heads, like the irresistible force meeting the immovable object: improving social values and equality versus our desire to win at sports. Unfortunately, you can't always have both.

If Australia wants to win the cricket, for example, forgiving Smith, Warner and Bancroft is inevitable. Even if Warner was the 'mastermind', his role will probably be overlooked if we lose enough games ahead of the Ashes.

What will happen more broadly is a tightening of the unofficial rules of forgiveness. Things that used to be forgivable, like family violence, homophobia and racism, will be harder to come back from, if it remains possible at all.

But we'll continue to cut our sporting heroes slack that no one else would ever receive. We can't help ourselves. Australians want to win and so we have an immense fondness for those who deliver victory. We'll always cherish their greatest moments, even if they don't deserve it.

ACKNOWLEDGEMENTS

When I sat down to write this book I actually had another idea in mind. When I ran it past my wonderful editor Andrea McNamara, she told me it was terrible and I needed to try harder. The result of me trying harder is this book you hold in your hands and, as always, she was right. I can't thank her enough.

I want to also thank Cressida, Antigone and Cillian Wall, who would regularly point out that no one would ever read this book and that I shouldn't stress about it too much.

I must thank the Twomey family, who supported me even though it was throwing good money after bad.

The team at Penguin Random House have been a delight to work with and have all gone out of their way to pretend to like me. I appreciate them all following the 'never look me directly in the eye' edict. Nikki Christer, Ali Watts, Louise Ryan, Jake Davies, Johannes Jakob, Jackie Money, Alex Ross and Ali Hampton have all at some point put up bail money for me, acted as an alibi and/or accompanied me to a court appearance.

Lastly, I'd like to thank everyone who's read my stuff over the years or come to one of my shows. Knowing there are others out there who love sport while also recognising how ridiculous it is makes me feel like I may not have completely wasted my life.

Titus

NOTES

FORGIVING THE GOOD BLOKES

2   'Their belief is fantastic . . .' David Beniuk, 'Meninga hails Maroons mateship', *Sydney Morning Herald*, 8 July 2010.

7   'In October 2015, Lodge . . .' Rachel Olding, '"Infuriating": New York family terrorised by Broncos' Matt Lodge speak', *Sydney Morning Herald*, 2 March 2018.

      'Lodge followed the two . . .' 'Former NRL player Matthew Lodge avoids jail in US over 2015 rampage', *The Guardian*, 20 December 2016.

8   'I don't know. We've let . . .' 'Paul Gallen posts video clarifying Matt Lodge position', *News.com.au*, 4 March 2018.

10   'Lodge had pleaded guilty . . .' 'NRL considered Lodge's DV guilty plea', SBS News, 28 March 2018.

THE WAYWARD CHAMPION

31   'No strings attached . . .' and 'Rob O'Regan QC . . .' Trevor Marshallsea, 'Warne at odds with himself over John the bookmaker', *Sydney Morning Herald*, 22 January 2007.

34   'When the ACB investigated . . .' Malcolm Conn, 'Live from the Warne-Waugh affair', *ESPNcricinfo*, 24 June 2010.

36   'Naive and stupid . . .' Jake Lynch, 'Cricket: Australia

shocked by Warne and Waugh', *The Independent*, 10 December 1998.

49   **'Warne's response . . .'** Martin Williamson, 'Shane Warne's World Cup shame', *ESPNcricinfo*, 14 February 2015.

'The ACB inquiry was not impressed . . .' 'ACB report slams Warne's "vague and unsatisfactory" evidence', ABC News, 26 February 2003.

50   **'A victim of the anti-doping hysteria . . .'** 'Devastated Warne banned for a year', *Sydney Morning Herald*, 23 February 2003.

'As much as the boys . . .' 'Warne knew risks: McGrath', *Sydney Morning Herald*, 17 February 2003.

'You cannot have an IQ . . .' 'Warne's fate lies behind closed doors', *Sydney Morning Herald*, 21 February 2003.

'Whether you hate me . . .' 'Warne admits he took earlier tablet', *The Age*, 26 February 2003.

53   **'Between 2011 and 2013 . . .'** Chris Vedelago & Cameron Houston, 'Shane Warne Foundation sought to block release of records by regulator', *Sydney Morning Herald*, 29 November 2015.

54   **'We have no problems . . .'** Rita Panahi, 'Shane Warne says charity foundation has given $4m to needy', *Herald Sun*, 19 November 2015.

'The audit found . . .' Chris Vedelago & Cameron Houston, 'Shane Warne Foundation unable to explain what happened to cash donations', *Sydney Morning Herald*, 11 March 2016.

55   **'Unwarranted speculation . . .'** 'Shane Warne Foundation shuts down amid funding controversy', ABC News, 29 January 2016.

'Shane Warne Foundation cleared . . .' Kara Irving, 'Shane Warne Foundation cleared of wrong-doing', 11 January 2017.

60 'Lieutenant Bill Schwartz . . .' Miki Perkins & Ian
Munro, 'Wayne Carey faces US assault charges', *The Age*,
30 January 2008.
'He has openly discussed . . .' Fiona Byrne, 'Wayne Carey
admits cocaine abuse and needs help', *The Advertiser*,
16 March 2008.

THE COLOURFUL RACING IDENTITY

67 'This is my first . . .' Kate McClymont, 'Colourful funeral
for colourful racing identity Jack Sparrow', *Sydney Morning
Herald*, 6 February 2018.

90 'Other material relating . . .' '$225m Drug Tsar Free After
Only Six Years', *Sun-Herald*, 3 February 2002.
'Mr C: We should all meet . . .' Kate McClymont, 'Revealed:
How Sydney races are fixed', *Sydney Morning Herald*,
7 April 1995.

92 'It may as well be . . .' Matthew Benns, 'The wrong side of
the track,' *Sydney morning Herald*, 8 November 2012.

93 'They said I tried . . .' John Silvester, 'Do crooks fancy horse
racing? You can bet on it!', *The Age*, 18 August 2012.
'You f—ing bitch . . .' Kate McClymont, 'Where angels fear
to tread,' *Sydney Morning Herald*, 4 May 2013.

95 'Jimmy Cassidy accepted . . .' Nick McKenzie, 'Top jockey
took Mokbel cash in return for tips', *The Age*, 14 June
2008.
'Breaking down the amounts . . .' Nick McKenzie, 'On the
wrong track', *Sydney Morning Herald*, 7 August 2012.

96 'Your paper can go . . .' Nick McKenzie, 'Top jockey took
Mokbel cash in return for tips', *The Age*, 14 June 2008.
'I've got nothing but respect . . .' 'NZ jockey admits
friendship with drug fugitive', *NZ Herald*, 16 October
2006.

97 'One of the most important . . .' Les Kennedy and Kate McClymont, 'Drug baron keeps his $500,000', *Sydney Morning Herald*, 31 May 2008.

98 'Oliver told Hunter . . .' Michael Lynch, 'Out for 10 months: Oliver banned for illegal bet', *Sydney Morning Herald*, 20 November 2012.

THE CASHED-UP BUSINESSMAN

104 'In 2013 Hawke was again . . .' Benjamin Millar, 'Bob Hawke drops the F-bomb', *Sydney Morning Herald*, 26 September 2013.

105 'It seems to be so . . .' 'Alan Bond: 10 things you need to know about the controversial tycoon', ABC News, 5 June 2015.
'We had gone through bad economic times . . .' 'Alan Bond dead: Australian business tycoon dies aged 77 in Perth', *News.com.au*, 5 June 2015.

111 'The club captain . . .' Patrick Carlyon, '10 tales of Tiger heartache: Richmond's pain from 1980 to today', *Herald Sun*, 29 September 2017.
'After much discussion . . .' Alex Heber, '11 telling quotes from Alan Bond, the businessman, fraudster, and America's Cup hero,' *Business Insider*, 5 June 2015.

113 'Enormous in its magnitude . . .' 'Bond's billion-dollar fraud plot "astonishing"', *Sydney Moring Herald*, 4 August 2004.

114 'I'd say it wasn't until the mid 1990s . . .' Julie-Anne Sprague, 'Alan Bond dead: Bond Corp's demise left bad taste in the West', *Sydney Morning Herald*, 5 June 2015.

116 'Well, let us at the outset acknowledge . . .' 'Alan Bond dead', *News.com.au*, 5 June 2015.
'For those people . . .' Paul Toohey, 'There is only Bondy in a lifetime', *Daily Telegraph*, 5 June 2015.

116   'He was a controversial figure . . .' Kate Campbell & Kara Vickery, 'Alan Bond tributes: Former tycoon remembered as a trailblazer who helped put WA on world map', *Perth Now*, 5 June 2015.

       'I think he himself has said . . .' Calla Wahlquist, 'Bob Hawke leads tributes to Alan Bond, America's Cup hero and jailed fraudster', *The Guardian*, 5 June 2015.

       'People have very polarised views . . .' Kate Campbell & Kara Vickery, 'Alan Bond tributes', *Perth Now*, 5 June 2015.

117   'He handed me the envelope . . .' Roger Vaughan, 'Oakley and the empty envelope', *InDaily*, 9 June 2014.

119   'I think his track record stands . . .' Jo Mazzocchi, 'The Life of Skase', The World Today, ABC News, 6 August 2001.

121   'Two Rolls Royces . . .' Patrick Barkham, 'Not the new Ned Kelly', *The Guardian*, 8 August 2001.

122   'Has Queensland ever . . .' Grantlee Kieza, 'Nostalgic Brisbane: Fugitive businessman Christopher Skase wanted dead or alive', *The Courier-Mail*, 20 October 2016.

123   'Few people believed . . .' and 'If he had done . . .' Patrick Barkham, 'Not the new Ned Kelly', *The Guardian*, 8 August 2001.

127   'Rumours that he was involved . . .' Garry Linnel, *Football Ltd: The inside story of the AFL*, Ironbark, Sydney 1995.

       'I believe it is a great investment . . .' 'Edelsten's $6.5m wins the Swans', *The Age*, 1 August 1985.

       'My manager came up to him . . .' 'A few regrets but Edelsten is still true Blue', *Sydney Morning Herald*, 1 July 2004.

129   'Bashing up people . . .' Kate McClymont, 'Tell him I love my husband, but not that much', *Sydney Morning Herald*, 12 September 2009.

129   'Mr Justice Lee ruling . . .' Peter N. Grabosky, *Crime in the Digital Age: Controlling telecommunications and cyberspace*, The Federation Press, Leichhardt 1998.

130   'In the respondent's appearances . . .' and 'That the applicant urged . . .' Medical Tribunal of New South Wales, no. 40018/00, 'In the matter of Geoffrey Walter Edelsten – Reasons for Determination', 31 July 2001.

131   'The media have . . .' Nick Tabakoff, 'Life and loves of man bucking his past, Geoffrey Edelsten on jail, Brynne Gordon', *Daily Telegraph*, 26 September 2009.

132   'Flannery was a complete pest . . .' Kate McClymont, 'Roger Rogerson's murder of Jamie Gao caps notorious career in and out of the law', *Sydney Morning Herald*, 15 June 2016. 'Admitted he had lied . . .' Medical Tribunal of New South Wales, no. 40018/00, 'In the matter of Geoffrey Walter Edelsten – Reasons for Determination', 31 July 2001.

133   'I'm absolutely obligated . . .' Jon Pierik & Chris Vedelago, 'Edelsten claims he fears for his life if he doesn't pay Carlton Football Club $150,000', *The Age*, 5 July 2014.

134   'Carlton's latest salary-cap breaches . . .' Greg Denham, 'Why AFL clubs live in fear of cheating the salary cap', *The Australian*, 11 May 2016.

142   'If you know something . . .' Michael Warner, 'Carlton Blues boot John Elliott over footy rape scandal', *News.com.au*, 16 August 2009.

144   'Palmer then gave an interview . . .' Marco Monteverde, 'Freedom of Speech slogan: FFA says Gold Coast United in material breach of its A-League agreement', Fox Sports, 26 February 2012.

145   'We intend to fight . . .' Ray Gatt, 'Gold Coast owner Clive Palmer loses A-League licence', *The Australian*, 29 February 2012.

146   **'Mr Palmer said . . .'** 'Palmer forms organisation to challenge FFA', ESPN, 1 March 2012.

        '[Football Australia] will publish . . .' Marco Monteverde, 'Queensland billionaire Clive Palmer establishes new body for Australian soccer Football Australia', *The Courier-Mail*, 2 March 2012.

149   **'Suddenly he's gone . . .'** Megan Doherty, 'Billionaire retailer and horse breeder Gerry Harvey says bankrupt miner Nathan Tinkler thought he was "a big shot"', *Sydney Morning Herald*, 4 March 2018.

152   **'News Limited revealed . . .'** Andrew Carswell & Amy Spear, 'Court documents reveal how Newcastle Knights owner Nathan Tinkler lost a fortune betting', Fox Sports, 30 July 2013.

153   **'*BRW* estimated . . .'** Andrew Heathcote, 'Tinkler toppled as Atlassian tech duo named richest young Australians', *Australian Financial Review*, 26 September 2012.

154   **'Tinkler blew up . . .'** 'Nathan Tinkler officially cited by FFA', *Newcastle Herald*, 24 April 2015.

        'The club owed . . .' Donna Page, 'The Jets had $21m in debt, $605 in the bank', *Newcastle Herald*, 19 June 2015.

155   **'HSG has behaved . . .'** Giselle Wakatama, 'Newcastle Jets' A-League licence cancelled after Nathan Tinkler places club in voluntary administration', ABC News, 20 May 2015.

        'Tinkler was caught up in . . .' Andrew Carswell & Amy Spear, 'Court documents reveal how Newcastle Knights owner Nathan Tinkler lost a fortune betting', Fox Sports, 30 July 2013.

        'Tinkler, the former CEO . . .' Australian Securities & Investments Commission, 'Three former co-directors banned from managing companies', 24 May 2017.

156 'There's something in his character . . .' Megan Doherty, 'Billionaire retailer and horse breeder Gerry Harvey says bankrupt miner Nathan Tinkler thought he was "a big shot"', *Sydney Morning Herald*, 4 March 2018.

157 'In 1988, Groves . . .' Liam Walsh, 'Eddy Groves fights to hold on', *News.com.au*, 1 March 2008.

158 'ABC Learning paid the Bullets . . .' Adam Schwab, *Pigs at the trough: lessons from Australia's decade of corporate greed,* John Wiley & Sons, Milton, Qld, 2010.
'In 2006, ABC paid a company . . .' James Thomson, 'Lessons learned from ABC', *The Australian*, 7 November 2008.

160 'Boats International director . . .' Phil Lutton, 'Conman sprung in Bullets bid', *Brisbane Times*, 24 June 2008.
'ASIC launched a seven-year . . .' Justine Parker, 'ABC Learning: ASIC probe ends; founder Eddie Groves exits bankruptcy', ABC News, 23 February 2016.

164 'It turned out he made no donations . . .' Gerard Ryle & Jacquelin Magnay, 'Firepower chief had dinner with Howard', *Brisbane Times*, 15 July 2008.

166 'It turned out the Kings . . .' Jacquelin Magnay & Gerard Ryle, with Mark Forbes, 'Owner of Sydney Kings faces arrest', *Sydney Morning Herald*, 20 June 2008.

ISSUES

181 'Luke notified the club . . .' 'St Kilda player Luke Dunstan was detained by police on Saturday morning', *Herald Sun*, 10 December 2016.

CRISES

189 'I've spoken with David Peever . . .' 'PM: Ball tampering news "beggars belief"', Cricket Australia, 25 March 2018.

192 'I'm embarrassed . . .' 'Transcript: The Smith and Bancroft

ball-tampering confession', *Sydney Morning Herald*, 25 March 2018.

192 **'No, I won't be considering . . .'** 'Transcript', *Sydney Morning Herald*, 25 March 2018.

193 **'Yes, I lied . . .'** Sam Ferris, 'I lied, I panicked – I'm sorry: Bancroft', Cricket Australia, 29 March 2018.

195 **'Given the admission . . .'** Australian Sports Commission, 'ASC statement on Australian Cricket', 25 March 2018.

197 **'Like the rest of Australia . . .'** Darren Gray, '"A shameful moment for Australian sport": Cricket sponsors hit out', *Sydney Morning Herald*, 26 March 2018.

200 **'No other players . . .'** David Davutovic & Ben Horne, 'Smith, Warner and Bancroft sent home in disgrace as Tim Paine officially named Test captain', *Daily Telegraph*, 28 March 2018.
'As I understand it . . .' Jane Cadzow, 'What turned Steve Smith into a cheat?', *Good Weekend*, 23 June 2018.

201–2 **'Sutherland had described . . .', 'Ugly verbal spat . . .', 'I don't think that's necessarily . . .', 'That's James' opinion . . .' and 'David has matured. . .'** Richard Gibson, 'David Warner calls being Australia's deputy captain a "massive honour"', *The Guardian*, 15 August 2015.

204 **'A conspiracy by the leadership . . .'** Darren Gray, 'Ashes sponsor dumps $20m naming rights deal', *Sydney Morning Herald*, 29 March 2018.

205 **'A culture is everybody's responsibility . . .'** Tracey Holmes, 'Ball-tampering scandal: Cricket Australia under mounting scrutiny over team culture', ABC News, 1 April 2018.

206 **'The feeling is that . . .'** Chris Barrett, 'Darren Lehmann quits as coach of the Australian cricket team', *Sydney Morning Herald*, 20 March 2018.

207 **'I'm here today to accept . . .'** Jacob Kuriype, 'David

Warner leaves key questions unanswered in emotional but disappointing press conference', Fox Sports, 31 March 2018.

210   **'I think we're all going to come under the microscope . . .'** 'CA chairman David Peever announces independent review into men's team 'culture', separate ex-player-led process', Fox Sports, 6 April 2018.

      'The integrity review . . .' 'CA chairman David Peever announces independent review into men's team "culture", separate ex-player-led process', Fox Sports, 6 April 2018.

211   **'A joke . . .'** Jane Cadzow, 'What turned Steve Smith into a cheat?', *Good Weekend*, 23 June 2018.

212   **'When I think about . . .'** Jacob Kuriype, 'Justin Langer reveals what banned Aussie trio have to do to get back in the team', *News.com.au*, 3 May 2018.

      'Actually, I've heard him say . . .' 'Australia cricket coach Justin Langer wants players to be good blokes who could "marry his daughters"', ABC News, 31 May 2018.

213   **'The game has never been . . .'** Andrew Wu, 'Cricket Australia CEO Sutherland announces resignation', *Sydney Morning Herald*, 6 June 2018.

SAGAS

219   **'WorkSafe Victoria began investigating . . .'** Mark Dunn, 'Essendon Bombers fined $200,000 for workplace safety breaches over supplements saga', *Herald Sun*, 28 January 2016.

THE DOWNRIGHT ODD

222–3 'You get wedgies . . .', 'It wasn't a wedgie . . .', 'It's disgusting . . .' and 'In forty-five years . . .' 'Rugby League: Lowe – kick Hopoate out for life', *NZ Herald*, 31 March 2001.

224–5 'There was just smoke . . .' and 'Mr Johnston said the incident . . .' Samantha Landy, Aaron Langmaid & James Dowling, 'Dwarf entertainer set on fire during St Kilda's Mad Monday party criticised for not entertaining players', *Herald Sun*, 4 September 2013.

FORGIVING AND FORGETTING

233 'Has Nick Kyrgios finally . . .' Sam Duncan, 'Has Nick Kyrgios finally grown up?', *The Age*, 22 January 2018.
'Fans heap praise . . .' Ebony Bowden, 'Australian Open 2018: Fans heap praise on former bad boy Nick Kyrgios', *Sydney Morning Herald*, 22 January 2018.
'Nick Kyrgios a role model . . .' Simon Cambers, *Nick Kyrgios a role model? You'd better believe it*, ESPN, 16 January 2018.

235–6 'Basically, she caught . . .', 'The family [of Alisha Horan] . . .', 'It's a load of rubbish . . .' and 'protect their young daughter . . .' 'Revealed: what took place in the hotel room', *The Age*, 1 March 2003.

237 'By any definition . . .' Lynn Bell, 'Gary Ablett inducted into AFL hall of fame', ABC AM, 7 June 2005.

239 'It feels too soon . . .' Alex Zaia, 'Is Warner's Commentary Appearance Too Soon?', SEN, 12 June 2018.

240 'I thought I was worthless . . .' Miranda Devine, 'Morality code kicked into touch', *Sydney Morning Herald*, 14 May 2009.

241 'I'm so ashamed . . .' and 'Those blokes at *The Footy Show* . . .' 'Matthew Johns accuse[d] of making anti-gay Footy Show skit', *News.com.au*, 28 May 2009.

243 'I'm keen to get into . . .' Larissa Nicholson, 'Glenn McGrath: Former cricketer regrets shooting wildlife on safari', *Sydney Morning Herald*, 21 February 2015.

246   'Joey was a bit disturbed . . .' 'Barry Hall sacked from Triple M radio after "inappropriate" comment', *News.com.au*, 1 July 2018.

249   'In the conversation that followed . . .' 'Eddie McGuire apologises to Adam Goodes for King Kong comment but will not resign', ABC News, 29 May 2018.

250   'In fact, I reckon . . .' Deborah Gough & Chloe Booker, 'Eddie McGuire in hot water over Caroline Wilson ice pool gibe', *The Age*, 20 June 2016.

252   'No one spoke of Caroline . . .' James Matthey & Olivia Lambert, 'Eddie McGuire joked about drowning a woman on Triple M radio', *Herald Sun*, 20 June 2016.

254   'I would like to say . . .' Alex Blair, 'Triple M host opens up on Barry Hall madness', *News.com.au*, 6 July 2018.

255   'When it comes to this . . .' Ewan Gilbert, 'NRL players may face life bans if found guilty of domestic violence', ABC News, 17 July 2017.

256   'To put it into some context . . .' Jessica Halloran, 'NRL players found guilty of domestic violence should face life bans from the game', *Daily Telegraph*, 23 June 2018.

257   'He told listeners . . .' Michelangelo Rucci, 'Jason Akermanis apologises after calling the late Jim Stynes "a nasty man in his day" during radio interview', *Herald Sun*, 23 March 2012.

258   'I'd say, "Jason . . ."' Sarah Olle, 'Open Mike: Justin Leppitsch discusses relationship with Jason Akermanis, St Kilda's multimillion-dollar offer', Fox Sports, 27 March 2018.
       'Western Bulldogs chief executive . . .' Peter Gordon, 'Aka's book nothing more than a nasty little rant', *The Age*, 14 September 2010.

260   'The staff member involved . . .' Caroline Wilson, 'AFL

had to let Simon Lethlean go: Gillon McLachlan', *The Age*, 10 August 2017.

260   '**I know our industry . . .**' Stephen Drill, 'AFL press conference days after affair claim', *Herald Sun*, 15 July 2017.

261   '**I would hope . . .**' 'Carlton hopeful former AFL executive Simon Lethlean applies for vacant CEO position', Fox Sports, 6 October 2017.

ARE GOOD BLOKES AN ENDANGERED SPECIES?

262   '**Of course it was . . .**' Anthony Colangelo, 'Simon Lethlean deserves a second chance, say Saints', *The Age*, 15 December 2017.

266   '**From my point of view . . .**' Nathanael Cooper, '"Say it to my face": Sam Newman takes aim at AFL star Patrick Dangerfield', *Sydney Morning Herald*, 30 June 2017.
       '**It's definitely a persona . . .**' 'Alex Rance: Tide Changing for Newman', SEN News, 20 July 2017.
       '**I can't go on TV . . .**' Danielle Gusmaroli, 'Political Correctness killing Australian comedy says comedic great Kevin Bloody Wilson', *Daily Telegraph*, 2 May 2018.

268   '**The AFL's integrity unit . . .**' Michael Warner, 'Former homicide squad detective heads growing AFL integrity team', *Herald Sun*, 3 December 2017.

273   '**The onus is . . .**' James Willoughby, '"I'm embarrassed": Michelle Payne suspended for positive drug test', *The New Daily*, 29 June 2017.

274   '**An independent review . . .**' Chris Barrett, 'I won't quit: Coates says he will stay on despite damning report of AOC culture', *Sydney Morning Herald*, 24 August 2017.

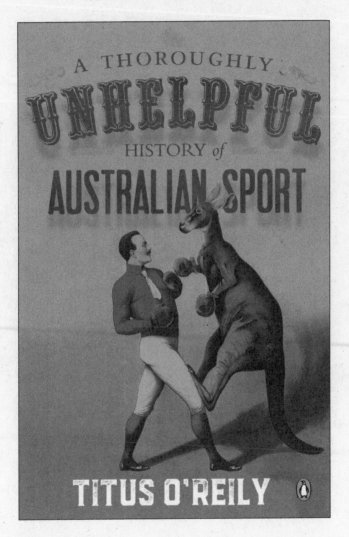

Discover a
new favourite